THE MEGACHURCH AND THE MAINLINE

THE MEGACHURCH
AND THE MAINLINE

REMAKING RELIGIOUS TRADITION
IN THE TWENTY-FIRST CENTURY

STEPHEN ELLINGSON

THE UNIVERSITY OF CHICAGO PRESS · CHICAGO AND LONDON

STEPHEN ELLINGSON
is assistant professor of sociology at Hamilton College.
He is a coeditor of *The Sexual Organization of the City*
(2004, with Edward O. Laumann, Jenna Mahay, Anthony Paik, and Yoosik Youm),
also published by the University of Chicago Press.

The University of Chicago Press, Chicago 60637
The University of Chicago Press, Ltd., London
© 2007 by The University of Chicago
All rights reserved. Published 2007
Printed in the United States of America

16 15 14 13 12 11 10 09 08 07   1 2 3 4 5

ISBN-13: 978-0-226-20489-5 (cloth)
ISBN-13: 978-0-226-20490-1 (paper)
ISBN-10: 0-226-20489-8 (cloth)
ISBN-10: 0-226-20490-1 (paper)

Library of Congress Cataloging-in-Publication Data
Ellingson, Stephen, 1962–
The megachurch and the mainline : remaking religious
tradition in the twenty-first century / Stephen Ellingson.
   p.   cm.
Includes bibliographical references (p.   ) and index.
ISBN-13: 978-0-226-20489-5 (cloth : alk. paper)
ISBN-13: 978-0-226-20490-1 (pbk. : alk. paper)
ISBN-10: 0-226-20489-8 (cloth : alk. paper)
ISBN-10: 0-226-20490-1 (pbk. : alk. paper)
   1.   Church renewal.   2. Church—History of doctrines.
   3. Tradition (Theology)   4. Big churches.
   5. Christian sects.   6. Protestant churches.   I. Title.
        BV600.3.E56   2007
   262.001'7—dc22   2006025444

♾ The paper used in this publication meets the minimum requirements
of the American National Standard for Information Sciences—Permanence
of Paper for Printed Library Materials, ANSI Z39.48-1992.

CONTENTS

ACKNOWLEDGMENTS

I OFTEN REMIND my methods classes that social research is a cooperative endeavor, built on relationships of trust. This book is no exception, and I have relied on the help of many. First and foremost, the members and clergy of the nine congregations where I conducted most of my research deserve my heartfelt thanks. They invited me into their churches and homes; served me numerous cups of coffee; shared their stories, hopes, and fears; and welcomed me to worship, Bible studies, barbeques, retreats, late-night drinks after hours-long church council meetings, seder meals, and church potlucks. At each congregation there were one or two members who made my task easier by introducing me to people, inviting me to events, and generally ensuring that the project succeeded. I owe a large debt to these unnamed informants.

The project was made possible in the first place by a five-year grant from the Lilly Endowment that was awarded to Pacific Lutheran Theological Seminary. The school's late president, Timothy Lull, and the faculty of PLTS hired me in the fall of 1999 and gave me free rein to design and implement the grant as I wished. PLTS proved to be a hospitable place to work and reacquaint myself with the Lutheran tradition. I owe special thanks to many of the faculty members: Carol Jacobsen was my regular sounding board and answered all my questions about Lutheran theology; Michael Aune shared his knowledge of Lutheran worship and American Lutheran history, as well as his library, with me; Tom Rogers, Martha Stortz, Jane Strohl, Bob Smith, and Gary Pence asked questions about the project at faculty meetings and around the copy machine that helped me clarify my ideas. Victor Gold read most of the manuscript and provided information about the history of Lutheranism in the American West that proved invaluable. The archivist of the Sierra Pacific Synod of the Evangelical Lutheran Church in America, Carol Schmalenberger, guided me to interviews, papers, and histories of West Coast Lutheranism that helped me contextualize my findings. Anne and Jim Carlson graciously let me stay in their guest house while I conducted research in the Silicon Valley and proved to be lively conversation partners throughout the course of the project. PLTS, the western synods of the ELCA, and numerous congregations in California and the Pacific Northwest provided opportunities to share my early findings. I also presented early versions of book chapters at the 2001 meetings of the Society for the Scientific Study of Religion and the 2002 meetings of the Association for the Sociology of Religion.

A number of other scholars and students helped me from the research design phase to the writing phase: Speed Leas, Roger Johnson, and Penny Edgel reviewed my research design and helped me refine it; Jerome Baggett, Penny Edgel, and William McKinney read the manuscript and offered helpful advice to clarify my arguments. I was ably assisted during the data collection by three research assistants: Ruth Lesher, Nancy Hanson, and Karen Perkins. They made it possible for me to be at two or three congregations at the same time on many Sundays. Several graduate students transcribed interviews, and I am grateful for their diligence and their questions and comments about what they were hearing on tape: Barbara Caine, Shelly Dieterle, Katy Grindburg, Bernt Hillesland, and Debra Koch. Finally, Veronica Carrillo, of Carrillo Business, quickly transcribed dozens of interviews near the end of the field period. At Hamilton College, Alexandra London tracked down missing citations, Meredith Scheiner identified all of the mistakes in my endnotes and then fixed all of them, and Robin Vanderwall, the sociology department administrator, provided much-needed assistance whenever I ran into trouble with Word and made sure I met my deadlines. My editor, Doug Mitchell, provided sage advice about framing the book and was a source of encouragement throughout the process. Thanks also go to Doug's assistant, Tim McGovern, for handling my many editorial queries with patience, and to copy editor Pamela Bruton, whose careful work improved my prose. I am grateful to the anonymous referees for their theoretical insights and editorial suggestions.

Finally, I must acknowledge the debt I owe my family. Zachary arrived as I began writing and provided comic relief and daily reminders that play was much more important than writing. My partner, Jennifer DeWeerth, helped me in more ways than I can possibly thank her for: she kept me honest in the field and allowed me to be AWOL during weekends for three years; she read and edited every chapter, usually twice; and she provided love and support every step of the way. I dedicate this book to her.

Chapter 1

THE RESTRUCTURING OF
AMERICAN RELIGIOUS
TRADITIONS

IT WAS A WARM and sunny afternoon as I pulled into the parking lot of Zion Lutheran Church[1] in the heart of Silicon Valley. I came to attend the installation of the congregation's new associate pastor. As I walked from the parking lot behind the church to the front entrance, I heard the rock-and-roll band playing loudly and I could smell the fatted pig being barbequed. As I rounded the corner, I saw the band setup on the front lawn in front of two or three hundred folding chairs under a large tent. I had just sat down near the back when Tom, a member I had met recently at the church's twelve-step Bible study, invited me to join him and his wife, and soon I found myself in the front row. The outdoor sanctuary filled up quickly as it neared the five o'clock starting time, and then the band launched into a set of simple "praise music" songs; the only one I recognized was an upbeat, jazzy rendition of the classic hymn "Joyful, Joyful We Adore You." Several clergy walked through the band and sat down on chairs in front of the band; all were wearing brightly colored Hawaiian shirts. The senior pastor of Zion welcomed everyone to the service and invited us all to the postservice luau. The service continued with another praise song led by the rock band, and then one of the pastors read two passages from the New Testament.

Then came the main event: several of the visiting clergy delivered three- to four-minute sermons on the question that the new pastor had posed to them some weeks before, "What keeps you going?" The first pastor spoke about the days when he is overwhelmed by the job—too many deaths and illnesses, too many meetings, not enough time or compassion to deal with it all. "When I want to quit I turn to the Living Word. Hear the word of the prophet Isaiah, 'The grass fades, the flowers wither, but the word of our God will stand forever.'" He gave a brief excursus on the centrality of daily Bible study for successful ministry and concluded with the following sage advice: "More often than not I am driven to my knees by the demands of being a pastor. Ministry is about living with bruised knees, and scripture is the one thing that is constant; it is what I turn to when God drives me to my knees."

A second pastor rose and began with a serious look on his face, "What keeps me going as a pastor? The minister's edition of *The Lutheran Book of Worship*? [*long pause*] No, that won't help." His opening lines were met with peals of laughter, but then he turned serious. He held up his leather-bound, floppy Bible, gestured with it, and solemnly said, "This is what I turn to when things get bad." He read a passage from the Old Testament book of Micah and instructed his junior colleague that the Bible contains everything we need to know about being disciples.

A third pastor finished the sermon time by reading two passages from works by the patron saints of orthodoxy and contemporary evangelicalism, C. S. Lewis and George MacDonald. In the story from MacDonald, God is likened to a master carpenter whom we invite to make some modest repairs on our house. Once inside, God starts doing repairs—unclogging drains, fixing the leaking roof. But then, like some contractor run amok, God starts the major renovations—tearing out walls, building turrets and new rooms. The pastor wryly noted that "we just want to live in a small cottage, but God wants to build a palace in order to live there with you. I keep going after thirty years of ministry because I want to find out what God will do with me and all the other Christians in my life."

The service rapidly concluded with the laying on of hands and praying for the new pastor, another up-tempo praise song, and then the youth group ambushed their new pastor and dressed him in all things Hawaiian—grass skirt, coconut-shell bra, straw hat. As they did so, the chairperson of the call committee informed us that the Hawaiian theme not only was good fun but had a serious side. He continued by regaling us with the story of how the Hawaiian shirt was created. Apparently, Western missionaries were so appalled at the nakedness of the native islanders when they arrived to convert them in the nineteenth century that they gave them shirts to cover up their nakedness. The natives, delighted by the gift of the shirts, made them their own by decorating the plain white shirts with bright colors and flowers. "We should be like the Hawaiians," he said, "obedient but joyful." The service ended and the luau began.

A few months later I attended the ordination service of a new pastor at Grace Lutheran Church in the Oakland suburbs. I entered the sanctuary to the sound of drumming. Eight young people were sitting in one of the four front rows pounding away on a variety of large African drums. The service began with a dozen robed clergy processing into the pastel-painted sanctuary arranged as a partial theater-in-the-round, singing a song from the contemporary Lutheran hymnal. The senior pastor of Grace welcomed us by using a traditional South African greeting (the newly ordained pastor would soon leave for a three-year stint at a South African Lutheran parish) and then asked us to greet one another in the same manner. All the men said, "Nda," and the women responded, "Ah" (making a glissando from high to low). We then followed one of the three regularly sung liturgies in the hymnal of the Evangelical Lutheran Church in America (ELCA). For the scripture-reading rite, a young woman sang the Shema for the Old Testament lesson, and a Roman Catholic priest and two faculty members from the local Lutheran seminary read a number of texts from the New Testament, all of which emphasized God's love, inclusivity, and justice.

The senior pastor read the Gospel lesson, from the fourth chapter of Luke, in which Jesus delivers his first sermon and identifies his own calling to be one in which he will bring good news to the poor, set the prisoners free, and make the blind see. The pastor's sermon drew parallels between Jesus' call and the new pastor's call. "Like Jesus," he said, "you are called to speak the good news: light, joy, FREEDOM!!" Next he reminded her and all of us about Luther's understanding of the call to be a Christian by quoting from two of Luther's most remembered writings, "The Freedom of the Christian" and his alleged speech in front of the Diet of Worms in which he ended his critique of Catholicism with the words, "Here I stand, I can do no other." He finished by applying Luther's ideas and the Gospel lesson to the soon-to-be-ordained pastor's call:

This is what you are called to. You are called to preach the cross and resurrection. You are called to speak about the mysteries of Christianity: how we are all called to forgive seven times seventy times; to attain the grand status of children; to proclaim the absurdity of it all! You are not called to make Christianity palatable. Your call is tied to Luke 4 [here he read it again]. You are called sometimes to poor the acid of the gospel on the corrosion of human nature, and it won't be a pretty picture. It will cause the death of the old self. You are called to preach mercy, the crucified, resurrected mercy—the way of the cross—and people will reject it. But continue to preach it. Your call has put you in your place [*pause*] the place of grace.

The bishop then led the official ELCA ordination service. We ended the service with a lively South African hymn, for which the newly ordained pastor taught us the words and hand motions and the senior pastor taught us a sort of line dance that involved a lot of foot stomping. Within minutes, the entire congregation was dancing and singing along with the incessant beat of the African drums.

Ordinations and installations of pastors are extraordinary rituals in the life of a congregation. They are moments when the foundational beliefs, distinctive theological worldviews, and the most important elements of a community's religious culture are displayed. If Clifford Geertz is correct that rituals are the vehicles through which we tell ourselves stories about ourselves, then these rituals should tell us a story about the nature and salience of the historic religious tradition that should govern the congregations.[2] At Grace Lutheran, the ordination ritual proved to be a moment in which the congregation's Lutheran theological and liturgical commitments were rehearsed but the tradition was opened up to include the social-justice concerns more central to liberal Protestantism as well as the ecumenical and global additions to the music and liturgy of the service. At Zion Lutheran, the tradition that was signaled was not Lutheran but a generic evangelicalism. The Lutheran tradition was dismissed as irrelevant and humorously outdated, and Lutheran theological ideas and liturgical practices were absent from the installation ritual. Instead, we heard the kind of music used at growing evangelical churches around the country; we heard about the centrality of the Bible for authentic Christian faith and saw how it was used instrumentally to solve problems; we heard about the important mission to convert people to Christianity (note that the ordained pastor at Grace was going to South Africa, not to convert the heathen natives, but to serve in a preexisting Lutheran parish); and finally we heard that foundational evangelical story about individuals' personal relationship with Jesus.

Two rituals in two Lutheran churches—one was grounded in the tradition, albeit one flavored by ecumenism, liberal Protestantism, and a much more emotive style of worship than customarily found; the other was not really Lutheran at all except that it took place on the front lawn of a Lutheran church. What was going on at these events? Why was the historic tradition being altered at one church and replaced with evangelicalism at another? Why was the tradition dismissed as an outdated joke at one church and blended with a variety of other traditions at another? More generally, these two events raise questions about the nature of religious change: How does the process of changing a tradition work? What parts of the tradition are saved, mined, or abandoned, and why? Under what conditions are attempts to revise the tradition met with approval or with resistance? What happens to a religious tradition and the community that bears it once it has been significantly altered?

These questions are at the heart of my ethnographic study of nine Lutheran congregations in the San Francisco Bay Area. Initially, the study's goal was to explain how and why some congregations were able to flourish amid a long-standing and pervasive loss of membership and participation within California Lutheranism. However, my observations and interviews during that first year revealed that several of the most successful congregations did not seem to be particularly Lutheran in theology, culture, or ritual practices. All of the congregations were intentionally reworking the inherited Lutheran tradition. Some were adopting the theologies, worship practices, and educational materials from evangelical and nondenominational megachurches;[3] others were borrowing practices and ideas from Eastern religions or a vaguely defined seeker spirituality.[4] Few of the clergy and even fewer of the nearly 250 members I interviewed expressed strong interest in retaining a distinctly Lutheran identity for themselves or their congregations. One pastor claimed that replacing the historic worship practices of Lutheranism with those from contemporary American evangelicalism was simply "changing the form but not the faith of Lutheranism." Why did he (and others) have this interest in altering the tradition, and is it possible to change forms through which the tradition is expressed without changing its content?

This is a book about how and why a particular religious tradition is changed, about how and why the logic and practices of evangelical religion, seeker spirituality, and the utilitarian, consumerist ethos of American society press upon and ultimately lead congregations to alter their received traditions. As such, it supplies a piece of the whole picture that is missing from sociological accounts of the restructuring of Protestantism within the United States. Much of the work on the restructuring of American religion focuses either on the macroshifts in affiliation and participation among the different branches of Protestantism or on microchanges in the religious lives of individuals. By focusing on the organizational level and closely reading the shifts in the cultural content and cultural work that occur within congregations (i.e., efforts to change their own denominational and congregational traditions), this study offers a new way of understanding the process and outcomes of religious restructuring at the outset of the new century.

This book also is about the more general process of religious and cultural change. Theoretical and empirical accounts of change within religious or cultural systems tend to understand change as an episodic phenomenon, driven by external social forces and resulting in a return to social order or stasis. Too often we conceptualize change as happening only during periods of "unsettled times" and overlook the ways in which organizations and individuals must create the unsettled times by interpreting events as crises.[5] This study offers a constructivist approach to religious and cultural change. I argue that congregational leaders selectively draw on experts' interpretations of congregational growth and decline and their models of successful organizational change to construct crises of meaning and membership that they then use to justify and generate support for their efforts to rework the Lutheran tradition. At the same time, I engage in an ongoing conversation with cultural, ecological, and market-based approaches to religious change as I explain how and why local congregations rework and redefine the tradition that provides them with meaning and identity.

Finally, this book is about the relationships among religious tradition, community, and moral authority discussed instructively by Bellah and his colleagues in *Habits of the Heart* and more recently in studies of boomer spirituality and religion, religious restructuring, Roman Catholicism, and Orthodox Judaism.[6] One consistent theme across this diverse body of scholarship is that religious tradition is necessary to create communities of memory—communities that provide enduring meaning, identity, and belonging to its members. However, the nine congregations in this study raise questions about the relationship between tradition and community. Does the creation of new traditions or the rediscovery of old traditions actually create more committed and stronger communities of faith or does it merely reinforce the move toward communities of limited liability? The data from the nine congregations also raise questions about the nature of moral authority in religious organizations. According to scholars of America's religious restructuring, individuals and congregations increasingly choose to align themselves with a given tradition or combine elements from different traditions as they create a new one. Yet the selected tradition or traditions are not considered authoritative within a congregation for its members. It appears that the very consumerist and utilitarian ethos of religious choice that has facilitated the creation and adaptation of religious tradition may be undermining the authority of the tradition. In the concluding chapters, I address these broader questions about community and authority. In the next section, I review the three broad themes of the book—religious restructuring, theories of religious change, and the relationships among tradition, community, and authority—in more detail and show how an analytic focus on the internal processes of meaning making at the level of the congregation can shed new light on some of the perennial stories of American religion.

TRADITION AND THE RESTRUCTURING OF AMERICAN PROTESTANTISM

The story of how American Protestantism has changed since the mid-1960s is now a familiar one. Sociologists of religion have charted the decline of mainline Protestantism and the ascendance of conservative and evangelical Protestantism; documented the privatization of religion and growing disenchantment with organized or institutionalized religion among Americans; and shown how choice has become a normative feature of American Christianity.[7] Rather than rehearse these accounts, it will be more fruitful to identify those pieces of the story that can help us understand how historic denominational traditions may be affected by this restructuring. In general, the restructuring literature suggests that since the mid-1960s congregations and individuals are less likely to consider a particular religious tradition important, meaningful, or binding than in previous decades. This is especially true for American Lutheranism.[8]

First, the common practice of dropping out of organized religion or switching from one church body to another suggests that commitment to a given denominational tradition has weakened. Even if the majority of switchers stay within the broad denominational family (e.g., switching from Lutheran to Episcopal), as Hadaway and Marler argue,[9] the old, former tradition is probably not very important, as individuals must abandon much of the unique history, theology, culture, and worship practices of their former denomination. Second, the rise of religious consumerism encourages individuals not only to switch from one church body to another but to pick and choose among doctrines, practices, beliefs, or values from different traditions and put them together to form a religion that meets individuals' interests. This religious eclecticism may undermine the authority and integrity of a given tradition because it pulls individuals out of the community that preserves and practices the tradition. Moreover, change in Americans' religiosity, namely, the search for spiritual experiences and the creation of "multilayered spirituality," takes place outside religious communities that can provide support and some degree of control over the creative process.[10]

The story of restructuring is not simply one of denominational decline but also one in which the tradition is rediscovered and reworked. Some scholars argue that denominational identities and traditions are alive and well by pointing to the individuals and congregations who actively seek to rediscover and hold on to their distinctive ritual practices and identity narratives or to develop new traditions from a burgeoning religious marketplace.[11] Although some congregations within mainline Protestantism are intentionally preserving and passing along their historic traditions, others have intentionally moved away from and seem indifferent or even hostile to the worship rituals and theological stories of the denomination. Ammerman argues that we need to look "to the agency of the congregations themselves, to what they are doing and how they tell their own stories," to understand why the tradition is preserved or discarded and how it is altered or reconfigured in particular ways.[12]

Finally, the proliferation of nondenominational congregations (including many of the new megachurches) and the growing importance of church growth consultants may be weakening the historic traditions of mainline Protestantism. Nondenominational churches self-consciously eschew many hallmarks of these traditions such as hymns, routinized liturgies, theological idioms and symbols, and recognizable church architecture. Nondenominationalism, especially the seeker church model created by prominent megachurches, is both sold by church growth consultants as the panacea for all that ails declining mainline Protestant churches and identified as the path to success by many leaders within mainline Protestant denominations who then push their congregations to emulate nondenominational churches. At the same time, many megachurches aggressively market their worship, educational, and leadership resources, and several have established quasi-denominational associations that expand the influence of the nondenominational evangelical tradition.[13] Some commentators suggest that we are seeing a shift from a diverse array of Protestant traditions to a more unified Protestant tradition that is grounded in nondenominational evangelicalism.[14]

While the restructuring literature confirms the decline of the historic traditions within mainline Protestantism, it has not investigated what is replacing those traditions nor how congregations are responding to or being shaped by this restructuring. Miller's claim that the movement toward nondenominational Protestantism constitutes a "second Reformation" or "Third Great Awakening" still has not been empirically substantiated.[15] One of the limitations of this body of scholarship is that researchers have given little attention to explaining how the major shifts of this restructuring have impacted the religious forms, beliefs, and practices of congregations within particular denominations. Are congregations altering or abandoning their inherited tradition in favor of the worship rituals, language, and leadership strategies of growing nondenominational churches, or has the nondenominational movement led them to rediscover their own tradition? Are they using their tradition to justify such changes or resist them? How extensive is this second Reformation, and is it really remaking Protestantism as predicted by Miller?

Major studies of congregations, in recent years, provide glimpses into the ways in which tradition is being transformed, but most of these studies pursue other agendas.[16] Studies of the new voluntarism also provide clues about the nature and direction of change within given denominational traditions, but because individuals are the unit of analysis, this literature does not explain the role that congregations play in the process of change.[17] If we are to more fully understand how and why American Protestantism is changing, then we must investigate the ways in which local congregations are reshaping the forms and meanings of religious belief and practice. It is vital to make congregations the focal point because they are the primary organizations that teach, practice, and remake religious traditions. Congregations are important, according to Bass, because "individuals can learn and participate in traditions only in the company of others; they do so by entering into the practices and institutions through which particular social groups, versed in specific activities and gathered into specific organizations, bear traditions through time."[18]

In short, we have few sustained investigations of the processes by which congregations rework or fundamentally transform the historic traditions that provide meaning and identity for the organization and its members. My contribution to scholarship on religious change in the United States is to examine how the form and content of one strand of Protestantism—one that has been relatively insulated from external pressures—have been transformed by the larger religious and cultural forces documented in the restructuring literature. In particular, this study examines what happens when the practices, beliefs, and language of a religious tradition that historically has emphasized the collectivity over the individual, doctrine over experience, and sacred ritual over practical moralism encounter and incorporate elements from a religious tradition that stresses the opposite features.

EXPLAINING RELIGIOUS CHANGE

Within the sociology of religion, three theoretical approaches have tried to explain ideological and structural changes within a religion over time as well as how and why new religions emerge.[19] Cultural explanations focus on the role of symbol, ritual, and meaning as the key explanatory factors. Ecological approaches stress the ways in which religions respond to changes in their immediate and larger social contexts, while market theories emphasize how shifts in the supply and demand for religious goods fuel religious change. While the three theories offer different understandings of the catalysts, processes, and outcomes of change, they share three features. First, the catalysts for change most often come from outside the religious system and force religious organizations to respond or suffer some form of decline. Second, they generally agree that the process of religious change involves some degree of redefining or re-creating religious ideas, practices, or structures to meet the demands of a new religious environment. Third, all three models share an implicit assumption that change is an aberration and that the usual state of affairs is social order. Thus, outcomes are often understood as a return to social order or stasis.

Cultural Theories of Religious Change

Cultural theories of religious change start with the question of meaning and expect religions to change when the system of symbols, values, rituals, or ideas no longer provide order in the face of fundamental human questions about suffering, evil, identity, or the purpose of life. Weber's "Social Psychology of World Religions" is the classic text within this paradigm. In this model, the catalysts for change are events in the world that challenge the coherence and power of a religious meaning system. Weber refers to this in terms of the recurrent problem for religions of having to face questions of suffering that create a "mis-fit" between the religious ethic and the lived experience of believers. The process of religious change is intended to solve this problem of misarticulation. Religious entrepreneurs (Weber's charismatic leaders) or organizations redefine or rework the religious meaning system to provide a new and more "rational" answer to the problem of suffering. The outcome is the formation of a new religious ethic or meaning system. The process of change in this model is often contested, as old and new religious elites struggle to control the emergent religious system or reestablish the old. In addition, Weber suggests that changing a religious ethic will be facilitated to the degree that the proposed changes articulate closely with the interests and ideas of key or targeted social groups.

One contemporary variation on this model is Roof's study of baby boomers. He argues that the catalysts for major changes within American Protestantism in the past few decades are to be found in a set of interrelated social and cultural changes (i.e., the consciousness reformation of the 1960s and 1970s, the shift from modernity to postmodernity, the rise of a therapeutic understanding of the self, new communication technology, and globalization). This set of large-scale shifts in practices, values, and attitudes has led to the creation of a "religious-quest culture" in which individuals intentionally seek to reclaim or rework existing congregational and denominational traditions to facilitate their spiritual quests. Roof finds that some individuals simply reaffirm the old traditions, others infuse the tradition with new meanings, and a few create new traditions altogether. These processes of change have led many denominational traditions to incorporate traditions from Eastern religions, Celtic and ancient Christianity, or self-help or therapeutic regimes. In particular, Roof documents how liberal and moderate Protestants are both rediscovering their own specific traditions and self-consciously borrowing liturgies, theologies, ecclesiologies, and vocabularies from Catholic, Jewish, Buddhist, and Hindu traditions.[20] Roof's account addresses the nature and directions of contemporary changes to religious traditions, and he identifies several mechanisms of change that will guide my analysis in chapter 4.

Another cultural approach can be found in Becker's work on congregational conflict.[21] In most of the congregations she studies, conflict arises from efforts to change worship, decision-making practices, or resource allocation patterns initiated by clergy or some group of members, and thus change is largely driven by internal causes. However, in many cases, the catalysts are indirectly related to larger shifts in values and attitudes in U.S. society regarding gender equality or sexual morality. In a few cases, the catalysts are demographic changes in the communities she studies.[22] The cultural models in operation at each congregation determine the process of change because they provide the rules and understandings that determine which issues get addressed, how they will be fought over, and how they will or will not be implemented.[23] These models channel efforts to alter a congregation's traditions by making proposed changes fit within the parameters of the model and thus tend to reproduce a congregation's culture and structure.[24] In short, cultural theories suggest that we should look for some external catalyst that creates a crisis of meaning and then investigate how religious elites alter, update, or rework the tradition to resolve the crisis and return to a state of religious order.

Ecological Theories of Religious Change

Ecological approaches to religious change start with the local and supralocal social contexts in which congregations are embedded. They stress that changes within the institutional, social, or demographic environment in which congregations operate force congregations to respond. Wuthnow's application of a population ecology model to explain the emergence of and change within religious ideologies and Ammerman's study of how congregations adapt to changes in their local communities are exemplars of the ecological model.[25]

In these two versions, the catalyst for changes in religious ideas, practices, or structures comes from external sources, often depicted as a crisis that a congregation or religious organization must address in order to survive.[26] In Wuthnow's account, some disturbance to the moral order leads to the production of new ideologies. In an uncertain environment, creators compete with one another for resources or potential followers as they attempt to adapt to the emergent environment. As in Weber's model, the winners of this competition gain support for their ideology because it resonates more closely with the needs or interests of target audiences than other ideologies. The change process concludes when the new ideology is institutionalized and a new moral order is established.

Similarly, Ammerman's study of congregational change in nine U.S. communities identifies external changes as the catalyst of religious change. In this case, demographic or economic changes in the different communities create crises for congregations as they lose members and resources. Her model is more descriptive than systematic but hinges on the ways in which congregations turn to their own culture, resources, and authority structures to adapt to the crisis caused by a change in the demographic or economic environment. For example, a congregation may recommit itself to a set of theological ideals that allow it to unite old and new members, especially across racial and ethnic lines, under a common identity.[27] Thus, ecological approaches suggest that we investigate how changes in the local economic, demographic, or sociopolitical context lead congregations to adapt. Such explanations show how congregations draw on their religious culture, decision-making structures, and resources to renew and create new traditions so they can more effectively adapt to a changed environment and thus appeal to and serve the new populations in their communities.

Market Theories of Religious Change

Market theories of religious change are generally used to explain individual religious behavior and larger religious shifts rather than changes at the organizational level, and they tend to rely on church-sect theory to explain the process of change.[28] Although market approaches identify internal organizational activities—mainly the lowering of religious demands and benefits as congregations accommodate themselves to the secular world—that are tied to change, they argue that the catalyst for change comes from outside the religious organization. Something has to happen that forces a "churchlike" organization to change its rituals and meaning system, and the most common catalysts for change are external events that create openings for new entrepreneurs or religious firms to enter the religious markets (e.g., the deregulation of the U.S. religious market). The supply-side version of the theory stresses how new firms enter the market with new religious goods and services and develop new demand for their goods. By offering more appealing religious benefits, perhaps in the form of new or reclaimed traditions (e.g., the sect that promises a return to a pure form of Christian worship and morality), new religious firms attract adherents and thus force other religious congregations in the market to innovate or face the loss of current and prospective members.[29] From the demand side, consumers' preferences and their acceptance of new religious goods and services shape religious change, as religious producers have little choice but to abandon unpopular religious products and innovate on tradition in order to broaden or keep market share.

Once a religious market is open to competition, the process of change follows the sect-to-church cycle in which more exclusivist and demanding groups create new religious practices and ways of life that pull members away from more established and worldly churchlike congregations. Some of the churchlike groups will respond by adapting their own traditions or adopting those of the more successful sectlike groups in order to compete for members and resources, while others will refuse to adapt and slip into organizational decline. In the end, the market returns to a steady-state equilibrium until the cycle begins anew.

Enlarging the Theoretical Windows

Theory can be thought of as operating like a window insofar as it lets us see out into the social world. Just as I have a very different picture of my backyard depending upon whether I look out the large casement windows in the bedroom or the small window in the bathroom, theoretical windows show us different perspectives on the same phenomena. Theories, like windows, come in frames (e.g., sets of assumptions; analytic emphasis on culture, structure, or interaction), and those frames shape what we see and how we see things. Each of the three theoretical approaches reviewed above helps us to see different features of religious change, and when brought together, they provide a fairly clear view of the causes, processes, and outcomes of change. Yet they hide from view several important aspects of religious change. I wish to enlarge the theoretical windows on religious and cultural change by developing a constructivist approach.

In chapters 3 through 6 I develop this approach not so much as an alternative but as an additional theoretical window that may give us a different perspective on religious change. I draw not only on insights from cultural, ecological, and market theories but also on ideas from symbolic interactionism and neoinstitutionalism. I use the conceptual tools from these different approaches to shift our focus onto the ways that changes in a religious tradition result from how congregational leaders interpret and construct their religious worlds. In particular, I argue that congregational leaders use the broader shifts in the American religious landscape as resources from which they construct crises of meaning and membership. How the crisis is defined and what strategy each congregation proposes to address the problem depend on several internal features of a congregation: its existing culture, its history and relationship to the tradition, its resources or access to resources, and its "negotiated order."[30] Therefore, the constructivist approach I develop emphasizes, not external causes of change, but internal processes of meaning making that direct change down specific paths, and it emphasizes the organizational conditions that affect how congregations adapt, preserve, or transform their traditions.

In general, cultural, ecological, and market approaches see the catalyst for change as coming from outside the congregation. Shifts in American religiosity, demographic change in the community, or the entrance of religious entrepreneurs with new and more appealing traditions into the market will force congregations to respond as they face declines in their membership, attendance, or resources and struggle to make their own tradition relevant to the changed environment. This emphasis on external causes of change comes as no surprise, as sociologists of religion have been influenced by cultural and organizational theories of change that stress external catalysts. For example, many accounts of religious change rely on Swidler's notion of the cultural tool kit in which change occurs only during unsettled times.[31] Similarly, research on organizations from various perspectives tends to start from the assumption that organizations are "rife with inertia" and will resist change until external shocks arising from market shifts, changes in technology, or economic downturns create organizational crises of efficiency or legitimacy and thus force organizations to change in order to stay competitive.[32]

External social trends, events, or market forces, however, do not automatically cause congregations to change their inherited traditions. Events, models of successful megachurches, or rock-and-roll worship services must be signified as salient to the congregation if they are to have any impact. Fligstein contends that, while organizational change usually arises from some "exogenous shock," how that shock is interpreted and framed for the organization is critical if the organization actually tries to change its way of doing business.[33] Thus, change is not a sudden response to the onset of "unsettled times" but a response to a socially constructed crisis of meaning and organizational survival that is tailored to articulate with a congregation's history and extant tradition, as well as the religious needs and interests of members who govern the organization. In other words, congregational leaders interpret external events and larger religious trends through the lens of the inherited denominational and congregational traditions and then use the events to construct a crisis that can be resolved only by remaking the tradition.

A constructivist approach shifts the focus of analysis and explanation away from external sources of change toward the internal processes of interpretation and meaning making. It offers a new window through which we can see how leaders of congregations identify some set of broader religious changes as a threat to the continuing vitality of the congregation, define some set of religious goods and services as the means to address the threat, and then devise strategies to adapt the tradition to these outside forces. My goal is to show how congregational leaders, who are embedded in different networks of church growth experts, use the information provided by these outside experts to construct crises of meaning and membership and then to change their inherited tradition in ways that defuse the alleged crises—for example, by adopting the rock-and-roll music and casual dress of the megachurches or by incorporating non-Western traditions into the Lutheran tradition. An emphasis on the construction of congregational crises helps us identify the internal mechanisms and the external social forces that together propel religious change.[34]

The three prevailing approaches also provide different ways to understand the process of change. While all three perspectives expect that congregations will respond to the external catalyst by altering the tradition in some way, each emphasizes a different feature of the process. Market theories help us see how declining congregations will adopt the traditions of more successful churches to become more competitive. Ecological approaches emphasize the ways in which congregations in a local religious ecology respond by mimicking successful newcomers, by rediscovering their tradition to become niche churches, or by combining elements from a variety of traditions to meet the diverse interests of both old and new populations. Like ecological approaches, cultural theories also focus attention on the ways in which congregations or their leaders reach back into the archive to rediscover the tradition or find ways to make the tradition applicable and relevant to a new religious situation, such as trying to attract a population unfamiliar with a particular denomination's traditions. Roof's discussion of the strategies of "reconnecting" and "reframing" illustrates this practice, as does Becker's case study of congregations that "mine their traditions" to develop new congregational identities, worship practices, theologies, and authority structures.[35]

Despite these important insights, the three theoretical frameworks obscure an important aspect of the process of change: identifying the organizational or environmental conditions under which a given strategy of change will be selected and successfully implemented. Although we know from ecological and cultural theories, for example, that congregations may mine the tradition or create a new one, it is not clear under what conditions they will do so. Similarly, market theories alert us to investigate the entrance and impact of new competitors and suppliers into the market, but they do not specify how congregations decide to follow the practices of a "successful congregation" or decide that some entrepreneur's prescription for congregational growth or revitalization is relevant, legitimate, and applicable for their church.

Although my analysis of the processes of change at the different congregations relies on Roof's concepts, I address this concern about the general conditions that facilitate and constrain change by showing how the nature and degree of each congregation's embeddedness in particular institutional spheres (e.g., the local set of congregations or the denomination) and religious markets shape the way in which it defines and resolves the specific crises of meaning or membership it faces. Embeddedness in particular religious worlds enables and constrains congregations as they attempt to remake the tradition. A congregation's embeddedness in a given religious world provides it with new material and ideological resources and locates it in alternative religious and cultural codes or systems of meaning that may help the congregation redefine the tradition.[36] For example, congregations embedded within networks of evangelical church growth experts and nondenominational megachurches are exposed to worship practices and theological ideas that emphasize conversion. Conversion is not a core component of the Lutheran tradition in part because conversion is so closely aligned with broad cultural codes of individualism, pragmatism, consumerism, and experience that are not congruent with Lutheran theological priorities, which place God and the community of faith over the individual. But this embeddedness in the larger evangelical world allows Lutheran congregations to delegitimize at least part of the Lutheran tradition and replace it with elements from this alternative tradition.

I also argue that congregations are not free to change the tradition however they wish. They are constrained by the congregation's existing culture and the process of change itself. Each congregation in the study had a particular relationship to the tradition and expressed some commitment to retaining particular elements such as the liturgical order, the theological emphasis on grace, or the weekly ritual of Holy Communion. Leaders of the congregations tried to buffer these core elements from change, even as they discarded or altered other aspects of the tradition. Failure to buffer these core elements or respect the commitment to Lutheranism of key constituencies within the congregation often led to conflict. Finally, the process of change may limit the direction and degree of change. Changing a religious tradition also means that a congregation must change its "negotiated order"—its formal and informal rules, myths, and founding narratives, power arrangements, and operating practices—because the tradition is part of this order.[37] For example, the Lutheran tradition historically has combined Episcopal and congregational polities; which polity is emphasized in a congregation will determine who will be authorized to change the tradition (clergy or lay members). Because changing one element of the tradition often has unintended consequences, such as alienating powerful subgroups, the process takes on an experimental nature. Leaders implement one change, assess the congregation's response, and then try additional changes, reverse course, or slow or speed up the process, depending on the feedback they receive from members. In summary, the approach I develop emphasizes endogenous, rather than external, catalysts of change; the constructed nature of religious change; and the constraints placed on change by institutional embeddedness and the interactive processes surrounding change.

TRADITION, COMMUNITY, AND AUTHORITY

Ideally, traditions are intimately related to community and should exercise authority over members of the community. Traditions, especially religious ones, tie individuals to communities and guide action because they provide individuals with stories, beliefs, and assumptions about identity, belonging, and purpose that act as normative guides to action.[38] Voicing the prevalent view of tradition, Carroll notes that "traditions provide a genealogy, real or imagined, that connects individuals with ancestors, contemporaries and successors. . . . Because traditions connect us with larger narratives from the past in which we can locate ourselves, they also give us perspectives and precepts that guide our understanding and behavior in the present."[39]

However, the decline of specific denominational traditions and the ways in which traditions have become disembedded or disconnected from their original organizational carriers in the last fifty years suggest that the relationships among tradition, community, and authority needs to be reexamined. Under the regime of religious choice, both individuals and congregations now have access to a wide variety of religious traditions. In particular, congregations, as carriers of tradition, may feel pressure to piece together new traditions or at least improvise on the old in order to compete in a religious environment where few individuals possess strong ties to any one denominational tradition and where the shaping of religious identity and belonging is seen as a project of self-development.[40] The authority of traditions may be weakened in this environment of choice in several ways. First, if specific beliefs, rituals, or symbols are pulled out of the larger meaning system of the religious tradition and faith community that uphold them, individuals may lack the support and guidance of a knowledgeable community that understands the tradition. Similarly, traditions must be interpreted or placed within an interpretive system to be meaningful, and when they are disconnected from communities, they may become meaningless and thus easily discarded. Finally, faith communities are constituted by their past. They are "communities of memory," to use the term of Bellah and his colleagues,[41] that transmit and reenliven traditions as they tell the stories and enact the rituals of those traditions. Yet when communities borrow others' traditions and when individuals move in and out of different church bodies, they may have a looser sense of ownership of those traditions and hence a weaker imperative to preserve and transmit them. As a result, congregations may lose the ability to operate as communities of memory as their commitment to an inherited tradition diminishes.

Although there are strong environmental pressures weakening specific traditions, the process of altering or improvising on an inherited tradition may also weaken its authority and undermine the ability of congregations to constitute themselves as communities of memory. As I interviewed members and clergy and observed worship, Bible studies, and church council meetings within the nine Lutheran churches I studied, I began to hear and see how language, theology, and practices from non-Lutheran religious traditions were becoming commonplace in these organizations. In particular, several congregations were adopting ideas and practices from the broader pan-Protestant tradition in the United States that understands the Christian life and the purpose of church very differently from "traditional" Lutheranism.

One prominent strain of Protestantism within the United States is grounded in revivalism and stresses individual conversion and the ongoing effort of individuals to lead lives of moral purity. It is a religion that stresses emotion over intellect, the authority of personal experience over the authority of the institutionalized church with its doctrines and creeds, and the practical application of faith in all arenas of social life.[42] This is the type of Protestantism that gave birth to American evangelicalism and Pentecostalism, as well as Baptist and nondenominational church bodies, and that has heavily influenced Presbyterianism and Methodism. Hart labels this revivalist Protestantism "Pietism" and summarizes its legacy in the following way:

> Clergy, creeds, rituals, and church order did not matter since they did not affect the heart noticeably. Instead, what mattered were preachers who could convict sinners of their wrongful ways and lead them to conversion, converts who studied the Bible for daily guidance, and Christians who led personal lives that were obviously different from those who had not experienced conversion. Going to church and participating in public worship, to be sure, were fine activities and should not be neglected. But these acts of devotion had no real bearing on one's personal salvation. Like a vitamin, the institutional church was merely supplemental.[43]

Conversely, American Lutheranism, part of what Hart calls "Confessionalism," has stressed the intellect and individuals' subscription to doctrines and creeds.[44] The Christian life was understood, not in terms of individual conversion and devotion, but in terms of corporate worship and education in which the individual slowly grows to a deeper understanding of the faith and is guided by a professional clergy. Hart notes: "For confessional Lutherans, the walk of church members was tied to the minister's acts of declaring corporate forgiveness and in administering the sacraments. Lutheran creeds defined the significance of these rites and participation in them was at the core of Lutheran identity."[45]

The attempts of congregations in this study to graft pietism onto Lutheran confessionalism provide a unique opportunity to investigate the consequences of religious change, especially how these attempts affect the nature of religious authority and community. Are congregations that adopt pietism's pragmatic orientation to tradition and religious life forced to abandon many of the ritual practices and meaning systems that have been central to Lutheran identity? Can tradition and doctrine continue to function as sources of religious authority when the primary source for congregational change is a tradition that eschews doctrine and denominationalism in favor of individual experience? Does the shift away from confessionalism toward pietism help congregations create new or rerooted communities of memory or does it lead toward the creation of communities of interest?[46]

This study looks at how nine congregations manage the tension between the two meta-Protestant traditions of pietism and confessionalism as they attempt to make the Lutheran tradition relevant and meaningful to members and nonmembers alike. It pays special attention to the relationship between form and content because many of these congregations struggle to maintain some aspects of Lutheranism's content but allow it to be expressed in different cultural forms. I am interested in exploring how the essential or native characteristics of a tradition—the theological, hermeneutical, and spiritual practices that provide identity and worldview—can be retained if a congregation relies on new or imported ritual and symbolic forms to convey meaning. Are cultural forms merely vehicles that carry religious information, or do they contain meaning themselves that intrinsically limits what religious content can be transmitted? If cultural forms are more than vehicles, then it will be important to attend to the ways in which the form and content both play a role in the transformation of tradition.[47]

However, this book is not just about the Lutheran tradition or how several West Coast congregations struggle to redefine and rediscover their heritage. The particular cases offer a window into larger sociological questions about solidarity, order, and the nature of community in a postmodern, posttraditional world. Congregations are one of the few remaining social institutions that connect individuals to larger narratives about origins, identities, and value commitments. They provide individuals and groups with a moral language and ethic that may inform everything from citizenship to child raising. In a world in which identities are plastic, stable employment is elusive, and civic associations are in decline, religious traditions offer individuals a stable mooring point. One of the most common reasons against changing the tradition that I heard from my interviewees was that they wanted church to be the one place in their world that would not change.

Yet the Lutheran tradition is being transformed and in some cases abandoned at the congregations in this study, and in the final chapter I discuss the larger social consequences of these changes. What holds a community together when the religious tradition that is embraced, whether nondenominational evangelicalism or an eclectic spirituality, emphasizes expressive individualism over collectivism, choice over an inherited history, emotional experience over time-honored doctrine and ritual? Does the move toward evangelicalism, on the one hand, or a common spiritual-quest culture, on the other, provide the once-insular Lutherans with the grounds of solidarity with larger religious groups in the United States? How can a congregation constitute itself as a community of memory or ground its members in a unique moral language if the tradition is lost or diminished? Ultimately, this book is a Durkheimian-inspired investigation into the possible ways that religious tradition can provide the basis for solidarity and meaning in a social environment where tradition is less able to bind individuals into a single moral community.

PLAN OF THE BOOK

The book is organized around the central themes of religious and cultural change. In chapter 2, I discuss my understanding of tradition and provide an overview of the Lutheran tradition. I also describe the nine California congregations, their context, and the ways in which each is attempting to transform or revitalize the Lutheran tradition. Chapters 3, 4, and 5 explain the catalysts and processes of change. I draw on and critique cultural, ecological, and market explanations while offering a constructivist and interactionist account of the causes of these congregations' efforts at retraditioning. In these chapters I develop the argument about how pietism, religious choice, and the larger cultural forces of American pragmatism and consumerism shape religious change at the nine congregations. In chapter 3, I discuss how several congregations use the model of the megachurch and the ideas from the church growth movement to construct hypothetical or fictional crises of membership for their congregations. In chapter 4, I identify several strategies that congregations employed to reframe or reorient the Lutheran tradition and that pushed them in the direction of liberal Protestantism and the religious-quest culture described by Roof and, surprisingly, toward a form of liberal sectarianism.[48] In chapter 5, I explore how two congregations in particular adopted the worship practices and theological ideas of evangelicalism. I show that, while both tried to integrate evangelicalism into Lutheranism, they became locked unwittingly into the theologies/ideologies and practices of the alternative tradition from which they borrowed.

In chapter 6, I examine the outcomes of the various efforts to alter, redefine, or reclaim the Lutheran tradition. To explore the relationships among authority, congregational cultures, and tradition, I use a series of case studies in which the process of change results in either conflict, compromise, or consensus. Specifically, I develop an explanation that combines the concept of articulation with interactionist ideas about the negotiated order and definitions of the situation to show how different configurations of organizational conditions led to different outcomes. This chapter also returns to the book's larger theme of exploring how some of the key shifts in American religion and forces within the broader culture are implicated in efforts to remake religious traditions.

The final chapter explores the connections among the process of transforming a religious tradition and several broader issues in American religious and public life: individualism and privatization, consumerism and pragmatism, and the continuing search for community. The first section of chapter 7 explores how changes to tradition in the San Francisco Bay Area congregations fit within the larger story of the restructuring of American Protestantism. By shifting attention to the organizational level, I offer a new chapter in the restructuring story that shows how the macroshifts in affiliation and religiosity are affecting congregations within one mainline Protestant denomination. I argue that religious restructuring in the United States is not only about shifts in affiliation or attendance but also about the power of both evangelicalism and seeker spirituality to remake mainline Protestantism in their own images. The second section of the final chapter looks at the question "Does changing the tradition impact the nature of community in the congregations? And if so, does it strengthen or weaken community?" I discuss how the changes to the Lutheran tradition create barriers to maintaining the congregations as communities of memory. The chapter ends with a discussion of the ways in which this study challenges and builds on existing explanations of change that are dominant in cultural and religious sociology.

In the following pages, I have tried faithfully to tell the congregations' stories as I heard them from members, knowing that my lenses as sociologist, outsider, and lapsed Lutheran shaped how I heard and interpreted those stories.[49] As suggested by the brief chapter summaries, I have not organized the book to tell each congregation's particular story, but instead I have used the interview and observational data to tell a more general story about cultural and organizational change and provide a more detailed account of how larger changes in American religion play out in several congregations of one denomination in one specific region of the United States. Hawaiian-shirted clergy making jokes about the Lutheran hymnal while they rely on the language of evangelicalism in their sermons; African rhythms juxtaposed to Luther's "Freedom of a Christian" at an ordination service; seeker services that rely on rock-and-roll bands belting out the latest praise music song—these are not idiosyncratic events but patterned responses of congregations that tell the next chapter in the ongoing story about the restructuring of American religion. The book now turns to the telling of this story.

Chapter 2

THE TROUBLE
WITH TRADITION

"SO, IN WHAT WAYS would you say that Faith Lutheran Church is a Lutheran church?" I posed this pointed question to John Lincoln, the congregation's senior pastor, in hopes of finally getting an answer to a question that had been puzzling me. I had been attending worship, new-member classes, and a men's Bible study for several weeks, but I was still having trouble connecting the congregation with the Lutheran tradition. I kept hearing members talking about being born again and having a personal relationship with Jesus—idioms more commonly used by evangelicals, not Lutherans. Bible studies and small groups relied almost exclusively on materials from Willow Creek Community Church, one of the first nondenominational megachurches in the United States.[1] Two of the three Sunday morning worship services used rock and roll and praise music rather than organ music and hymns from the Reformation.

We sat at a table in Pastor Lincoln's office and talked for nearly two hours about his congregation, the church growth movement and evangelicalism, the state of American Lutheranism, surfing, music videos, and sports cars. Many of his comments revealed the struggle of a congregation trying to preserve the essentials of the Lutheran tradition while searching for a language, style of worship, and theology that transcend Lutheranism and resonate with an increasing number of members and potential members for whom the Lutheran tradition is inaccessible or irrelevant. Lincoln offered the following answer to my initial question:

"I think the centerpiece of our theology is the Lutheran understanding of *simul justus et peccator* [i.e., simultaneously saint and sinner]. I think it's the ready admission [*pause*] that I am born again, filled with the spirit, perfectly sinful. I'm all that stuff at once. And it's just easier to live one or the other; it's easier to just say, 'I'm a flake' or 'I'm a sinner.' But to come to terms with 'No, I'm a mix of all this stuff.' And that absolutely is one of the bedrock pieces for why I'm a Lutheran Christian. And I think that's where the community is. I think that's where the people we're trying to reach are. They either think too much of themselves or think too little of themselves. They're always in that place. And to try and help them find a 'Tao'—to find a middle. And that dialectic tension, that's the paradox that Jesus brings—that's my theological perspective right there: Law and Gospel. And again as a Lutheran I have to say that's us. This is precisely us."

I followed this up by asking him for more information about the church's Lutheran identity: "Okay, but now help me understand why that theological message and language are not the first things I hear when I attend a Bible study or participate in worship at your church. I hear more members talking in the language of American evangelicalism than traditional Lutheranism, and worship doesn't follow the structure and practices set out in *The Lutheran Book of Worship*."

He responded, "I don't want to dismiss the born-again experience as illegitimate. At Faith, we want to encourage the person to explore what that experience means and to go deeper. They may not have a language except this born-again stuff. I disagree with evangelicals who see born again as the sine qua non event. Each day I must be born again as I struggle with the condition of sin. We Lutherans have driven thousands of people away from Lutheranism and into evangelical and fundamentalist churches because we have rejected the born-again experience and language out of hand. Let me just say this: if Faith or any of our other congregations are going to start to enlarge the discussion of how do we bring not only unchurched but unbelieving people into the church, then we have to figure out how to maintain the culture of the church in light of these people who are coming in who say, 'What does being Lutheran matter?' Last year for the first time we really saw a third of those 151 new members come from nowhere. And we're seeing it even more in this last new-member class and the one that starts up this Sunday. People are literally coming to us with no church background. That's going to change the culture of this place almost whether we like it or not. As those kinds of people come to church, the church has got to shift. Why should we teach everybody the green book [i.e., *The Lutheran Book of Worship*]? That's completely ludicrous to me anymore."

"Well, are you still trying to teach them the historic traditions of the Lutheran church in some way?" I asked.

"Sure. We do the confession and forgiveness of sins—that kind of thing. But this particular form being absolutely the only way to do it—that's gone."

"When we first spoke about the possibility of Faith's participation in the study, you mentioned that you were trying to change the form and not the content of Lutheranism—is that what I hear in your approach to the tradition?"

"I think that's true. I think we have to be willing to experiment on the form side. And we're not advocating throwing babies out with bathwater. But the content has got to continually be repackaged—and particularly as we move into the postmodern age. We have tried to learn some of the best stuff we could from church growth, to be as seeker—consumer-friendly—as possible. OK? But we're not trying to become Willow Creek. We follow Willow Creek's model for our Sunday school, support Young Life, and use Alpha Bible Studies. When I talked about that at a leadership conference last year, three ELCA staffers came up to me and said, 'You know that's not Lutheran?'"

"How did you respond?"

"I said, 'What you mean is that they're not Lutheran by origin. In other words—Alpha is Church of England, Young Life is whatever it is, and I would probably argue that it's Presbyterian, and of course Promised Land [i.e., a Sunday School program] is Willow Creek. So because these things did not originate with us—and that's the old Lutheran mentality, if we don't own it and control it, it's not Lutheran. It's no wonder that 95 percent of our congregations are in decline or plateaued. Most of our leaders don't have a clue how to grow a church."

This conversation highlights one congregation's relationship to the Lutheran tradition and identifies several tensions most of the congregations in the study experience as they attempt to preserve or alter their inherited tradition. First, there is the struggle in every congregation to identify what exactly Lutheranism is and what the core or essential elements of the tradition are. For some members of a congregation, the tradition includes only those elements whose lineage can be traced back to the Reformation, while others see the tradition as a set of immigrant practices (like lutefisk suppers) that are unwelcome and irrelevant. Pastor Lincoln speaks about the congregation's commitment to a Lutheran understanding of sin and forgiveness, while at the same time he identifies several elements of the tradition that are nonessential and hence dispensable: liturgical and ritual forms, use of the official hymnal, the theological language of Lutheranism. Second, he identifies the problem of how to use the tradition in a congregation that includes members to whom the tradition "doesn't matter" as well as members who wish to pass along the tradition, unaltered, to their children and grandchildren. Third, in his discussion of church growth, Pastor Lincoln underscores the tension within the denomination and in many congregations about the legitimacy of using religious practices, ideas, and resources from non-Lutheran sources.

My conversation with Pastor Lincoln first alerted me to a variety of troubles Lutherans seem to have with tradition. Members of the nine congregations in the study define "tradition" differently and wish to use it in divergent ways. Within most congregations there are members for whom the inherited tradition is inaccessible or meaningless, while for others, the tradition carries great authority and it is vital that it be preserved and transmitted intact. In short, I began to see that the tensions within congregations over tradition were grounded in questions (often unarticulated) about authority, legitimacy, relevance, and ultimately power—power to define what the tradition is and is not. I also began to ask myself and members of congregations what may have triggered the troubles Lutherans experience with their tradition.

The answer to that question can be approached by a closer investigation of three contexts: the broader socioreligious context, in which religious traditions appear to lack authority, relevance, or stable institutional mooring due to the primacy of a consumerist ethic; the history of American Lutheranism, in which the tradition has always been malleable; and the specific context of the irreligious western United States. That investigation, as discussed below, identified a more central theoretical issue that animates my analysis of religious change in the San Francisco Bay Area congregations: namely, religious traditions are in a constant state of change, and our existing explanations of the change process need to be retooled to help us grapple with the normalcy of change.

TRADITION IN A POSTTRADITIONAL WORLD

Tradition is intrinsically problematic. That is because tradition is not simply ideas and practices passed down from the past to the present in which the form and meaning of a tradition are locked into place. Instead, change is a built-in feature of tradition. In his classic text *Tradition,* Edward Shils argues that traditions are "constellations of symbols, clusters of images received and modified. They change in the process of transmission as interpretations are made of the tradition presented; they change also while they are in the possession of their recipients. . . . As a temporal chain, a tradition is a sequence of variations on received and transmitted themes."[2]

This suggests that tradition has two faces, or two temporal dimensions. One face looks to the past and views religious tradition as a set of religious beliefs, doctrines, values, worship practices (e.g., rituals, liturgies, hymns), and educational and decision-making practices that are passed down historically and stored in a denomination's or congregation's collective memory. This understanding of tradition emphasizes its archival nature. Understood as an archive, tradition is a repository of symbolic forms and practices that individuals and groups selectively access in order to understand what it means to be and how to act as a member of a particular religious organization. Carroll calls this "tradittium" or the "core deposits of the collective memory." The second face of tradition looks to the present and refers to the current religious activities and vehicles of expression in use by a given religious group. Carroll labels this dimension of tradition "tradittio"—the adaptations on the core made by successive generations.[3]

Carroll notes that the balance between archive and activity, tradittium and tradittio, has been weakened in a posttraditional world. Whereas we once wore tradition much as we wear our own skins, today we tend to wear tradition like clothes. And we are quite willing to change clothes to conform to the latest fad or express ourselves. Such an approach to tradition creates problems of preservation, transmission, and meaning. When activity is emphasized at the expense of archive, congregations may remake the tradition to such an extent that it no longer resembles the original tradition and, in doing so, alienate life-long members for whom the historic tradition grounds their identity and sense of religious belonging. On the other hand, when too much attention is placed on the archival face of tradition, religious communities run the risk of turning it into a dead relic and thus making the religion inaccessible or inhospitable to people who did not grow up in the tradition. Balancing archive and activity has always been a tricky undertaking; American Protestantism has always struggled to maintain an authentic self-identity and boundaries while at the same time making itself relevant and open to outsiders and the society.[4] Accomplishing this task in a posttraditional world becomes difficult because religious traditions seem as ephemeral as the latest fashion trend.

To say that we live in a posttraditional world is not to imply, however, that tradition at some point in the distant past was important and is now dead. Instead, "posttraditional" refers to the situation in late modernity in which traditions have become disembedded or unmoored from their institutional context and in which individuals locate moral authority in the self and not in the tradition or the organizations that bear them.[5] Roof suggests that in late modernity, organizations' and individuals' hold on tradition weakens because "connections to the past and to overarching systems of belief and practice are fractured."[6] Tradition is now treated as a resource or commodity that religious individuals and organizations choose to use as they attempt to find or construct authentic selves and communities and then abandon when they no longer prove to be useful. Carroll contends that we are not "beyond tradition," but we have moved to a situation in which traditions remain central in religious life only because "we *choose* to follow them; we *choose* to acknowledge their importance; we *choose* to seek their guidance in the changed and changing contexts in which we live. And we often reinterpret and change them in the process."[7]

Carroll argues that religious traditions are only loosely anchored in their original institutional homes as people and congregations freely borrow one another's traditions. Once this happens, a tradition may be more easily altered and may not be securely reanchored in the American religious culture of choice. This creates the potential for the misarticulation between archive and activity. For example, at Zion Lutheran in San Jose, the congregation has been self-consciously adding practices and ideas from nondenominational bodies (much like Faith Lutheran has) while minimizing its Lutheran heritage. Comments of members collected in a survey identify the problem of the mis-fit between archive and activity. For some members, the problem is that the archive is not being accessed enough and activity overshadows archive: "I am concerned at what appears to be a push toward making the worship experience at Zion similar to the big nondenominational churches that have grown very large. If I wanted that type of environment, I would join one of those churches." Another member urged the church to not abandon the worship traditions of Lutheranism: "I have loved the Lutheran liturgy since I was old enough to sing. It is loaded with excellent biblical material, and as a believing Lutheran, I always want to see it available and promoted in my Lutheran church. The most powerful worship experiences I ever had are high-church worship with robes, sung liturgy, pipe organ, choirs, hand bells, trumpet fanfares, red hymnal, Reformation-style services." For these members the problem of articulation is one in which they cannot find the archive in the activity and thus experience worship as alien, meaningless, and non-Lutheran. Conversely, many other members of Zion say they find these older and allegedly more traditional worship practices boring and meaningless. For them, there is no problem when archive and activity do not fit very closely as long as activity overshadows archive. In other words, these members do not mind if the worship traditions in use do not rely on or clearly reflect elements from the Lutheran tradition.

The articulation problem is not the only challenge to tradition in a posttraditional world. Religious communities also face a problem with the continuity of tradition, especially when the archive is not regularly accessed. In the seeker-sensitive, growth-oriented, religious-quest culture of the turn of the century, tradition becomes the object of continuous revision, not always for the sake of preserving and transmitting the tradition (albeit in some altered form) but in order to create new possibilities for encountering the sacred or constructing a spiritual self. In *Spiritual Marketplace,* Roof claims that contemporary religiosity in the United States is characterized by a restless and deliberate search for religious identity, meaning, and belonging in which individuals "cobble together a religious world from images, symbols, moral codes, and doctrines."[8] Under the conditions of religious bricolage, it becomes difficult for a congregation to maintain strong ties to their historic tradition as it adds on and sometimes replaces older beliefs and practices with those from different traditions or redefines core theological concepts (such as sin) in the language of psychology.[9] The continuity problem arises when too many elements or the essential elements of the inherited tradition are abandoned, altered, or unrecognizable. Shils notes that, even though a given tradition will change, "its essential elements persist in combination with other elements which change, but what makes it a tradition is that what are thought to be the essential elements are recognizable by an external observer as being approximately identical at successive steps or acts of transmission or possession."[10]

So if Tradition A is transformed into Tradition B or Tradition B/A, is it still the same tradition? In other words, is a tradition Lutheran simply because a group that calls itself Lutheran follows that tradition, or must there be some continuity with the elements of the Lutheran past in order to remain within the denominational fold? If the latter, how many elements must continue and which ones? This became a central question at several congregations in the study, and it fueled a serious conflict at one congregation. Three young pastors at Good Shepherd Lutheran began to change the liturgy and the theological language they used in sermons. They eliminated certain time-honored elements of the Lutheran order of worship such as the recitation of the Apostles' Creed, switched to gender-neutral terms for God, and abandoned Lutheranism's historic theological language of sin, atonement, and justification. They also abandoned any pretext of interpreting the Bible literally and spoke publicly about their symbolic interpretation of Jesus' miracles and resurrection from death.

Many members (perhaps as many as 20 percent) believe that the church is no longer practicing Lutheranism; the new practices were unrecognizable to them as Lutheran. One woman who left the church over these changes rebuked the clergy in her resignation letter: "Martin Luther would not be as offended that you used his name in this church's name as he would be incensed at your use of 'Christian' in a place where you feel the need to curtail the worship of the Trinity in order to draw people. Your result is a kind of Unitarian church with an emphasis on good works. Any service organization or club could meet the same objective." Another member concerned about changes in worship summarized the problem as a switch to Unitarianism during our interview: "You know, the pastor of worship talks about the love of god, the mercy of god and light too. Which kind of, you know, it kind of raises my hackles a little bit because it smacks a little of [pause] how Unitarians talk and all. And he hardly ever mentions Jesus and the forgiveness of sin. We don't hear about sin. No. 'Sin' is a bad word." Similarly, at a congregational meeting organized to defuse the ongoing conflict over changes implemented by the pastors, one member complained, "This congregation would never look to a Unitarian seminary or university to call a pastor. A Lutheran church wouldn't do that, but in essence that is what we've done. Pastor Curt's beliefs are closer to Unitarianism than to Luther and Lutheranism."

As suggested in the example from Good Shepherd Lutheran, a third problem of tradition in a posttraditional world concerns how it operates. Thompson suggests that tradition historically has served four important functions. First, it has a hermeneutic function insofar as tradition provides an interpretive framework that individuals and groups use to understand their social world. Second, the assumptions, beliefs, and patterns of action within a given tradition serve as a template to guide action in the present day. He notes that "material handed down from the past can serve as a normative guide in the sense that certain practices are *routinized*—that is, things are done as a matter of routine, with relatively little reflection on why they are done in that way—. . . and in the sense that certain practices can be grounded or justified by reference to tradition."[11] Third, tradition offers legitimacy for and support of the exercise of power and authority. Finally, tradition provides raw materials (i.e., beliefs, values, and stories) out of which individuals and collectivities form identities and a sense of belonging.

However, in a posttraditional world, tradition often fails to operate fully in these four ways. Most apparently, the legitimation and normative functions have weakened as modern or postmodern societies ground authority in the self or in expertise rather than in tradition.[12] Once the authority and legitimacy of a tradition become questioned or contested, it is less able to provide identity or a guide for action.[13] It is difficult to ground one's individual or collective identity in the stories of a tradition when they cease to be passed down, or when the stories change substantially as congregations and individuals try out, add on, and experiment with traditions from different strands of Christianity. This struggle is evident at Good Shepherd Lutheran. For some members the Lutheran tradition is seen as providing the norms that should govern congregational life, and it provides them with a sense of their identity as a particular type of Christian. Yet for the clergy and seemingly many other members of this one-thousand-member congregation, the Lutheran tradition is not considered authoritative, nor do they believe that the church's theology or ritual practices should necessarily conform to that which has been passed down from previous generations of Lutherans.

In general, the data from the nine San Francisco Bay Area congregations suggest that, in addition, the identity and interpretive functions of tradition also are in decline. Many members of these congregations self-identify as "Christian" and deliberately avoid identifying as "Lutheran."[14] Among the informants who self-identify as "Lutheran," most are unable to speak about how Lutheran theology, ritual practices, history, or ethics shape their self-understanding or provide a lens through which they make sense of the world. Even those who claim to be the true preservers of the Lutheran tradition often possess limited knowledge about the contents of the tradition. For example, the self-proclaimed "traditionalists" at Good Shepherd routinely cited *The Book of Concord* or the Augsburg Confession to support their charges of heresy against one of the ministers, yet they never quoted from those documents, cited the chapter and article, or showed any evidence that they were familiar with the contents of those documents.

Several scholars claim that "lived tradition" (tradition-as-activity) refers to a willingness to explore the tradition, argue with it, and mine it to make it one's own.[15] Following McIntyre, Bass argues that a congregation takes the archival material of a tradition and "extends the tradition itself [by] adding unfamiliar combinations of people and practices to its embodiment in that place."[16] In the process of extending and exploring a tradition, congregations and individuals reclaim or discover their religious identity and determine which practices will guide their community. However, this understanding of religious tradition and its ability to confer identity, to provide the means to make sense of the world religiously, and to direct actions assumes that individuals and congregations are both willing and able to argue with their inherited tradition. To what extent does tradition ground identity when individuals and congregations are uninterested or unwilling to engage the inherited tradition in conversation, let alone intentionally claim much of it as their own? Several congregations I study are wrestling with this question, and, as the Good Shepherd interviews suggest, this question creates the possibility for conflict.

Bass correctly points out that conflict is always possible because participating in a tradition or engaging in retraditioning compels members of congregations to argue about "the very goods the tradition pursues" and because they "will encounter some elements that disturb its [i.e., the congregation's] localism and particularity."[17] Some of the congregations in this study are fighting to determine if the "goods" of the Lutheran tradition are worth preserving or even serving as a point of departure as the congregations reconstitute their lived tradition. Others struggle over the legitimacy of borrowing from other traditions and deciding which traditions—Roman Catholic, evangelical, nondenominational, or liberal Protestantism—are the legitimate ones from which to borrow. And all of them experience some degree of conflict over the degree to which the community will hold itself accountable to the tradition or traditions to which it is aligned. Yet for Lutherans in the United States conflict over or about the tradition has been a normal part of denominational life since the 1800s.

THE PLASTICITY OF THE LUTHERAN TRADITION

The Lutheran tradition in the United States has been marked by malleability, diversity, and conflict. Much of the history of American Lutheranism has been a struggle to define the content of the tradition and make it authoritative for all the various ethnic groups that identify as Lutheran. It is a history of foundings, schisms, and mergers as different Lutheran church bodies tried to steer a course between the lure of Americanization and the duty of preserving their Northern European roots. Current struggles to transform the tradition have a lineage that can be traced back directly to the mid-nineteenth-century fight to support or resist a thoroughly Americanized Lutheranism (i.e., a brand of Lutheranism that adopted the theology of conversion and perfectionism from revivalism and more closely resembled American Baptist and Methodist theologies than Old World Lutheranism) and indirectly to two strands of Lutheranism that came with the early colonists in the seventeenth and eighteenth centuries.

Both the immigrant history of American Lutheranism and the structure of Lutheranism itself have made it difficult to speak of a pure or unified Lutheran tradition. Between 1637 and 1790, small numbers of German, Swedish, and Dutch settlers established a handful of Lutheran churches and institutions in the colonies. At the founding of the United States, there were only 120,000 Lutherans in a population of 2.8 million. However, the waves of immigration in the nineteenth and early twentieth centuries brought over 6 million Germans and 2 million Scandinavians to the States.[18] Each of these groups brought different pieties, forms of worship, and theological orientations that made it impossible to ensure denominational unity and uniformity. Moreover, many of the immigrant groups formed their own, ethnically homogeneous governing bodies (called synods), each with its own understanding of what constituted true Lutheranism. Between 1840 and 1875 fifty-eight different synods were established, often the result of inter- and intra-Lutheran disagreements over worship practices, the authority of the Lutheran tradition, and polity.[19] Throughout much of the nineteenth century, Lutherans fought over everything from the use of revival practices and hymns in worship to arcane interpretations of doctrines regarding baptism and the Lord's Supper, millennialism and predestination, the authority of scripture and the office of ministry. These fights over doctrine and worship were framed by a larger struggle about the legitimacy and necessity of Americanizing the tradition.

Lutherans' problems with their tradition have been exacerbated by the polity and history of the denomination. The sixteenth-century reformer Martin Luther did not set out to establish Protestantism, and despite his many theological treatises, sermons, and letters, he did not leave written instructions defining the new tradition. Luther's works, thus, have been used to support conflicting positions about what belongs in the tradition and how the various elements should be preserved and transmitted. Moreover, Luther appropriated music, ideas, and images from various sources, including popular culture of the sixteenth century, and this fact is often cited to justify contemporary adaptations of the tradition.

A number of twentieth-century Lutheran historians claim that there never has been one pure tradition and suggest that the Lutheran tradition has few essential elements: recognition of the authority of the sixteenth-century confessional documents to guide church life, commitment to a small set of theological principles (e.g., justification by grace through faith), and agreement to follow the principle of *adiaphora* (a Greek term referring to rites and practices that are neither commanded nor forbidden by the Bible), which allows for diversity in many matters of church governance and worship.[20] Article VII of the Augsburg Confession, one of Lutheranism's foundational documents, established the *adiaphora* principle and thus created the framework for a malleable and minimalist tradition when it declared, "The Church is the congregation of saints, in which the Gospel is preached and the sacraments administered. And to the unity of the Church it is enough to agree concerning the Gospel and the sacraments. But it is not necessary that the ceremonies or other human observances should be everywhere alike."[21] Klein describes the effect of this confessional principle for American Lutheranism in the following way: "Lutherans in every American generation, bereft of state churches rooted in Christendom, have to engage in massive extrapolation to create an order for themselves in which to accomplish their ministry."[22] Similarly, Jordahl argues that Lutherans, like followers of other nonindigenous types of Christianity in the United States, have always been pragmatic adoptionists.[23] They have altered or abandoned pieces of the received tradition to make Lutheranism relevant to the American context despite claims by some Lutheran groups that they alone have faithfully preserved the core elements of the tradition.

Despite ethnocultural differences and the apparent plasticity of the tradition, American Lutheranism gradually came generally to share a common set of ritual practices and theological commitments. From the mid-1870s through the late 1980s, Lutherans worked diligently to overcome differences in doctrine and worship practices to create a more uniform and unified Lutheranism. One result of these efforts was the creation of an American Lutheran tradition, or at the least the identification of the core of the Lutheran archive.

CREATING THE AMERICAN LUTHERAN TRADITION

Over the course of three hundred years, there has been considerable difference of opinion about what belongs in the Lutheran archive and how important that tradition is in the American context. Internecine battles have raged over how to interpret and apply the confessional documents and how closely to follow the inherited liturgical form, theological themes, and ritual practices within the archive. The struggle has been over exactly what belongs in the core, what belongs in the periphery, and what practices, beliefs, and ideas do not belong in the archive.

American Lutherans began to disagree about the content and authority of the tradition almost as soon as they arrived in the seventeenth century. Lutherans who settled during the colonial period (primarily Germans, Swedes, and Dutch) were split into two camps that mirrored the divisions in Europe: "orthodoxists" adhered to a strict interpretation and application of the Lutheran confessional documents and emphasized the importance of correct doctrine, and "pietists" held to a looser interpretation and use of these documents in church life and stressed instead heartfelt belief in the embodiment of those beliefs in acts of charity, service, and reform. This early split prefigured later conflict among three groups of Lutherans: those seeking to Americanize and thus fundamentally to rewrite the tradition; those wishing to preserve the pure tradition; and those seeking to hold on to some elements within the archive while making a space for Lutheranism within the dominant revivalistic form of Protestantism. It also fueled early efforts to downplay both the structure and the content of worship carried over from sixteenth- and seventeenth-century Europe and minimize a narrowly defined Lutheran theological sensibility in favor of the emergent form of revivalistic and individualistic Protestantism taking root in the new land.

Pietists quickly became the dominant group in the colonies largely due to the monies and clergy sent in support of the fledgling congregations from pietist centers in Germany and Sweden. German pietism sought to reform Lutheranism by giving greater importance to personal conversion and the process of growing more mature in one's faith (i.e., the process of sanctification), which was made evident in a life of missionary and benevolent service. What this meant for Lutheranism in America is a faith that de-emphasized doctrine in favor of ethics and emphasized the importance of Bible study and prayer over the corporate liturgical worship of the sixteenth and seventeenth centuries. These shifts freed Lutherans in the colonies to abandon European structures and practices and adopt those in use by other colonial Protestants that fit more closely with their understanding of Christianity.[24]

Throughout the eighteenth and into the nineteenth century, American Lutheran pietists reshaped Lutheranism in the image of the emergent form of Protestantism in the new nation. They embraced many of the innovations in worship and theology introduced by revivalists. The most visible changes in the tradition were seen in worship practices, as many Lutheran churches adopted the "frontier" tradition of revivalism. By adopting the frontier tradition, Lutherans redefined the purpose of worship and its organization. In this emergent American tradition, the purpose of worship was to bring about conversion by fomenting an intense emotional experience of a person's sin and need for God's forgiveness in order to lead a moral life and attain salvation. In practice, this meant a shift away from the Lutheran emphasis on the sacraments of baptism and the Lord's Supper toward greater emphasis on prayer and preaching. It also entailed a shift away from the corporate and intellectual nature of Lutheran worship toward an emphasis on individuals' emotional experiences.

Above all else, the frontier tradition was pragmatic. Its practitioners used any and all means in worship to bring about conversion and developed a basic order of worship. This order was very simple and consisted of three parts: a warm-up of singing hymns to touch the heart and raise excitement; followed by a sermon in which the preacher called for people to repent and convert; and concluding with an altar call, when participants came forward to the altar rail to pray for repentance or demonstrate the authenticity of their conversion. A variety of strategies, called "new measures," were developed during the Second Great Awakening (such as the protracted meeting and the "anxious bench") to win converts.[25] Lutherans increasingly adopted the worship form and strategies of revivalism during the antebellum period. Many churches abandoned or shortened the liturgical part of the service and adopted the generic model of prayer, song, and preaching since the Lutheran liturgical structure did not seem to promote conversion or personal spirituality as did the revivalistic format. Orthodoxists, later known as "confessionalists," opposed these changes, especially the adoption of revival techniques. Kuenning notes that most often they decried the betrayal of historical Lutheranism by pietists and berated them for their "capitulation to the ways of the Methodists and other Protestant revivalists."[26]

Pietists also altered the theology of American Lutheranism, and this especially drew the ire of Lutheran immigrants (German and Scandinavian) who began to arrive in large numbers during the 1830s and 1840s. These European Lutherans had experienced a revival of a different sort—a new self-consciousness of their Reformation roots—and carried it with them to America. This meant a renewed commitment to the theological principles and documents of the Reformation and the historic liturgies and worship practices of the sixteenth and seventeenth centuries. This group, the "confessionalists," was especially concerned that the Americanized Lutheran pietists had abandoned the core Reformation theology about sin, grace, and salvation. In its place, they argued, Pietists had adopted the doctrine of postmillennialism espoused by revivalism (i.e., a belief that humans could work gradually to improve living conditions on earth by promoting justice and peace, which would usher in the return and millennial reign of Jesus Christ) and the concomitant Arminian doctrine of human free agency, which claimed that individuals could become perfect by their choice to repent, convert, and live a sinless life.[27] As the number of confessional Lutherans increased during the 1850s, the pietist Lutherans (now in the minority) continued to press all Lutherans to unite in a form of Lutheranism that was closely aligned to the revival-based Protestantism of Methodism. In 1855 leaders of the Americanized pietists issued a document to clarify their position and redefine the core of the tradition. The controversy that followed effectively ended the dominance and legitimacy of the pietists and the wholesale process of Americanization.

The focus of the dispute became the Augsburg Confession and the degree to which it should set the norms for Lutheran belief and practice. Written by

Philipp Melanchthon, one of the leaders of the Protestant Reformation, in 1530, the Augsburg Confession contains eighteen articles of faith that lay out the basic Lutheran beliefs about God, Jesus Christ, human sin, salvation by God's grace, the sacraments of baptism and the Lord's Supper (which are the visible means of God's grace and forgiveness), and a basic organization for the church.[28] Since the Reformation, the Augsburg Confession had been the unifying document that defined Lutheran identity and set Lutherans apart from other Christians. And now the pietists had issued the American Recension of the Augsburg Confession, in which they argued that the original version of 1530 contained five errors, including the approval of the ceremonies of the Mass (i.e., the traditional structure and content of Lutheran worship) and the affirmation Jesus Christ's real presence in the bread and wine used in the sacrament of the Lord's Supper (revivalistic Protestantism argued for a symbolic presence and did not treat the ceremony as a sacrament; thus, it was no longer necessary for salvation). Thirty-three of the thirty-nine synods in the United States refused to accept the pietists' document, and many reaffirmed their commitment to the unaltered Augsburg Confession.[29]

This event shifted control of American Lutheranism and thus of the tradition to the confessionalists. The explicit attempt to make Lutheranism resemble the rest of American Protestantism ended and would not be renewed until after World War II. One commentator has offered the following analysis of confessional orthodoxy's triumph:

A more adequate explanation for the triumph of conservatism probably lies in the observation that Lutherans in America found themselves in a totally alien culture. The problems of survival and self-identity became intense on the frontier, where the forms of Protestantism that one encountered in the nineteenth century were overwhelmingly of a low church, revivalistic, decision-centered Evangelicalism that was coupled with a "methodist" ethic. The Lutherans had never before lived in a pluralistic society with a free church tradition dependent upon persuasion. The Lutherans therefore were faced with the problem of gathering together the scattered immigrants, largely uneducated in religion, and molding them into a cohesive and loyal group. And here, . . . the need for self-identity could be served by the highly articulate, precise, logical, and unambiguous orthodoxy of the seventeenth century. This orthodoxy gave easy answers and a system that could be taught for purposes of indoctrination and self-identification.[30]

Confessionalists moved quickly in the latter half of the nineteenth century to codify the tradition and push the pietistic Lutheranism to the periphery. The emergent tradition looked back to the theology and worship practices of sixteenth- and seventeenth-century European Lutheranism.[31] In 1855, several synods produced a German liturgy intended to "recapture confessional clarity and the responsive features of traditional Lutheran worship."[32] In 1888, several

Lutheran synods cooperated to produce a new hymnal, the *Common Service*, which became the standard hymnal used by nearly all American Lutherans and which has "provided the essential framework for Lutheran worship in America from 1888 to the present day."[33] Thus, by establishing a worship tradition grounded in models first produced by the sixteenth-century Lutheran reformers, American Lutherans were able to overcome the ethnocultural differences of American Lutheranism's many strands and the pressure to fit Lutheranism into the mold of revivalistic Protestantism, as suggested by the following comment:

> The *Common Service* struggled to give a common voice to disparate groups, but all hailing from Scandinavia and Germanic areas. The Germans might have sung rhythmic chorale settings of Luther et al., while the Swedes and Danes sang pious triple meter tunes, but the cultural content and cultural expressions were at least related by their North European origins. . . . The Protestant Episcopal Church in America and not a few Methodists taught them prayerbook piety and the hymns of Watts and the Wesleys. Still, despite anglicizing and accommodation, the official liturgical material of North American Lutherans clearly reflected its North European roots. This resulted in the stereotypical "organ/choir" settings of this common rite. The *LBW* [*The Lutheran Book of Worship*, published in 1978] merely continued the tradition.[34]

Similarly, the theological component of the tradition was reaffirmed after the 1855 controversy over Americanization. At the heart of the tradition is a set of theological documents collected in *The Book of Concord*. The most important documents include the Augsburg Confession, Luther's *Small Catechism*, and the three historic creeds of the Christian church (Apostles', Nicene, and Athanasian). Lutherans came to agree that membership in the denomination required formal adherence to the unaltered Augsburg Confession and the other confessional documents. These documents and commentaries on them provide the theological foundation for the Lutheran tradition, which includes a commitment to the following beliefs: justification by faith through grace; original sin and the existential human condition of being both saint and sinner; the priesthood of all believers; the call to respond to God's grace by acting as a "little Christ" to one's neighbor; and an understanding of the cross as God's entering human history to suffer for the sake of humanity. Perhaps the phrases "Word Alone" (to emphasize the primacy of the Bible), "Grace Alone" (to emphasize God's central act of saving sinful humanity through the death and resurrection of Jesus), and "Faith Alone" (the human response to God's forgiveness through acts of thanksgiving and service) best summarize the theological tradition of the Lutheran church.[35]

Even though the trend of the last 125 years of American Lutheran history has been toward establishing a more uniform and unifying tradition, differences still exist and internal debates have raged over worship, doctrine, and a host of issues in American religion that cut across denominational lines (e.g., fundamentalism and liberalism, inclusive language and gender roles, homosexuality, and the authority of the Bible).[36] Despite the confessional claim that unity on doctrine or beliefs allows for liturgical diversity, Lutherans have continued to fight over the meaning and the context of the tradition.[37] The "double debate" over the degree to which the form of worship defines Lutheran identity and about which forms are authentic and essential to the tradition that started during the colonial period continues today.[38] As we will see in the following chapters, Bay Area Lutheran congregations struggle with questions of self-identity and relevance in a postdenominational, secular world and respond by remaking and revitalizing the inherited tradition.

CALIFORNIA LUTHERANISMS IN THE IRRELIGIOUS WEST

"Things look sad around here. It is a wild, tough, and reckless life; everyone only wants to get rich quick. California is a veritable picture of hell. People of all nations are mixed together here, and most of them have no faith at all. . . . It will be a most difficult office . . . to establish a congregation here."[39] This commentary on the religious state of affairs during California's Gold Rush by a Lutheran minister seems to be as applicable today as it was in 1859. Historically, California and most of the western United States have been characterized as being less religious than the rest of the country. The 1890 census of religions found that the lowest rates of church attendance were in the western states and regions. At 23 percent, California's churchgoing rate was higher than rates in Colorado, Nevada, Nebraska, Oklahoma, Oregon, and Washington, but it was still quite low; one California minister noted that "there is a tacit conviction cherished by many that religion is not so important but that one can get along very well without it."[40] According to the 1950 census, church membership in California had climbed to 40.7 percent, but this was still 9 percent below the national average.[41] The 1990 National Survey of Religious Identification (NSRI) found that 13 percent of the state's residents reported having no religious affiliation (among the highest rates in the United States, and 5 percent higher than the national average), and the follow-up survey, the 2001 American Religious Identification Survey, found that the rate had climbed to 19 percent (which, again, is nearly 5 percent higher than the national average).[42]

A second key feature of religion in the western United States, and California in particular, is pluralism. Since the late nineteenth century, the Pacific Northwest and California have been hospitable environments for utopian communities, cults and new religious movements, evangelical Protestantism, and Roman Catholicism.[43] Yet no one religion has assumed numerical or cultural dominance in the West (except for Mormonism in Utah and in parts of the other Mountain West states). The denominations of the old mainline have struggled to establish congregations and keep the members they have.[44] Quinn notes that by 1940 less than one-third of the West Coast's Norwegian Lutherans remained Lutheran, and only 9 percent of Danish Lutherans remained Lutheran.[45] In 1962 there were 232,137 Lutherans in 310 congregations in California; by 2000 there were only 177,291 Lutherans in 479 congregations.[46] Currently, Roman Catholics are the largest religion in the state, but they represent less than one-third (32 percent) of California's religious population in the 2001 American Religious Identification Survey. The denominations within the old mainline represent only 10 percent of the state's religious population, down from 12.5 percent in 1990.[47] Lutherans have declined from 3.7 percent of the state's population in 1990 to 2 percent in 2001.

This struggle to establish and maintain congregations has been created, in part, by the distance of the western churches from the denominational centers in the Midwest and East Coast, in part by the dominance of religious diversity and irreligiosity, and in part by the strong culture of religious choice that flows from the religiously pluralistic and decentered context of the West. Kosmin and Lachman argue that historically people have moved west to escape the bonds of tradition and a lifestyle overly regulated by religion.[48] The process of migration has undermined religious affiliation and the maintenance of religious traditions because it severs ties to social networks and, for Lutherans, the ethnic cultures the embed people in religious organizations and a given tradition. Some historians argue that the geographic distance and pervasive individualism and pragmatism in the West have produced congregations less interested in following or reproducing the doctrine, theology, and ethics emanating from denominational centers and more interested in creating church life to fit the local context.[49]

The effect of the larger religious culture in the West has been to create contradictory pressures in congregations and denominations. The distance from the national religious centers and the emphasis on choice have freed congregational leaders and members from upholding "the historic traditions of doctrine and practice . . . that eastern centers have cared more to preserve" while also encouraging innovation and a spirit of entrepreneurship.[50] At the same time, the absence of sociocultural reinforcement for participation within a particular type of Christianity or identity as a particular type of Christian has pushed some congregations to create denominational enclaves of high and rigid commitment in which some ideal-typical version of the tradition is reproduced.[51]

This history of California Lutheranism follows the general patterns described above. Lutherans have faced a nearly continuous battle to establish congregations and hold on to members since the early missionary days in the 1850s. Although the denomination grew during World War II, when significant numbers of midwestern Lutherans migrated to California to participate in wartime industries, the period of growth was short—only until about 1965, when the larger decline of mainline Protestantism began. Minutes from the annual meetings of western Lutheran church bodies and interviews with former leaders of the churches that eventually merged to form the Evangelical Lutheran Church in America provide a glimpse into the rapid growth and decline of California Lutheranism.[52] For example, the South Pacific District of the American Lutheran Church (ALC) established, on average, thirteen new congregations each year between 1963 and 1967, but only three per year from 1967 through 1979. One former denominational leader claimed that membership grew at an annual rate of 10 percent during the late 1940s and the 1950s but then sharply declined in the late 1960s and the 1970s.[53] A former bishop of the South Pacific District summarized the twentieth-century history of California in the following way:

> So, you come out here, and of course, Lutheranism was practically—well, it wasn't non-existent, but I think in all of California at that time [1946] of the churches making up the present ALC, there were probably 50 congregations at the most in all of the Southwest. So we were very much in the minority. Lutheranism was not known well. But, of course, the things that made it possible to start a lot of missions at this point was that a lot of people were moving out here from the Midwest. Some of them had worked in defense plants during the war. Some of them had been stationed here during the war. And they came flocking back to California and later on to Arizona to work in these plants, to set up some new roots, establish homes. And a lot of them found their way into the churches.[54]

Lutheran congregations in California also felt the tension between innovation and reproduction. Many congregations simply reproduced the Lutheranism they brought with them from the Midwest and created Norwegian or German Lutheran enclaves. Often clergy were more interested in gathering up the diaspora than in opening the church up to the non-Lutherans and unchurched people who made up the majority of the state's population. A former missionary leader of the ALC claimed that in the postwar years, the Lutheran church was seen as a "foreign" church and often confused with Roman Catholicism because of its liturgical worship style. Another denominational official from the 1960s noted that the Lutheran church in the West too often reproduced the worship practices, theology, and church structures inherited from the Midwest and that, during the decline of the late 1960s and 1970s, the most committed, and often conservative (in the sense of preserving the tradition), Lutherans remained in the church.[55]

In the interviews I conducted with retired clergy who lived in the San Francisco Bay Area during the 1960s, 1970s and 1980s, I repeatedly heard accounts of two types of congregations: those that adapted the tradition to fit the informality and irreligiosity of California and those that tried to duplicate the midwestern church.[56] These clergy also reported that the Lutheran church has struggled in California because Lutheranism and even the general practice of going to church never were part of the region's culture, as both were in the Midwest, and because Lutherans failed to reach out beyond the narrow ethnic populations that the church had always served. Too often, they suggested, Lutheran congregations in California either hold on to the tradition so tightly that they become irrelevant to everyone but life-long Lutherans or adopt the traditions of other

Christian groups but in the process lose the strongest parts of their Lutheran heritage. One retired pastor wryly commented that the Lutheran church in the West is like Dagwood Bumstead, the cartoon character: "Dagwood is always late; always chasing a car, a bus, a train. And he never catches it. The church in the West is like that; always chasing the promised thing that will lead to growth but we never quite get it. At best, we get a pale imitation of the original program." In short, Lutheranism in California has been and remains a minority religion. Some congregations are nostalgic for the one golden period of growth and yearn to be Lutheran just as they once were, while other congregations remake themselves in the guise of other traditions in the hopes of growing, or just surviving. Most congregations are caught in a struggle to be both relevant to an irreligious audience and reproduce a religious tradition that creates barriers to being relevant.

THE LUTHERAN TRADITION IN BAY AREA CONGREGATIONS

The nine congregations in this study struggle to hold on to the tradition and to modify it. Several congregations are adding elements from evangelicalism as they attempt to make Lutheranism relevant in a religious market dominated by the revivalist tradition. A few are adding elements from liberal Protestantism and Eastern religions to meet the religious sensibilities of spiritual seekers. One is replicating the tradition closely and intentionally, much like the confessionalists of the nineteenth century. The urban congregations are trying to contextualize the tradition for a racial population that has not historically been Lutheran by adding music, theology, and programs more commonly found in the historic black churches.

However, the nine congregations face a difficult challenge in making the tradition relevant to Bay Area residents, even to Bay Area Lutherans, due to the demographics and religious culture of the region. The congregations are located in the most religiously pluralistic and the most irreligious area of California. Compared to Orange County and Los Angeles, the San Francisco Bay Area has more residents who report having no religious affiliation and fewer Christians.[57] Moreover, the Lutheran church in northern California has been losing members steadily—nearly 8 percent since 1994—which creates greater pressure to modify the tradition in order to grow.[58] Recent reports from the bishop of the Sierra Pacific Synod claim that about one-third of the congregations are in decline, one-third are stable, and one-third are growing. The largest congregation in the synod has 2,648 members, and the average church size is 347 members. I studied congregations in Oakland, the suburbs east of Oakland, and in the San Jose area (Silicon Valley). There are seven congregations in Oakland, with an average size of 136 members and with an average of 55 attending services on a given Sunday. In the seven contiguous suburbs east of Oakland, there are eight congregations,

Table 1. Profiles of Congregations

Congregation	Location	Size[a]	Race/Ethnicity	Church Model[b]	Theological/ Political Orientation	Relationship to Tradition[c]
Faith	East Bay	1,255	White	Evangelistic	Conservative	Weak
Good Shepherd	East Bay	787	White	Community	Conservative to liberal	Weak
Grace	East Bay	406	White	Activist	Liberal	Moderate
Emmanuel	Oakland	238	African American	Worship	Moderate to liberal	Strong
Christ	Oakland	78	Mixed	Worship/activist	Moderate to liberal	Moderate
St. Luke's	Oakland	189	White (14% nonwhite)	Worship/activist	Liberal	Strong
Zion	Silicon Valley	1,023	White	Evangelistic	Conservative	Weak
St. Peter's	Silicon Valley	1,142	White	Evangelistic	Conservative	Strong
Resurrection	Silicon Valley	547	White	Community/ worship	Moderate	Moderate

[a]"Size" refers to membership, not attendance.

[b]"Church model" refers to the patterned ways in which congregations answer the questions "Who are we?" and "How do we do things here?" See Penny Becker, *Congregations in Conflict* (London and New York: Cambridge University Press, 1999); and David A. Roozen, William McKinney, and Jackson W. Carroll, *Varieties of Religious Presence* (New York: Pilgrim Press, 1988).

[c]"Relationship to tradition" refers to the degree to which a congregation follows the tradition and sees its preservation as important.

with an average size of 452 and an average attendance of 172. In the Silicon Valley, the average size among the twenty-five congregations is 390 and the average attendance is 155. Table 1 provides an overview of several key organizational characteristics of the nine congregations that I studied.

The Oakland congregations are among the smallest in the region and state. They are the most racially and ethnically diverse congregations in the study. Most of the congregations in the study are aging and in decline. Nearly all suffered significant membership losses in the 1970s and 1980s as the white population moved east to the suburbs. The three study congregations in Oakland represent the diversity of the city's population and types of Lutheran congregations. Emmanuel Lutheran is an African American congregation that members call their extended family. It has 238 members, 95 percent of whom are African American, and it is not uncommon to find families with three and four generations in attendance on Sunday mornings. The church is located a few miles from downtown Oakland in an area that is marked by racial and ethnic diversity and poverty. Fifty percent of the population is African American. 26.6 percent is Asian, 12.6 percent is Hispanic, and 7 percent is white. The median household income in 1999 was $21,124, less than half that for the entire state.[59] Many of the church's members, especially the younger and more active members, live outside the neighborhood, some traveling longer than an hour to attend church, but that has not prevented the church's active involvement in the local community. The congregation hosts a charter school, houses a computer academy to train community residents in the basics of word processing and data entry, and provides health-screening services.

Emmanuel was founded as a black Missouri Synod church in 1929 but split from the synod in the early 1970s and joined the more socially and theologically liberal Association of Evangelical Lutheran Churches, and finally became part of the ELCA in 1987. Its members, largely middle-class professionals, are either lifelong Lutherans or switched from one of the historic black churches to Lutheranism as young adults. The church reached its peak in terms of membership, participation, and involvement in city politics under the leadership of a nationally known minister in the 1970s and 1980s. When he left in the early 1990s, the church rapidly lost members and never fully recovered. Members repeatedly reminded me that Emmanuel is "not a shoutin' church," and worship, while more emotive than most Lutheran services, is sedate in comparison to black Baptist or Pentecostal services. Emmanuel tries to contextualize the Lutheran tradition by integrating the call-and-response preaching style, gospel music and spirituals, and an emphasis on liberation theology commonly found in other, non-Lutheran black churches.

Christ Lutheran Church is located in the Oakland hills, a new merger of two small, aging churches, one white and liberal, the other predominantly African American and oriented to local community needs. During the merger process (which included the resignation of the pastor), the church lost members and now has only 78 members and averages 33 at worship services. The church is roughly

70 percent white and 30 percent African American and Asian, but it does not mirror the demographics of the neighborhood, which is 15 percent white, 60 percent African American, and 21 percent Hispanic and Asian. Most of the congregation's middle-aged and elderly members are lifelong Lutherans but are open to change. They gave the pastor who led them through the merger carte blanche to change the programs, worship service, and decision-making structures to help the church attract new members. Its current pastor is a young African American woman who has brought an Afrocentric perspective to worship and who uses the advice of church growth experts and her experience of faith-based organizing to develop outreach and community-service programs.

St. Luke's Lutheran, with 189 members, is the most ethnically homogeneous of the three Oakland congregations, as 86 percent of the congregation is white. It is also located in a neighborhood of Oakland that has a higher percentage of white residents (40 percent) than the neighborhoods of the other two churches. St. Luke's is unique insofar as it has an openly gay minister and is one of the few Lutheran congregations in the city that is a "Reconciled in Christ" congregation (this is the ELCA term for congregations that welcome gay, lesbian, bisexual, and transgendered persons). St. Luke's is the most visibly Lutheran church of the three. Worship follows one of the three denominational hymnals, and the church is becoming known for its excellent music program. New members are instructed in Lutheran theology; and preaching usually follows the Lutheran emphasis on grace, the freedom of the Christian, and one's identity given in baptism.

The congregations in the suburbs east of Oakland and Berkeley are larger, almost exclusively white, and rich in material and human resources compared to the churches in Oakland. Faith Lutheran is the largest of the three, with over 1,200 members. It is located in a suburb that is 80 percent white but has a growing Asian population (11 percent), and where the median household income (in 1999) is two to three times greater than the median household income for the Oakland congregations. Faith has grown steadily since its new pastor arrived in the mid-1990s, and while its members are primarily lifelong Lutherans, roughly one-third of new members in the past few years are coming from unchurched or non-Lutheran backgrounds. Since the 1980s, the church has drawn on the worship music and practices of evangelicalism, and in the 1990s, it slowly replaced much of the content and structure of Lutheran worship with that of evangelicalism. The church also has been using educational resources, Bible study guides, and governance models from non-Lutheran megachurches. At Faith, the language of born-again Christianity is commonly heard, and the theology expressed at Bible studies and from the pulpit mixes Lutheran understandings of sin and grace with a revivalist emphasis on conversion and the god of twelve-step programs.

Good Shepherd Lutheran, in the neighboring suburb, was about the same size as Faith when the study began, but by the end of the field period it had lost over five hundred members.[60] Like Faith, Good Shepherd is almost exclusively white

(98.7 percent) in a suburb that is nearly as white (84 percent of the population is white). It is also in an affluent community with a median household income of $101,555. The church has a historic identity as a "civic" church, providing a variety of services for the community, catering to families with children, and known as a good place to meet one's neighbors. Members also speak fondly and proudly about their high-quality music programs (shortly after I first visited the church, I was sent a tape that their choir had made in the 1980s). During the study period, this congregation actively fought over the tradition as the older members tried to defend a very doctrinally rigid, almost fundamentalist version of Lutheranism that was being replaced with a liberalized version. The church's pastors, with the support of many of its elected leaders and rank-and-file members, were replacing Lutheran theology, language, and worship practices with those from liberal Protestantism (e.g., a de-emphasis on sin and atonement, an emphasis on the life of Jesus rather than on his death and resurrection, and the addition of Buddhist language and prayer practices to worship).

With just over four hundred members, Grace Lutheran Church is the smallest of the three suburban congregations. Like its suburban counterparts, it is almost exclusively white (97.5 percent of the congregation) in a predominantly white and affluent neighborhood (74 percent White with a median household income of just over $142,000). Grace has many of the characteristics of liberal Protestant congregations: it has an active peace and justice ministry; it is a Reconciled in Christ congregation; its worship life and programs emphasize spirituality and incorporate practices from Zen Buddhism; its leaders are involved in the local interfaith organization; it supports a pastor who serves sister congregations in Latin America and Africa as part of the congregation's commitment to global Christianity; members are involved with Amnesty International and Bread for the World; they support a battered women's shelter, as well as homeless and feeding programs, host a PFLAG meeting,[61] and engage in AIDS justice advocacy.

Grace's Lutheran identity is visible in its public theology and organization of worship (e.g., a consistent message of God's grace, the Lutheran order of worship, and emphasis on the sacraments on Sunday morning), but it is a Lutheranism tempered by a commitment to a theology of liberation and an emphasis on various spiritual practices from Roman Catholicism, Anglicanism, Eastern Orthodoxy, and Buddhism. Many of its members self-identify as seekers or people who had dropped out of organized religion but found Grace's worship and theology to be welcoming for individuals who have been alienated from church, who have unanswered faith questions, or who hold progressive or liberal social and political views in a largely conservative community.

The last three congregations in the study are located in Santa Clara County, home of Silicon Valley. These congregations are more similar to the East Bay suburban parishes than to the Oakland churches insofar as one has an evangelical persona, like Faith Lutheran, one is more liberal and incorporates practices from Roman Catholicism, like Grace Lutheran, and one defends a more conservative form of Lutheranism, like the minority group at Good Shepherd.

Zion Lutheran Church is located at the northern end of Silicon Valley and has a membership of slightly over one thousand. The congregation is predominately white in an area becoming increasingly Asian (according to the 2000 census, nearly 45 percent of the population is Asian). Many members work in the high-tech industry and in some ways replicate the engineering culture of the industry at church. It had two new, young (thirty-something) pastors at the start of the field period, both of whom self-identified as evangelicals, and the church has a mix of like-minded evangelistic members, lifelong Lutherans, and former Roman Catholics. It has a historic identity as a mission church more interested in sharing the Christian faith with nonbelieving residents of the community, but that identity, according to the church's leaders, is in abeyance, and they are trying to revive it. Like Faith Lutheran, it freely borrows resources, worship practices, and theological ideas from the megachurch and church growth movements. While its worship follows the typical Lutheran structure, its content tends to emphasize an evangelical approach to Christianity, and Zion was one of the early adopters of contemporary praise music and rock and roll among northern California Lutheran churches.

St. Peter's Lutheran Church, in San Jose, is also a large congregation (1,142 members). It is self-consciously and unashamedly Lutheran. It sees itself as a true defender of the Lutheran Confessions against the ecumenism of the ELCA and of Lutheran morality against the pro-homosexuality position it sees as dominant in Bay Area Lutheranism and in the national church.[62] Most of its members are lifelong Lutherans who appreciate the Lutheran theological emphases on "law and gospel" and "saint and sinner" that they hear in sermons, adult education classes, and Bible studies. St. Peter's offered only Sunday worship services that followed *The Lutheran Book of Worship* until the end of the field period, when they began to develop a new service that relied on evangelical praise music mixed with the liturgy found in the other service. The congregation generally takes an instrumentalist approach to the governance models and educational resources it borrows from nondenominational megachurches, but the Baptist theology that undergirds much of this literature is evident in the sermons and the teaching of its clergy and lay leaders.

Resurrection Lutheran Church is located at the southern end of Silicon Valley where the population is more Hispanic than Asian (nearly 30 percent of the population is Hispanic) and where the median household income, while substantial ($79,008), is smaller than in the census tracts of the other two congregations. While the congregation has a small number of Hispanic and Asian members, the vast majority of members are white middle-class professionals, most of whom have some background in Lutheranism. Throughout its brief history (founded in 1973) the church has experienced the regular turnover of approximately one-third of its members every two to three years due to the job switching and loss of employment in the dot.com start-up sector of the high-tech industry, yet nearly everyone I met or interviewed called the church home.

In 2001 Resurrection's associate pastor took over from the retiring senior pastor. The congregation was in the midst of a cultural and structural change during the field period, as the pastor and the church council struggled to redefine the church's mission and follow the advice of some church growth experts about empowering the lay members to be responsible for the majority of programs or ministries at the church. Although the church reproduces the Lutheran theological tradition in its preaching and teaching, emphasizing the themes of grace and one's baptismal identity (as is done at Grace Lutheran), it is open to altering the tradition if it will further its new mission. Currently, the church uses a Catholic hymnal and is interested in finding ways to reach out to the growing Hispanic population, most of whom are Roman Catholic, and learning how to become a resource for the larger community in which it is located.

The histories of American Lutheranism and Lutheranism in the western United States reveal several important trends regarding the tradition and its transformation, and suggest, first, that the tradition is dynamic. It has been changed in radical and incremental ways since the colonial period, and the efforts to change it have been driven by how religious elites have tried to make Lutheranism fit with or stand against the prevailing social and religious context. The histories thus indicate that we should expect change to be the normal state of affairs in the study congregations and that it is fueled by how congregational leaders define and use the tradition. Second, the content and form of the tradition have been contested, and it is more accurate to speak about Lutheran traditions rather than one unified tradition. In particular, some Lutherans periodically have tried to reshape the tradition in the image of the evangelical, pietist, or revival tradition, but they have not been able to marshal the institutional resources necessary to successfully legitimize this more fundamental transformation of Lutheranism. While there has been a move toward greater uniformity, especially regarding worship and theology, the current push toward evangelicalism more broadly within American Protestantism, Lutheranism, and several of the study congregations suggests that the heterodox evangelical tradition offers a substantial challenge to orthodox Lutheranism.[63] Finally, I expect that the western context of irreligiosity and experimentation will encourage some of the study congregations to be more open to remaking the tradition and others to more firmly embrace and preserve a distinctly Lutheran approach to religion.

The following chapters explore in more depth why these nine congregations seek to change or reproduce Lutheran tradition, how they go about it, and what happens organizationally and religiously when the tradition is altered. Several of these nine congregations have been more active in playing with the tradition, and they will serve as the primary case studies in the remainder of the book.

Chapter 3

CONSTRUCTING THE
CATALYSTS OF CHANGE

"WE HAVE TO CHANGE OR DIE." That phrase, or some variation of it, served as a mantra in seven of the nine congregations I studied. It was often pronounced with heartfelt conviction, sometimes laden with regret, fear, or uncertainty, by clergy and lay leaders. I was puzzled that both growing and struggling congregations commonly invoked this phrase and used it to explain why they were altering worship practices, programs, and more generally the Lutheran tradition. In those congregations with an aging and dwindling membership, the phrase seemed to ring true—the old ways of being Lutheran were not attracting new members in great enough numbers to offset the losses of members and resources over the last ten or twenty years. But why try to change now when they had experienced decline for years? In several large, growing congregations, the phrase, on first hearing, seemed hollow, especially since they were adding members, filling their Sunday school classrooms, and even looking to build. So why did these seemingly successful congregations act as if their future survival was at risk? And why did they believe they needed to change their tradition to stem decline or continue to flourish?

Prevailing theories of religious and organizational change provide some important clues about the answer to these questions. Recall from the discussion in chapter 1 that the different theoretical approaches—cultural, ecological, and market—argue that external events force congregations to change. Yet the kinds of catalysts these theories identify, such as demographic shifts or new competitors in the local religious market that seem to directly threaten the viability of congregations, were not at issue in the California churches. Instead, congregational leaders whose churches faced no immediate or new threat drew on explanations for the larger mainline decline and models of congregational success from religious entrepreneurs to create a crisis of meaning and membership to mobilize change. I will show how the expected catalysts for change failed to materialize and then discuss how congregational leaders created a rationale and plan for change as they imagined how larger cultural and market changes in American religion might affect their congregations.

ECOLOGICAL, MARKET, AND CULTURAL CATALYSTS

Ecological approaches suggest that the catalyst for congregational change often is a major shift in the population—the arrival of new racial or ethnic groups to the neighborhood or the out-migration of former church members. While there was some evidence of population shifts in communities surrounding several congregations, none of the organizational changes were made to meet the needs or interests of new populations or reach out to them. For example, Zion Lutheran is in a Silicon Valley city that saw its Asian population increase from 23 percent of the total population in 1990 to 45 percent in 2000 and its white population decrease from 74 to 51 percent of the total population. This should be an important demographic shift, because Lutheran churches in general, and this church in particular, are overwhelmingly white and primarily draw new members from the white middle class. Yet the actual changes and rationale for the changes at Zion made no reference to this significant shift in the area's population. Instead, the loosening of the congregation's commitment to its tradition was made to make the church more appealing to young, unchurched white families in the community, and not to the growing Asian and Asian American population in the community.[1] Congregations did not appear pressured to change the tradition to meet the needs and interests of new ethnic or racial groups in their communities.

Ecological approaches also suggest that changes in the sociocultural environment may push a congregation to become a "niche" church, which largely maintains the tradition but attempts to draw members from a wider geographic area. Doing so helps a congregation evade the social or demographic changes within the immediate environment that challenge the saliency or appeal of a particular tradition.[2] For example, St. Mark's Lutheran Church in San Francisco adopted this strategy by providing professional-quality classic church music and high-church liturgy (i.e., a liturgy that follows the historic form of the Lutheran Mass from the Reformation period). It is the one Lutheran church in the Greater Bay Area that draws its members from across the region. However, none of the congregations in the study were attempting to become niche congregations by reproducing the tradition in order to draw Lutherans from a broad geographic area. Although two of the congregations occupied particular niches (Grace Lutheran was a "peace and justice"/activist church, and St. Luke's catered to a gay, lesbian, and transgender population), their status was not the result of retooling or reproducing the tradition.[3]

Market theories begin with the premise that social changes outside the congregation create opportunities for new religious groups to emerge in local religious markets, which in turn forces existing congregations to respond to the increase in competition. While I found that the congregations were responding to external religious pressures (e.g., information about seeker worship services or outreach strategies from nationally known megachurches), they were not pressures within the local market that arose from the entrance of new religious competitors. First, I was unable to identify any specific event or changes in the institutional, political, or cultural environments that made the local religious markets in the three communities more open to new religious competitors. Second, none of the congregations cited the emergence of new congregations or growing churches as an important factor in the decision to change the tradition. Few clergy and lay leaders talked about other congregations in their communities, and when they did, they had little information about the programs, worship styles, or constituencies of those congregations. Instead, they spoke about evangelism programs at Willow Creek Community Church, the latest book from a church growth expert, or growing churches outside California that had abandoned their historic tradition and that served as the inspiration for prompting innovations at their own churches. This suggests that, rather than the local religious market, national shifts in religious practice mediated by church growth experts, megachurch ministers, and denominational officials were the catalysts for change.

Market theories assume that congregations or members of congregations will act rationally and implement change in ways that will maximize membership or resources. While it was clear that the study congregations' leaders were responding to the larger decline in mainline church membership and the growth of evangelicalism and nondenominationalism, they did not always act rationally. For example, the leaders I discuss in chapter 4 altered the tradition, in part, by adding non-Christian elements and a focus on therapeutic spirituality, while also pushing the congregation toward liberal Protestantism. They pursued this transformation despite opposition and organized resistance by members, and at least in the short run these innovations did not make the congregation more efficient or able to attract new members. Market theories contend that such strategies make a congregation less competitive.

However, leaders in most of the congregations were interested in successful nondenominational seeker churches and megachurches as models for their own congregations, and they relied heavily on church growth experts' analyses and explanations of the causes and solutions to congregational decline. They also believed experts' claims that religious consumers are no longer interested in denominational religion and that this fact should be considered when churches seek to reach out to new members. It is important to recognize that the openings in the religious market (e.g., megachurches and nondenominationalism) were not new or directly impinging on the local markets of the study congregations. This all suggests a relationship between market processes and congregational change that is more complicated than is described in the literature. Openings in the market are important, but they do not automatically compel organizations to change and do not alone explain the timing of the change efforts in the study congregations. Instead, we need to look at how religious experts and entrepreneurs mediate information about religious trends, strategies and rationales for change, and other religious goods to local congregational leaders, who then package this information in ways to motivate change.

Finally, contemporary cultural explanations argue that shifts in the religious attitudes, values, and beliefs of the wider U.S. population have rendered denominational traditions inaccessible or irrelevant for many and have motivated some Americans to reclaim and rework various traditions in an effort to make sense of postmodernity. The evidence in support of these newer cultural approaches is stronger, but problematic. Leaders at every congregation in the study, when citing reasons to alter the Lutheran tradition, listed some of the key shifts in late-twentieth-century religiosity that have been well documented by social scientists and church growth experts (e.g., decline in denominational identity and loyalty, interest in spirituality). Yet these broader shifts in American religion have been going on for years, and in some cases for decades. We need to identify the organizational mechanisms to account for the timing of congregational responses to broad cultural shifts, especially when the responses come years after the external changes have occurred.

In short, I could not find solid evidence of some set of objective external crises that compelled these congregations to rework or change the Lutheran tradition. External events are not catalysts in the sense that demographic shifts or trends in religious participation, for example, automatically cause congregations to change their identities and practices. That is not to say that external events are irrelevant, just that such events or social trends such as the decline of mainline Protestantism and the rise of evangelicalism and nondenominationalism are the raw materials from which congregational leaders construct arguments for change. Congregations' leaders sift through a vast amount of information from church growth experts, denominational offices, the popular press, and conversations with leaders at other churches to try to make sense of the forces that may be related to real or potential congregational decline. From these diverse data and perspectives, church leaders then construct a rationale and plan of action to stave off the threat of decline.

The immediate catalyst for change that emerges from this interpretive work is an organizational crisis that is constructed by congregations' leaders, who create a crisis of meaning or membership whose cause and solution center on the Lutheran tradition. According to their rationales, the Lutheran tradition and, more generally, denominational religion are no longer seen as meaningful or relevant to members and potential members alike, and therefore the tradition is blamed as the cause for membership loss or the threat of membership loss. Since the tradition is blamed, it must be altered or abandoned to save the congregation. Thus, external events provide the resources church leaders use to construct crises of membership and meaning that in turn fuel intentional efforts to alter the tradition. In the next section, I combine insights from symbolic interactionism, social constructionism, and cultural and market theories to develop a more refined explanation of how traditions change that emphasizes the role of endogenous structures and dynamics.

CONSTRUCTING CRISES OF MEANING AND MEMBERSHIP IN BAY AREA CONGREGATIONS

Leaders of the congregations in the study drew on church growth experts' explanations and interpretations of congregational success and failure to create crises of membership and meaning that served as the immediate catalyst for change in six of the nine congregations in the study.[4] Nearly all of these congregations had clergy and a small group of lay leaders interested in altering the tradition that governed life at their church. Some congregations believed that the only way to appeal to non-Lutherans, who were the vast majority of people living in their communities, was to minimize the tradition. Some congregations saw themselves as havens for individuals damaged by the strict moralism of 1950s and 1960s Lutheranism and thus sought to downplay the exclusionary aspects of the tradition while emphasizing its more inclusive features. Some were looking for techniques to make the congregation run more efficiently and to more effectively meet the religious needs of members and thus were willing to let some elements of the tradition go in order to meet these goals. Yet each group of leaders could not simply implement change at will, as each congregation operated according to a democratic decision-making process. Thus, each church had to develop a set of arguments that identified the reasons for change and the congregational benefits that would follow from the proposed changes.

The arguments for change were couched in larger narratives or causal stories in which the leaders of these churches defined the problem facing their congregation, identified the cause of the problem, and offered a solution.[5] Causal stories are the mechanism by which conditions, events, or issues are transformed into problems and framed as amenable to corrective human action. They also are a tool by which church leaders suggest solutions to the problems, identify the people who are best equipped to implement a desired solution, and more generally set the standards used to gauge the moral ordering of organizational life.[6]

Leaders at each congregation first identified the fundamental problems they were facing as the real or potential loss of members and the threat of organizational decline. These problems in turn were fueled, they said, by the loss of interest and meaning in the Lutheran tradition among members and nonmembers alike. In other words, their congregation faced a membership and meaning crisis because they were following a religious tradition that was out of step with the religious needs and interests of people. They couched this crisis in several causal stories that tapped into larger cultural accounts about seeker spirituality, conservative, nondenominational, and evangelical Christianity, the decline and revitalization of the inner city, and the supremacy of the market.

These congregations' causal stories drew heavily on the accounts provided by organizations and experts in the church growth industry—organizations from the conservative and mainline sides of Christianity that provide consulting services and advice to congregations about the strategies and methods that can help a congregation grow. This is not surprising, since most of the clergy and lay leaders had been reading the books and attending seminars offered by church growth experts. Despite differences in size, cultures, histories, location, and membership demographics, all six churches defined the problem as actual or potential membership loss because worship, programs, and congregational life in general were not meaningful, important, or authentic to members and potential members. However, the specific details about the definition of the problem, attribution of blame, and organizational solution were shaped by the differential access congregations had to experts in the church growth industry as well as by the unique histories, cultures, and decision-making structures of each congregation.

Three causal stories emerged from my analysis of the data. Usually each congregation had one primary account, although they sometimes combined elements from the other stories as well. I have named these stories based on how they diagnose the problem and suggest the means to resolve it. One story defined the problem and solution in terms of *evangelism;* another in terms of offering seekers *authentic religion;* and a third stressed the disconnect of the church from the *community.*

The Evangelism Causal Story

From all outward appearances Faith Lutheran and Zion Lutheran should not be worried about dying in the immediate future or losing members to competing churches in their communities. Both congregations are among the largest in the synod, have full parking lots and sanctuaries on Sunday mornings, and are filled with young families. Yet Faith, and to a lesser extent Zion, see themselves on the brink of decline, and leaders from both congregations developed a similar causal story that identified the crisis or problem as the failure of mainline Protestantism to reach out intentionally to the unchurched. They placed the blame on churches that were more interested in reproducing the Lutheran tradition or taking care of their members than in bringing about the conversion of non-Christians.

The evangelism causal story frames the problem facing congregations as the failure to follow Jesus' command to spread the Christian faith. Lutheran churches are dying because they are more interested in maintaining the tradition and providing services to members than in converting the unchurched. In this account the tradition is blamed, often indirectly, either because it has historically downplayed the primary task of evangelism or because the core elements of the tradition—the theological language and doctrines, rituals, and ethnic practices—prevent Lutheran churches from making their worship accessible and appealing to non-Lutherans. The solution is to shift the focus of the church from serving members to recruiting nonmembers, and this will be facilitated by adopting the worship practices and theological approach of "seeker-friendly" churches that successfully reach out to the unchurched.

This story is widely used by Faith and Zion (roughly one-third to one-half of the pastors' letters in each church's monthly newsletter invokes this story). Sometimes the stories emphasize how the problem of membership loss stems from an overcommitment to the Lutheran tradition, while on other occasions, the accounts stress how evangelism will help the church adapt to America's post-denominationalism, and the cause of the problem is left implicit or ambiguous. The following excerpts illustrate two versions of the evangelism story. The first is from an essay in the monthly newsletter of Faith Lutheran:

> Less than 5% of the churches of the ELCA grew during 1999. It is a startling statistic, but indicative of the general decline of denominational churches for the past thirty years. But I would like to hazard my opinion as to why we are in such a steep decline. The mantra of Willow Creek Community Church (one of the fastest growing and largest churches in the US) is "Lost People Matter to God." It is the passion that drives their pastors, church leaders, and their members. The Bible is clear, it is the Church's mandate to reach out to those who are lost. Churches that care enough to invite and share the Good News will grow. Those who care primarily about themselves and keeping "religious" will continue to decline. All people matter to God, but especially the lost. The only question now is, "Do they matter to us?"

In this letter to his members, Faith's senior pastor aligns his church's mission with that of the flagship seeker megachurch and uses statistics to heighten the dilemma facing Lutheran churches. The minister frames the decline of Lutheranism and mainline Protestantism as a crisis of meaning and organizational practice that threatens the existence of the church (in a 1999 article, the same minister suggests that the continued existence of the church, and his church specifically, cannot be ensured unless they follow the lead of churches that successfully bring in the unchurched). In particular, the problem of membership loss is seen as a symptom of an even greater problem—namely, the Lutheran church's inability or unwillingness to engage in the practice of evangelism because too many churches are more interested in "keeping religious" or preserving the ritual practices, doctrines, and theological language of the tradition. The logic of this story is that nearly all Lutheran churches in America are not growing because they are primarily interested in preserving their religious system (i.e., the tradition): we are a Lutheran church; ergo, unless we refocus our mission toward evangelism, we too will die.

The senior pastor of Zion, in the following account, aligns the church's new mission with the task of evangelism and focuses more on the solution than identifying the problem. Here he defines the problem in terms of larger trends toward irreligiosity as well as the tendency of mainline Protestant churches to ignore the needs of nonmembers, and he does not directly connect the problem to the congregation. Instead, he treats the problem as a larger crisis facing Lutheran churches and uses it to mobilize support for a shift in programs and resources at the church:

> Our mission is to INVITE & Welcome people into a relationship with God. The INVITE & Welcome portion of our Mission is a response to Jesus' Great Commission in Matthew 28:19: *"Go therefore and make disciples of all nations . . ."* From the beginning of Christianity, being messengers of the Gospel has been at the heart of God's calling for his people. Some churches today have lost sight of this central calling and have slipped into an inward focus rather than an outward focus. Too often our churches have developed a "country club" mentality rather than a "mission outpost" mentality. In a country club, the institution exists exclusively for the benefit of its members and the concerns of outsiders carry no weight. By contrast the Mission Outpost exists for the fulfillment of the mission and a concern for the context, culture, and needs of those outside the institution guides the methods and efforts of those inside the institution. . . . It [i.e., the new mission] moves us beyond a focus on our own preferences and needs to focus on how we can be more effective in reaching that growing segment of our population that is outside the Church and for whom the Gospel is like a foreign language. Part of fulfilling this aspect of our Mission is to discover how we can translate the language of the Gospel into forms of ministry that are relevant in our rapidly changing culture. In a culture where institutions are suspect and the majority of people are unfamiliar with the Church, personal invitation is the crucial vehicle by which we can carry out this aspect of our Mission. By building authentic relationships with unchurched people, we will have the opportunity to share our faith and invite them to join us in a worship experience that is comfortable, meaningful, and life changing.

Both congregations also frame their causal stories in terms of larger shifts in the American religious environment, as suggested by references to the unchurched and renewed interest in spirituality among baby boomers. For example, in his article entitled "God Is Party-Giver," the new pastor of congregational life at Zion begins by contrasting two images about churches today. First, he describes Van Gogh's painting *The Church at Auvers,* in which the church is lit up but has no doors: "We must dare to admit that this is how most people in our society view churches, even our church." Then he describes a Christian rock concert, what participants call "positive partying," attended by 50,000 young people. The pastor then taps into the evangelism theme and calls on the church to change in order to meet the needs of today's spiritual seekers:

> Something happened in 1998 that may surprise you: The United States became the third largest mission field in the world. Only China and India

have more not-yet-believers than the United States. At the same time, a recent Gallup Poll shows that 8 of 10 Americans want to grow spiritually. What are all those spiritual sojourners out there searching for? . . . Spiritual sojourners in our society are looking for a place where hope is not only talked about, but also acted upon; a place where people sing through their tears and dance with contagious joy. . . . My role is to continue to transform this community of faith from a church with no doors to a church of positive parties with God as the host.

In this case, evangelism is invoked as the solution in the code language of American pietistic religion. In addition, this story frames the larger crisis in American religion (the growth of irreligiosity and the inability of churches to meet the growing interest in spirituality) and Zion's opportunity to offer spiritual seekers a religious home.

Two years earlier, the senior pastor at Faith began his monthly letter to the congregation with the same statistic about the U.S. mission field and then turned to spiritual seeking. Like his colleague at Zion, he uses evangelism to set up the problem—the large number of nonbelievers—and connect it to the fundamental causes—mainline churches' inability to meet the spiritual seeking of believers and nonbelievers. Again, the tradition is attacked obliquely (in the phrase "doing church") and the story suggests that Lutheran churches will need to change their tradition and focus their energies on evangelism (the solution to the problem) in order to minister to the growing ranks of seekers:

> It officially happened early in 1998. The United States is now the third largest mission field in the world. . . . Several recent polls suggest that church is one of the last places people *outside* the church expect to find God. But would it surprise you to learn that this attitude exists *within* the church as well? Of the 75 million who attend church weekly in the U.S., less than one-third say they regularly feel God's presence there. . . . Notice the widespread interest in angels, miracles, and Hollywood bankrolling projects on the afterlife lately. Some researchers say this is evidence of a cultural shift due to baby boomers, now in their 40's and 50's, seeking answers to spiritual questions. Their search (again, often outside the church) is driving a new interest in "spirituality." A Gallup poll shows that 8 out of 10 Americans want to grow spiritually. . . . Mainline churches are seeing a severe decline in membership and attendance while the general population is seeking for God. This should suggest that how we are "doing church" has not been meeting people's heart (or head) needs.

Finally, the evangelism story is informed and shaped by the advice of experts and organizations from the conservative and mainline church growth industries, including several prominent megachurches. Faith's and Zion's accounts are peppered with references to Willow Creek Community Church (especially its motto of "lost people matter to God") and Saddleback Community Church,[7] church growth training programs (e.g., the Beeson Institute, at Asbury Theological Seminary, a conservative United Methodist school), and a host of individuals (e.g., Max Lucado, William Easum, Thomas Bandy, or evangelical pollster George Barna). For example, the following newsletter article reveals Faith's ties to the church growth industries and its belief in the central role of evangelism:

> Two buzzwords for 2000 are Invitation and Communication. We want to see everything we do as an opportunity to INVITE people to faith in a living God (the first part of our Mission). We want to make our worship more inviting (to ourselves and friends). We want every special event to be a chance to say to someone for whom we are praying, "Why don't you join me?" That's where it all begins—WITH PRAYER. Who can you be praying for, that God might give you the opportunity to be an inviter?
>
> We continue to define church growth as "going deeper" as much as getting bigger. Let me share with you Five Principles of Effective Ministry (By Dr. Gary McIntosh):
>
> 1. The Principle of Visionary Leadership—a church grows when decisions are made based on the intention of bringing new people into the church
>
> 2. The Principle of Human Resource Allocation—a church grows when decisions provide the staff, leadership, and resources needed to focus on outreach
>
> 3. The Principle of "Open Doors"—a church grows when decisions create opportunities for new people to enter into the life of the congregation
>
> 4. The Principle of Incorporation—a church grows when decisions spawn ways to incorporate new people into the social circles of the congregation
>
> 5. The Principle of Finance—a church grows when decisions adequately finance local outreach activities.

In this article, the pastor defines the problem in reference to the solution—namely, overcoming barriers to growth by refocusing the congregation on the task of evangelism by reworking worship to make it "inviting." Although the pastor does not directly indict the Lutheran tradition or argue for changing it, such a course is implied in the call to change the congregation's worship. The solution comes from a book by an evangelical church growth consultant (and professor at Talbot School of Theology, an evangelical seminary in southern California) who contends that mainline decline can be overcome only by an intentional effort on the part of the congregation to "invite new people into church."

Rank-and-file members were less likely to offer complete or complex stories, but the ones they told relied on the basic structure and components of the evangelism causal story: a concern for growth and the need to not slide into decline, accompanied by a solution that entailed reworking the tradition to make it a more effective tool for evangelism. For example, one member during our interview complained that Faith Lutheran "is obsessed with change right now and change just for the sake of change. We see churches around us with a lot of problems and maybe we might be afraid of having those problems too. . . . I think our vision is to grow; to become another Willow Creek or Community Church of Joy. That's the goal for some people, but it's not necessarily a shared vision. I'm not sure it's my vision. Do we need to be a church of 5,000 or 10,000 people?" Her comment alludes to the larger problem of decline among Lutheran churches and Faith's solution (according to this member) of becoming a megachurch like nondenominational Willow Creek. It also reflects the sense of an impending crisis of growth and membership that many leaders of her church believe they can fend off by following the example of a successful megachurch.

One of the elected lay leaders of Faith echoed the causal story articulated by the senior pastor when I asked him to describe how efforts to redefine the church's mission were progressing:

I was at a meeting with other members to discuss the new mission document in 1998, and when the discussion bogged down, I asked people if they wanted to have young people at church. An older member answered, "Yes! It's absolutely critical." Then I posed a second question, "If we are to reach young people, would the church be willing to do multimedia, video-based worship used at successful churches like Willow Creek?" The same older member said, "Absolutely not. They can worship the same way we worship."

This attitude about not changing worship, he said, is the reason that so many Lutheran churches are "old and gray" and irrelevant to younger people. This lay leader identified the cause of the problem as Lutherans' unwillingness to change their tradition to meet the religious needs and interests of young people and suggested a solution that entailed altering the tradition by using worship practices and techniques from outside Lutheranism—in this case, Willow Creek Community Church.

In these accounts, evangelism becomes the answer to the perennial problems of membership loss and irrelevance to the growing non-Christian and/or unchurched population of America. The Lutheran tradition is blamed, often implicitly, for these problems as the leaders of both congregations advocate a return to a foundational task of Christianity and search for ways to make Lutheranism understandable, accessible, and meaningful to the unchurched. This causal story carries traces of more widespread religious narratives about post- or nondenominationalism, seeker spirituality, and the growth of America's unchurched population framed in the theological language of evangelicalism rather than Lutheranism. Surprisingly, the evangelism story is remarkably acontextual; there are few references to local demographics or religious trends in northern California;

it could be used by almost any church in any community in the United States. That these churches used this generic story without contextualizing it to fit their particular situations suggests that the evangelical entrepreneurs and experts who provide the template and information for the causal story wield significant power among congregation leaders.

The Authenticity Causal Story

The authenticity causal story bears some resemblance to the evangelism account insofar as both define the problem facing congregations in terms of the growth of nondenominationalism, the unchurched, and an emergent population of spiritual seekers. But the authenticity story is less concerned about membership loss and more concerned about making Christianity relevant and meaningful to non-Lutherans.

Good Shepherd Lutheran Church, another suburban church east of Oakland, is the primary advocate of this story. Like Faith and Zion, it is a large church, filled with young families and empty nesters, and it had been growing through much of the 1990s. Attendance and membership dropped during the field period, but it was more the product of the crisis the pastors created than an indication that the congregation itself was in serious decline. Thus, the story has less to do with a crisis of membership and more to do with a crisis of meaning. And like Faith and Zion, the account is decontextualized, framing the crisis in terms of national religious trends rather than local ones.

In general, this story defines the problem in terms of the inability or failure of the Lutheran church to make religion relevant and meaningful to people under age fifty who distrust organized religion or who are looking for help navigating the moral waters of postmodernity. Young people are looking for an authentic religious experience, and too often, according to this account, Lutheran churches operate more like "a little religion club with a cross on top" than "a community that helps people experience the sacred," according to Good Shepherd's pastor of worship and music. This problem arises from the tendency for churches to be more concerned about reproducing the tradition than in helping people make their faith relevant to daily life. This story places the blame on the Lutheran tradition and the congregation itself and conceptualizes the solution as getting rid of those parts of the tradition that keep the unchurched or formerly churched away and that make religion irrelevant or not meaningful to young people. The goal is to transform Good Shepherd from a denominational religious club or a "provider of religious services" into a community that "experiences God's way of being in the world" and "who strive to live out being sent with new way of love into the world."[8]

Good Shepherd's authenticity story is illustrated in the following account from a congregational dinner meeting at which the three ministers tried to explain to members why they were pushing the church to change its tradition. One member asked Dave Richards, the senior pastor, to explain what he meant by the cryptic phrase "imperialistic doctrine" that showed up in his last newsletter. Pastor Richards replied:

The church has often followed doctrine and introduces church to new people by giving these people doctrine and hitting them over the heads with it. Doctrine, like our theory of atonement, is not part of our common culture anymore. You may know what it all means but the unchurched don't. Part of being a missional church is to start by listening to where people are at and to ask them what God is up to in their lives and help people live a life of faith together. Church isn't about agreeing to a set of beliefs or doctrines.

Another pastor chimed in then and described what older and younger people were looking for in church. His answer highlighted the generational shift away from doctrine to experience and the way in which seeker spirituality has come to overshadow the 1950s pattern of religiosity grounded in church membership and intellectual assents to dogmas and creeds:

The World War II generation looks for a church with order and provides clear answers based on the Bible. Gen X'ers and younger are looking for what's really real. They say to me, "Don't tell me who or what God is—help me experience God. How does religion help me make sense of my life right now?" The modern church struggles with the challenges of science and postmodernism that rejects biblical literalism and doctrine. Younger generations want to discover God and not be told about God. They want a pastor who won't tell them what to believe but who will be a companion with them on a journey—they want us to be real.[9]

In this exchange the two pastors provide a complicated definition of a problem for which the Lutheran tradition is blamed. The problem facing this congregation and most other Lutheran and mainline churches is that young people do not attend or join (the argument implies that young people are the future of the church) because church operates like a club with rules, a set of theological ideas, and a language only insiders understand. Moreover, young people do not want an intellectual religion; they want one that is fundamentally relational and experiential. In the end, the problem is that many Lutheran churches too closely adhere to historic doctrines and theology, and this not only makes it impossible for non-Lutherans to participate but keeps them out because doctrine-based religion is not meaningful to young spiritual seekers.

This account also levels a specific charge of exclusivity against this congregation, as many members informed me that it has a history of acting like the local country club. The solution entails a radical rethinking of what the church is and who the church serves. It should be, not a club where you have to have special knowledge to join or be prepared to intellectually agree to a formal set of beliefs, but a community of people figuring out how to live as Christians and struggling together to find answers to questions of ultimate meaning. According to the second pastor, the old way of being or doing church is not appealing to young adults who want to place authentic relationships at the center of their religious lives. Thus, the pastors seem to be making a subtle anti-institutional argument—namely, that young people are not interested in organized or institutionalized religion. And this argument was picked up and reproduced by members during our interviews. For example, when I asked the outgoing church council president to describe Good Shepherd's new mission, he replied, "To establish ourselves in a challenging culture. People shy away from the institution. They don't go to worship because it's an institution. They don't give because it's an institution, and they have friends who have been turned off by the institution of church. And so we have a large number of our population who want to hear a [spiritual] call, but they don't want to put it in place in this institution. What is our mission? I think it's something we don't know yet." This member's comment and the authenticity story also identify the target audience of the church—people in their twenties, thirties, and forties who have been alienated or uninterested in church—which indicates a clear shift away from its core membership of longtime and older Lutherans.

This way of understanding the problem is elaborated upon and framed in terms of a larger crisis of meaning within American Christianity by the senior pastor in one of his newsletter articles. He first identifies the shift in American religiosity from the universality of churchgoing in the 1950s to the current emphasis on religious choice and then introduces the authenticity solution with a favorite concept of Good Shepherd's leaders, "faith in daily life."

> I've been trying to wrap my head around how the church might help you be a deep and spirit-filled human being. How might it assist you in living out such an orientation in your everyday life? For too long, the church has been obsessed with itself. Clergy are often trained to maintain the institution and programs that make church, church. . . . We at times forgot that the way of Jesus is not about institutional longevity, but the personal and communal vibrancy of a people who journey as little Christs in the world. Over the years, churches got lazy, resting in the confidence that they were BIG players in the social fabric of North American Culture. Church took itself for granted. It assumed that when it spoke, everyone listened. It assumed that the culture would always understand church language, and was interested in the historic ritual and dogma that had been its cornerstone. Those days have gone! Today we realize that the role of the church must shift. . . . For at its core, the church is people in mission and ministry in their daily lives.

Thus, the problem is irrelevant churches in a culture of religious choice, and in particular, the problem is caused by churches that are more interested in maintaining themselves than in helping people live authentic religious lives. The solution is to first understand how American religious culture has changed, to speak the saving message of Christianity in a language people can understand, and thus to alter the tradition in ways that will help the church meet the needs of a postdenominational, post-Christian population.

Good Shepherd's causal story also linked the problem of inauthentic religiosity with the general decline of mainline Protestantism and the possible loss of members. At a council meeting early in the process of change, one pastor defended the shift in theological language and worship practices (e.g., dropping the Lutheran theological emphasis on sin, the cross, atonement, and images of blood and sacrifice) as an attempt to adapt to a new religious environment: "Our goal is to be a mission-oriented church; to bring the gospel to a wider circle of people who aren't in church right now. We need to be intentional about reaching out to the unchurched. We can learn to speak meaningfully to the society at large in which we are, or we can die slowly."

Nearly two years later, the pastor for worship and music echoed the crisis of membership loss and tied it to a crisis of meaning. After attending a day-long seminar led by William Easum, a Methodist church growth expert, Pastor Mark Thompson wrote a long article in the February 2002 newsletter reporting on what he learned. First, he defined the problem in terms of decline due to the church's failure to adapt to postmodern religiosity: "The speaker said that 85% of mainline denomination churches would be closing in the next 15 to 18 years because they were not responsive to the changes in our culture. This reminded me of statistics from the ELCA that nearly 50% of ELCA churches would be gone in the same time frame." Second, he identified a long list of characteristics of "vibrant" or authentic churches that should be the models for Good Shepherd. In his words, these are "churches who reach out to a world that does not recognize God; who focus on discipleship instead of membership; who emphasize 'Who do I serve?' and not 'What do I get?'" He concluded on an anti-institutional note and argued that authentic churches stress spirituality over religion, relationships over buildings—a not-so-subtle challenge to the older members of the congregation who literally built the church and who expressed a great deal of confusion and concern over the language of spirituality and the spiritual practices the clergy were introducing into worship.[10]

In short, for Good Shepherd the problem is defined as a crisis of meaning that will lead to membership loss and eventually organizational death. The authenticity story stresses that the church must offer the unchurched an authentic faith—one that is meaningful—or else it will follow the majority of Lutheran and other mainline Protestant churches and close its doors. The church is blamed for the problem because it has insisted on following its tradition, which only lifelong Lutherans find important and meaningful. Thus, the solution is to get rid of doctrine and the insider language of Lutheranism and to develop alternative styles of worship that, as one pastor said, "will reach out beyond our familiarities and comforts to be true church to people who resonate with worship that is not centered on European art music."

The Community Causal Story

While the community causal story shares some of the elements of the other two accounts, it offers a more contextualized diagnosis and solution and a softer indictment of the tradition than the others. Like the evangelism and authenticity accounts, the community story frames the problem in terms of denominational and congregational membership decline, which is more generally understood to be caused by the inability of mainline congregations to adapt to changes in American religiosity. However, in the community account, the problem of decline is associated with a disconnect between a congregation and its local community in terms of demographic representation or service. That is, the congregation's loss of members is blamed on its inability or unwillingness either to make Lutheranism meaningful and appealing to populations that have not been the denomination's primary audience (e.g., African American, Asians, and Hispanics) or to make the congregation a resource for the community. The solution is to contextualize the tradition by incorporating pieces of ethnic populations' cultures (e.g., gospel music).

Three congregations in the study rely on this story: Emmanuel Lutheran and Christ Lutheran in Oakland and Resurrection Lutheran at the southern end of Silicon Valley. Not surprisingly, these congregations have experienced more demographic change in their communities than the other congregations, and thus an emphasis on reconnecting to the community makes sense. Yet each congregation constructed its community story also as a way to respond to internal dynamics. New pastors and revitalized lay leaders at the two Oakland churches tried to finally respond to the long, slow loss of members, while the Silicon Valley church struggled to deal with two pressing organizational concerns: filling up the pews in a new sanctuary (and hence paying for the new building) and the perennial problem of membership turnover in a volatile area of the Bay Area's high-tech corridor.

A good example of the community causal story is from the following pastoral letter from the minister of Christ Lutheran on the eve of its merger with a neighboring Lutheran church. In it the pastor defines the problem in terms of mainline Protestantism's history of racial segregation as well as the merging congregations' own flagging numbers and claims that both of these problems can be solved by serving the Oakland community. The Lutheran tradition and the congregation are not attacked as directly as they were in the other two types of causal stories. The community causal stories are not as coherent or complete as the evangelism and authenticity causal stories because the congregations were just beginning to develop their stories and thus had not finalized or even fully considered how changing the tradition figured into the problem definition, blame attribution, and solution. Indeed, in the following excerpt, no details about how the solution will be implemented are given:

Over the past four and a half years, I have committed myself to understanding the shifting paradigms of our culture and their significance for ministry in the 21st century. Together we have explored the need for change. . . . We have explored options and have come together with a common mission and vision. Our vision is to build a church for the 21st century, reflective of the community of Oakland. Among the most important words in our vision statement are the words, "reflective of the community of Oakland." Oakland is one of the most diverse communities in America. It is also a community that suffers from racial and class divisions. If the vision of Christ Lutheran is to build bridges between the various ethnic and economic groups in the city, it will not happen by default. . . . It will be because we as a people of faith, heed our Lord's command to *"go to the other side."* . . . Eleven O'clock on Sunday morning is the most segregated hour in America. If all we have accomplished is to merge two dying congregations into a new dying congregation we have not done much. We have a tremendous opportunity to do something new and something reflective of the reign of God. We have an opportunity to build a new community of faith that is inclusive of race, sexual orientation, and class.

Leaders at the church, especially the female African American pastor hired in 2000, refined the story over the next two years after attending workshops by church growth experts and faith-based organizers. In 1999 the pastor and some lay leaders often spoke about the need to revamp worship to attract the generations of the digital world—baby busters, Generation X'ers, and the millennialists[11]—but by the summer of 2000 this group was no longer mentioned in the causal story. Instead, a multicultural and multiclass constituency became the focus of the story. For example, at a council meeting in August 2000, one of the pastors rearticulated his vision for the church during a discussion of how to use the space of the second church after the merger: "We need to build bridges across racial cultures and economic cultures. Don't expect poor flatlanders to come up, but for the church to go down. We need to be a community of faith among the hill people who serve and do ministry with people in the flats who are poorer and different from us." The themes of diversity, both racial and economic, would become the key tropes in Christ Lutheran's causal story during the next two years. In particular, ordained and lay leaders would continually return to the call for this church, which is located in a wealthy neighborhood in the Oakland hills, to serve and partner with poorer and darker people down the hill.

When I interviewed Pastor Barbara Nelson, the African American pastor, in the spring of 2002, her vision for the church repeated these themes and highlighted the solution the church borrowed from the Gamaliel Foundation and faith-based organizing experts. The following excerpt is from the notes I took during the interview:

Q: What is your vision for this place?
A: I'd really like to see the church in use twenty-four/seven. I want kids here and for it to be a real multicultural, intergenerational place—where the elders work with young kinds and high schoolers and college

students mentor young kids. I want us to concentrate on poor people, and they won't come here unless they feel welcome.

Q: It sounds like you'd like the church to be a true center of the community?

A: Yes. A place where politicians will come and speak.

Q: How will this vision become a reality?

A: We will continue to canvass the neighborhood, asking residents what they think the church could do for the community, and then try to develop programs, like a preschool in the church basement or a tutoring program at the middle school down the road. It's not an approach to get lots of new members in the short-term, but a long-term strategy to make the church a servant of the community.

In this account, the pastor defines the problem of decline and revitalization in terms (indirectly) of the church's disconnect to poor(er) and nonwhite groups in the area who do not see the church as a friendly or helpful place. The solution is to convert the church into a social-service provider of sorts and to rely on the techniques of faith-based organizing as identified in the reference to canvassing the neighborhood.[12] In addition, the congregation began experimenting with new styles of worship that could attract non-Lutherans from nonwhite populations. For several months in 2000 they offered a Sunday evening gospel service and over the next two years slowly added Afrocentric practices (e.g., the use of African drumming during worship) and traditions from the historic black church (e.g., use of the call-and-response style of preaching and gospel music).

Emmanuel Lutheran, far down the hill from Christ Lutheran, also yoked community service and the incorporation of African American worship traditions as the means to revitalize the congregation after thirteen years of decline. Under a former pastor in the 1970s and 1980s the church was a "flagship for urban ministry" among Lutheran congregations according to its council president, and more generally it was a seen locally as an important player in Oakland politics. However, conflict near the end of the former pastor's tenure and his move to a new position resulted in the loss of significant members. At the same time the neighborhood itself began to further deteriorate during the recession of the 1990s, and with the continued loss of employment opportunities, safe housing, and commercial services, the remaining members of the black middle class exited, thus exacerbating the church's decline, as many members followed jobs and housing away from Oakland. Currently, the neighborhood is undergoing gentrification and the reentry of not just the black middle class but the white middle class as young professionals look for relatively inexpensive housing near San Francisco and the Silicon Valley.

When I asked Pastor Lawrence Cooper to describe the church's vision and future, I heard a causal story similar to that used by members of Christ Lutheran. Pastor Cooper also stressed the need to reconnect to the community in order to revitalize the church and offered a strategy based on making the church a center for community services and a place where African Americans, who tend to be unfamiliar with Lutheranism, feel welcome:

> When Pastor X left, we lost members and lost the congregation as a major player in Oakland. So what we're trying to do is to re-root. We're trying to find meaningful programs; meeting needs via our charter school; meeting needs in terms of the neighborhood, which plays out in terms of programs like our health ministry but also plays out in terms of worship. We understand that. More than likely—and we're assuming this—there are not a whole lot of Lutherans who live in the neighborhood. And so we're trying in terms of our worship to have some kind of cultural hook for the congregation. Neighborhood folks to walk in, who don't know Lutherans from a hole in the ground, but they know "Blessed Assurance" when they hear it. And so they say, "OK, this might not be all bad here. We'll come back and see what is this Lutheran thing about?" You know, Steve, I thought I had a vision of it being an African American church, you know? And I think now that I think I have to change. In the past year the neighborhood is radically changing again. White folks are moving in here in droves—snatching up the old houses. I think the Holy Spirit has to change that—it might mean, the vision might be a truly multiracial congregation. And it could have been the Holy Spirit saying, "You've got to change your vision" because who joined in 1999 were mainly white folk, you know? And so I think now the vision is to be a congregation to represent the neighborhood, to reflect the neighborhood. So however West Oakland looks, that's how we should look.

As in the story developed at Christ Lutheran, reconnecting with the community and authentically reflecting its demographic composition are problem and solution. Emmanuel also recognizes that service programs alone will not solve the problem of persistent membership loss and congregational stagnation. It is vital to alter the worship traditions at Emmanuel in order to bring in African Americans for whom Lutheranism is a great unknown. But rather than follow a faith-based organizing model, Emmanuel appears to be following the emergent model fueled by the rise of an activist neo-Pentecostalism within the black church. Gilkes discusses how black churches within the historically white Protestant denominations and established black denominations have begun to adopt worship traditions with a Pentecostal flavor (e.g., more emotional expression and shouting) in addition to becoming key providers of social services in neighborhoods with poor schools, inadequate housing and health care, and high rates of crime and unemployment.[13] Under the leadership of Pastor Cooper, Emmanuel developed a health ministry (it provides simple services like blood pressure screening to members and neighborhood residents) and a computer-training academy and houses a charter school. In addition, he has tried to add such worship traditions as gospel music but has met some resistance from long-time Lutheran members who insist their church is "not a shoutin' church."

The third version of the community account is used by leaders at Resurrection Lutheran Church, which is located at the southern end of Silicon Valley. This version sounded similar concerns about growth and the need to match the demographic and cultural diversity of the community. Yet it is a less-developed story than the ones advanced by the other congregations. It reflects a congregation negotiating its way through the opening stages of change. Four consistent themes emerged from the interviews with lay leaders of the congregation: an interest in growing more diverse; an interest in becoming a resource for the community; a growing commitment to outreach or evangelism; and an uncertainty about if and how to alter the Lutheran tradition to promote growth.

For example, one council member's answer to my question about the vision of the church touched on diversity, referring to the growing Hispanic population as well as the influx of newcomers looking for housing near new dot.com industry jobs located at the southern end of San Jose. She also suggested that the solution will require the church to change its tradition but offered no details about what such an alteration would look like:

> Right now we say that we want to increase diversity; reach out to more folks. It's not growing for the sake of growing, but the community is growing quicker than we are and what percentage aren't attending any church at all? . . . If we truly do want to expand who we target, then we need to start thinking outside the box and remember that we may be targeting people that aren't us. It may be uncomfortable for us.

A former council member's response to my vision question also expressed a concern with reaching out to a nonwhite audience and claimed that this is a turning point for the church; either it will grow more diverse or it will stagnate in the future. However, he recognized the difficulty of altering the tradition and was uncertain about how to do it and not lose the "richness" of Lutheran theology and liturgical practices:

> We do a good job of proclaiming the gospel and teaching, but if half the people in our audience are not Lutheran by birth or even longtime Christians, then we could make worship a little more user friendly. We could be more open to the unchurched families in our community. People like the friendliness of our church but worship isn't user friendly. But the Lutheran tradition is rich in liturgy and the history of the Reformation, and it is very comfortable and you don't want to lose that, but there's no easy way to share that richness with our neighbors so that they understand it. . . . We're at a fork in the road as a congregation. Not to overinflate where we're at but when we look back in ten or twenty years we will either remember this as a time when we stepped up to team leadership, a program-driven church, involved lay ministries, or not. We aren't currently growing as fast as the community is growing. How do we measure effectiveness? I don't think growth is the only measure or worship attendance; it's got to also

include how we reach out into the community. If we're still ninety-nine percent white Anglo-Saxon midwesterners with names like Hansen, then we've missed our opportunity.

This concern with changing versus preserving the tradition peppered many members' interviews. Some were ready to add a new worship service that resembled a typical evangelical or nondenominational service, but most wanted to keep the best of the Lutheran tradition while learning how to be more evangelical, as evident in the following comment from the church's music director:

> We try to be an outreach church but I think we have a long way to go. I've seen churches like this and it's a two-way pull. It's either outreach or member maintenance. How do you do both? You can go totally outreach to the point of losing your Lutheran identity. I've seen churches dumb down their service and adopt a praise chorus mentality, which I think is just awful. The participation in worship goes away and you become a spectator. Some churches lean toward maintenance of existing members and those churches don't grow. There has to be a good balance. I'm fanatic about the importance of the balance and of keeping the Lutheran tradition and not having to dumb down to attract new members.

Alternatively, some members strongly emphasized the community-service aspect of the church's vision as a way to grow and did not connect growth with the imperative to alter the tradition in order to make the church open to or appealing to non-Lutherans. Thus, they often described the vision simply in terms of "working on how we fit within the community and how best we can use our facilities with the community." The different emphases and lack of consensus on the solution in accounts at Resurrection suggest that their causal story was still a work in progress. In some ways this should have been expected because there was no consensus among the elected leaders about how to implement the church's new mission statement. The council had developed a new statement prior to the field period but struggled during the field period to articulate how the vision would be realized. During my last site visit, I attended a congregational meeting at which the implementation plan seemed to be crystallizing around a plan that would slow efforts to reach out to the Hispanic and unchurched populations within the community and thus table efforts to change the tradition. The plan called for members to engage in internal community building and to identify their own spiritual gifts that could be used for outreach and community service. One leader defended that plan at the meeting in the following way:

> We talk about outreach as something we need to do a much better job with; however, we're setting ourselves up for doom if you launch a program and there's nobody in the church that is really passionate about it. You're not going to do any good; it's going to end up being a lose-lose. Before starting to

launch a whole bunch of outreach programs, we're going to be a better servant to the community figuring out that our ministries are driven by the resources and the talents and the hearts of the people behind it. I think there's
a ton of stuff—the potential is enormous as far as what we could do—but we
need to figure out where the critical mass is so that we're successful.

At first glance, the community causal story, as it plays out at these three congregations, not only seems congruent with the ecological explanations of change
but appears to provide evidence in support of such explanations. The stories at
the three congregations take into account changes in the demographic makeup
of each community and suggest that each church's loss of members or potential
to go into decline would be addressed by responding to the population shifts. Yet
the congregations were responding to old and enduring threats, not new ones:
Resurrection regularly loses one-third of its members every two to three years
due to the volatility of the high-tech job market; the predecessor congregations
that now make up the merged congregation of Christ Lutheran in Oakland had
been losing members since the 1970s; and the African American congregation,
Emmanuel, had experienced declining rates of membership and participation
since the late 1980s.

The questions are, why did these three congregations decide to respond now
and why did they turn to the community causal story? First, each congregation
had leaders who were interested in changing the culture and practices of the
congregation and saw new opportunities in the early 2000s to pursue change.[14]
Second, Christ and Resurrection were newly connected to professional claims
makers in the church growth industry and faith-based organizing world and
were eager to try out their solutions.[15] Third, each congregation was committed
to preserving the Lutheran tradition in some ways and thus was reluctant to engage in the more radical changes undertaken at Faith, Zion, or Good Shepherd.
The genius of the community causal story is to construct a novel interpretation
of long-standing threats, make them relevant to and pressing on the congregation, and connect them to innovative solutions that do not necessarily demand
that the congregation abandon or significantly alter the tradition.

EMBEDDEDNESS AND CONGREGATIONAL CULTURES

Why did these congregations construct crises of meaning and membership in
order to catalyze organizational change? And why did they construct the particular causal stories reported on in the previous sections? Why did the churches
blame the Lutheran tradition for the larger, pan-mainline problem of decline,
and why did they believe that changing or abandoning the tradition would solve
the problem?

My answer to these questions, and more generally my explanation regarding the catalysts or triggers of congregational change, draws on theoretical work

about the collective construction of social problems, especially the public-arenas model of Hilgartner and Bosk and Stone's insights into the role that causal stories play in defining organizational problems.[16] Congregations face numerous situations or conditions that are potential problems, including membership decline, the loss of resources, or competition from nondenominational megachurches. However, these situations do not represent problems in and of themselves. They are "mediated by ideas" about what constitutes congregational success, growth, or vitality and about what are significant problem areas that need to be addressed by congregation leaders.[17] The public-arenas model is a helpful tool for understanding why certain situations become defined, or even manufactured, by congregations as crises that threaten a congregation's continued existence.[18]

A key insight of the public-arenas model is that social problems are constructed and made public by a community of claims makers, often within a specific institutional sphere (such as religion). In particular, the model stresses the role of professional claims makers in transforming social conditions into problems and then mobilizing public support to solve them. It is clear from the data that the six congregations (Faith, Zion, Good Shepherd, Christ, Resurrection, and Emmanuel) did not construct the problems they were facing by themselves but relied heavily on the problem definitions provided by professional claims makers who were alleged experts on church growth or church health from conservative and mainline parachurch organizations, nondenominational megachurches, and conservative Protestant seminaries.

Experts from the church growth industry first and foremost provide consulting services to congregations about strategies to help churches grow or revitalize themselves, but secondarily they are the key operatives within the congregational-problems arena. They routinely offer congregations generic causal stories (generic insofar as they are not specific to congregation, denomination, or social context) that define the problem of church decline, identify the cause of the problem, and suggest a solution. Claims makers within the religious arena create coherent narratives by identifying various putative conditions such as the decline of mainline Protestantism, identifying the root cause or blame for these problems, such as boring worship services, and then prescribing a remedy, such as replacing a church's historic worship traditions with those from one of the successful megachurches. The leaders of congregations learn about these causal stories from different claims makers and then shape the stories to fit their specific organizational context. Which causal story or stories a congregation advances depends on the specific religious network in which it is embedded because that provides access to specific definitions of the problem and solutions.

The congregational-problems arena comprises organizations and individuals from both the evangelical/nondenominational and mainline/liberal sides of Protestantism. The largest number of operatives come from nondenominational, theologically conservative, Biblicist organizations, including several of the nation's flagship megachurches (e.g., Saddleback Community Church, Willow Creek Community Church, and Community Church of Joy), conservative seminaries (e.g., Fuller Theological Seminary and Asbury Theological Seminary, both of which have church growth institutes), and a host of consulting organizations that primarily serve a multidenominational audience with a conservative or evangelical bent (e.g., NetResults serves independent, evangelical, and mainline churches with the goal of "helping congregations help people make a life-changing connection with Jesus Christ" by offering seminars, consulting services, and publications).[19] A smaller group of organizations and experts with strong ties to mainline Protestant denominations provide similar services. The Alban Institute, an ecumenical, nonprofit consulting firm, primarily serves a mainline and liberal constituency, as do Leonard Sweet (United Methodist) and such liberal theologians as Bishop John Spong and Marcus Borg (both Episcopal).

Although evangelical and mainline experts offer congregations different causal stories, their stories share a common way of defining the immediate problem. In general, many church growth experts' causal stories define the problem in terms of congregations' inability to grow with respect to membership, participation, depth of Christian faith, or organizational health. They blame this lack of growth on the failure of most mainline denominational churches to adapt to key changes in American society, religiosity, and Christianity. The changes they cite include the rise of evangelicalism and church switching or shopping, with a concomitant loss of denominational brand loyalty, and the new interest in spirituality.[20]

However, the conservative and mainline stories diverge when they specify the underlying cause(s) and suggest solutions. Groups from the evangelical/nondenominational side tend to favor a causal story that links the problem of church decline with the failure to engage in evangelism. The problem and solution are framed and justified in terms of the "Great Commission"—the last command a resurrected Jesus gave his disciples, which ordered them to proselytize. While the general framing of problem and solution suggest a return to an ancient and fundamental task of the church, it is a return that relies on the latest management and marketing strategies gleaned from the business literature and on the use of technology, pop music, and the idioms of therapy and pragmatism to effectively communicate the message of Christianity to a consumerist, postdenominational audience. Mainline and liberal church growth organizations stress authenticity in their accounts of congregational problems. In other words, they contend that many mainline churches are in decline because they do not offer people authentic religious experiences or credible ways to believe. The fault lies in churches' commitment to reproducing, seemingly for their own sake or uncritically, the theological language and ritual practices from their specific traditions that are inaccessible or meaningless to postmodern religious seekers.[21]

Leaders in congregations do not necessarily adopt the generic causal stories whole cloth but, like *bricoleurs,* select elements or claims from different generic causal stories and then put them together in ways that emphasize certain problem definitions and solutions they believe will generate members' support for new initiatives. Several organizational factors or pressures push congregations toward particular causal stories created by church growth experts and act as constraints and filters through which congregational leaders interpret and then apply the generic causal stories.[22] In other words, certain features of a congregation create an elective affinity between its self-understanding and setting and a causal story available in the congregational-problems arena. Which causal story or stories a congregation adopts and how its leaders rework it depend on several organizational contingencies: the nature and degree of the congregation's embeddedness within the congregational-problems arena; the history of the congregation and its relationship to the tradition; and the congregation's identity, resources, and decision-making structures. For example, a small congregation with few resources, like Christ Lutheran in Oakland, would be less likely to select a generic story that emphasized marketing and changing worship by adding a professional rock band and video screens (a common solution advanced in the evangelism causal story).

A congregation's connections to operatives within the congregational-problems arena expose it to particular generic causal stories and place the congregation within a discursive field that provides the vocabulary, lines of argumentation, and rationales for changing the tradition. In this way embeddedness within a church growth network pulls or channels the congregation toward some constructions of problem and solution and away from others. At the same time, the particular emphasis or spin a congregation's leaders give their causal story is influenced by the church's history, identity, and resources.

The nature of and degree to which congregations were embedded within the congregational-problems arena, especially in terms of their relationship to the church growth industry, reveal a great deal about the causal stories they constructed. All of the congregations were exposed to the causal stories coming from both evangelical and mainline church growth organizations through seminars sponsored by the Sierra Pacific Synod of the ELCA (a synod is the regional governing body for the denomination). Each year the synod offered clergy and lay leaders several opportunities to hear the latest ideas about congregational growth and revitalization from prominent experts from mainline parachurch organizations (e.g., William Easum, Ray Oswald, Leonard Sweet) on such topics as "Leadership on the Other Side of the CEO Model" and "The Culture-Friendly Church." Leaders at five of the six congregations were reading the same set of books during the field period, including William Easum's *Growing Spiritual Redwoods*, Gary McIntosh's *One Size Doesn't Fit All*, and Rick Warren's *The Purpose-Driven Church*.[23] Leaders at Faith, Zion, Resurrection, and Christ made pilgrimages to at least one megachurch during the field period (usually Saddleback Community Church, in southern California) in search of ideas and strategies to update their worship practices, educational programs, and decision-making structures. Two congregations relied almost exclusively and relatively uncritically on evangelical and nondenominational approaches to church growth and decline; two congregations viewed the ideas and strategies from evangelical sources with a great deal of skepticism; and one borrowed selectively while also drawing on a model from faith-based organizing.

Faith and Zion: Evangelical Connections, Evangelical Identity

Faith and Zion were the most tightly enmeshed in evangelical and nondenominational circles. Both are members of the Willow Creek Association and almost exclusively rely on educational resources from Willow Creek for their youth and adult classes. Both senior pastors were working on advanced degrees with a focus on church growth. One attended classes at Asbury Theological Seminary's Beeson Institute (a conservative United Methodist church growth training center), and the other was working on his doctor of ministry under church growth guru Gary McIntosh at Phoenix Seminary (a nondenominational seminary once affiliated with the Baptist Western Seminary in Portland, Oregon). In addition, both pastors are members of a small network of California Lutheran pastors who self-identify as evangelicals and who help each other design mission statements and programs to further the goal of evangelism.

During the field period Faith Lutheran's church council and several ad hoc task forces were reading various books about church growth and marketing and developing a number of programs inspired by or borrowed from nondenominational megachurches, such as a program to intentionally "assimilate" new members following the advice of Saddleback Community Church and following Willow Creek's plan of evangelism called "Becoming a Contagious Christian" (Zion also taught this course on a regular basis). Finally, Faith Lutheran regularly hosted video conferences on a variety of church growth issues led by clergy from Willow Creek Community Church and Community Church of Joy (the latter is a Lutheran megachurch that strongly de-emphasizes its denominational identity and heritage).[24]

Their strong connections to the evangelical and nondenominational side of the problems arena exposed these two churches to a generic causal story that stressed the lack of evangelism as the cause of church decline and the vigorous implementation of evangelism as the solution. One extended example illustrates the close connections between the conservative church growth industry and Faith Lutheran and how this embeddedness has influenced the causal story Faith developed.

Faith adopted many of the programs and ideas from e Saddleback Community Church as articulated in its pastor's book, *The Purpose-Driven Church*. The book begins with the claim that "God wants his church to grow; he wants his lost sheep found." This is the same starting presupposition used by the senior pastor at Faith. Warren urges churches to balance their mission around five congregational tasks: worship, evangelism, fellowship, education, and service, with worship as the primary means by which to bring the unchurched into church attendance and membership. In several chapters Warren offers advice about how to create seeker-friendly worship services and argues that worship is a vehicle for evangelism. Moreover, he argues that churches "must be willing to adjust our worship practices when unbelievers are present." In practical terms this means abandoning the religious language of Christianity ("the spiritual terminology that Christians are familiar with is just gibberish to unbelievers") and de-emphasizing denominational practices and ties because the "denominational labels carr[y] a lot of negative baggage for many of the unchurched."[25]

Faith has adopted the language of evangelicalism (e.g., being "born again" or "getting into the Word") and its emphasis on emotion rather than intellect in worship in order to appeal to potential members for whom such a language or practices are familiar. The senior pastor noted in one of our interviews: "People coming to this church may not have a language except born-againism. I don't want to dismiss that experience as illegitimate but encourage that person to explore what that experience means. We Lutherans have driven thousands of people away from Lutheranism and into the Evangelical Free Church or the fundamentalists because we have rejected the born-again experience and language out of hand." Similarly, Faith has adopted pop/rock Christian music in its worship services, also following the advice from Saddleback (and other church growth gurus) that most Americans born after the mid-1960s prefer contemporary pop/rock as well as church music that has an upbeat tempo.

Another way in which the southern California megachurch movement has influenced Faith is evident in the congregation's "mission strategy." As at Saddleback, Faith Lutheran's mission strategy begins with evangelism and focuses on worship as the means by which this will be accomplished ("We share our faith by building authentic relationships with unchurched people, living our lives of faith before them, and inviting them to join us in *Worship*"). Worship is organized at Faith so the unchurched "can experience people truly offering their hearts to God and can hear God's offer of a life-changing encounter with Him."[26] In other words, worship now is organized according to the pietist tradition insofar as it is intended to convert the unbeliever or unchurched person rather than being organized along the lines of the confessional tradition, from which Lutheranism traces its roots (i.e., to worship God corporately, proclaim God's saving acts in history, offer the means of God's grace or salvation in the ritual of Holy Communion).[27] Thus, Faith uses the language of American evangelicalism or the pietist tradition and indirectly criticizes the Lutheran worship tradition for failing to serve as a tool for evangelism.

Yet it is Faith's "pathway" toward fulfilling their mission statement that they most clearly borrow from Saddleback Community Church. The megachurch uses a developmental model in which individuals are moved from visitor to core member, or from unbeliever to mature Christian, and employs a series of courses to accomplish this task. The 100-level courses are for the unchurched and are intended to "lead people to Christ and church membership." The 200-level courses are for new members and should "grow people to spiritual maturity." The 300-level classes are designed to equip committed members "with skills they need for ministry," and the 400-level courses "enlist people in the worldwide mission of sharing Christ."[28] Faith offers a 101–401 series targeted toward new members that is intended to help them develop from novices to skilled evangelists. "You're Invited 101" introduces the Christian faith and extends an invitation to join the church. "Getting Equipped 201" introduces new Christians to the basic spiritual disciplines of the Christian life (e.g., prayer, Bible study, tithing, and small-group membership). "Created to Serve 301" helps people discover their unique gifts for ministry, and "Invite Others 401" trains church members in relational evangelism (i.e., learning how to talk about their faith with unchurched friends).

If Faith's embeddedness in the conservative church growth problems arena led it to embrace the evangelism causal story, then its history and weak relationship to the Lutheran tradition and the denomination reinforce this move and push the congregation toward non-Lutheran sources for understanding and addressing congregational problems. Founded in 1965, Faith has grown steadily throughout its life and more rapidly since its new pastor arrived in the mid-1990s. Members have been primarily lifelong Lutherans, although roughly one-third of new members in the past few years are coming from non-Lutheran backgrounds—mainly Catholic and Baptist. Since its founding, the church has had pastors more interested in evangelism (i.e., sharing the gospel with the community and bringing people into church) than in cultivating a distinctly Lutheran identity. It has a history of experimenting with worship practices, including an attempt to develop a seeker service in the late 1980s and early 1990s that was led by a charismatic Baptist musician. The church also has a long-standing group of members with evangelical or charismatic leanings, and many in this group now occupy positions of leadership in the congregation. In interviews with members I always asked if it is important to be Lutheran and what they appreciated about the Lutheran tradition. Few interviewees expressed strong interest in being Lutheran, and most referred to themselves as Christian, rather than Lutheran, or as Lutheran Christians. Moreover, few members could speak about the Lutheran tradition in detail, even those who had been lifelong Lutherans and/or longtime members of Faith. It appears that this congregation has cultivated a stronger nondenominational identity than a Lutheran one.

Similarly, Zion's history and identity predispose it toward the evangelism causal story. Founded in 1960 as a mission church, it has always seen itself as a church dedicated to evangelism. A former minister visited several megachurches in the late 1980s and returned with the idea of adopting some of the worship practices and educational programs he witnessed there. Zion was one of the early leaders among northern California ELCA churches to offer seeker- and evangelical-style worship, and it has been selectively indifferent to the tradition (i.e., it has retained some elements of the tradition but has been willing to abandon other parts in order to make worship and programs accessible and relevant to non-Lutherans). Current clergy of the church describe themselves as evangelical and claim that they hold more conservative views of scripture and theology than many of their peers in the ELCA. These factors have led Zion to favor an evangelical construction of its problems and a willingness to adopt some of the marketing and strategic management solutions advanced by consultants who urge congregations to act more like a for-profit business than an otherworldly community.

In short, the leaders at Faith and Zion constructed a causal story that echoed the generic causal story offered by evangelical church growth experts. It stressed the potential for congregational decline and death unless the church acted proactively to prevent decline. The way to do that was to modify the tradition to make it more accessible to the unchurched and people unfamiliar with the theological language and ritual practices of Lutheranism.

Resurrection, Christ, and Good Shepherd: Critical and Selective

Leaders at Resurrection, Christ, and Good Shepherd, while exposed to the evangelical and nondenominational side of the problems arena, tended to be more tightly enmeshed in nonevangelical networks or treat the ideas and strategies from evangelical operatives more critically than leaders at Faith and Zion did.[29] Moreover, in their construction of crisis and causal story, the histories, cultures, and resources of these congregations played a more central role than embeddedness in networks of church growth experts or in the church growth industry. For example, clergy and lay leaders at all three churches attended seminars led by William Easum, as did leaders at Faith and Zion, but rather than leaving the seminars with a new commitment to enact the solution of evangelism or even framing the problems facing their congregation in terms of evangelism, as did leaders at Faith and Zion, the leaders of these three churches selected nonevangelism elements from Easum's presentation about church growth and revitalization.

The seminars focused on congregational leadership for the twenty-first century. They began with an assessment of how American culture and American religious culture had been altered by postmodernity, in which the old rules of religion—propositional truths, linear thinking, print media, and credentialed professionals—are being replaced by embodied truth, fuzzy logic, and the embrace of chaos, digital media, and gifted lay leaders. Clergy are being called to replace the "institutional church" guided by the old rules with a "spiritual kingdom" guided by the new rules. And the way to revitalize old congregations is to become a "permission-giving" congregation in which lay people and not clergy or bureaucratic structures determine what kinds of ministries members will enact. The purpose of adopting these so-called new rules of religion is to make disciples and help save people from their sins and thus fulfill the core reason for the church's existence—a central claim of the generic evangelism causal story. At one point in the presentation Easum asks, "When you ask people for prayer requests, how many are for health issues and how many are for the salvation of someone? Leaders sense that the DNA of the church is to make disciples of Jesus Christ, not to take care of people. The reason churches are declining is that they have forgotten what business they are in."[30] He seems to be saying that, although leaders are aware of the church's primary mission, many forget about it in the day-to-day pressures of running their churches and, when the task of evangelization is neglected, churches will die. His rhetorical question and comment suggest that, ultimately, the purpose of engaging in congregational change is, not community service or helping people find an authentic religious life, but evangelism.

Leaders at Resurrection in Silicon Valley borrowed Easum's ideas about lay leadership and transforming the congregation into a "permission-giving" congregation in which lay people are empowered by the clergy to engage in the ministries based on their spiritual gifts rather than delegating ministry to professionals (like the pastors). However, as much of the literature on cultural reception suggests, consumers of ideas (among other cultural products) do not necessarily receive them uncritically or interpret them as intended by the producer. Rather, a variety of constraints, such as social location, influence how consumers assign meaning and use a given cultural object.[31] Pastor Barbara Williams response to my query about their use of church growth material and recent return from the Easum seminar identified the central role the congregation's culture played in shaping what they appropriated and how they used it:

> I'm skeptical about a lot of the church growth literature—mainly because it seems so dated. So much of it holds out a particular practice, like the use of praise music, as a key mark of vital congregations, but some of this stuff is from 1980s. We're more comfortable adding ideas or techniques that fit Resurrection's core values, but I want us to be careful to always do ministry that is informed by our theological perspective and not be driven by some technique that promises a quick fix. We're really struggling to figure out what it means to be Lutheran in the twenty-first century, but if I were to deviate from justification by grace [a core Lutheran doctrine] from the pulpit more than once or twice, I would hear about it at coffee hour.

Pastor Williams comments suggest that the congregation's commitment to Lutheran theology and an uncertainty about the fit between the congregation's values and certain ideas or techniques proposed to solve the growth problem limit how much or how far they are willing to follow the diagnosis and solution offered by Easum and others within the evangelical/nondenominational sector of the problems arena. Certain techniques, like becoming a permission-giving church, not only are congruent with one piece of the Lutheran tradition—namely, the emphasis on lay involvement in ministry, which follows from Luther's notion of the "priesthood of all believers"—but are safe. They do not require the congregation to radically change the tradition.

Similarly, leaders at Christ Lutheran in Oakland also adopted Easum's solution of becoming a permission-giving church without connecting it to the fundamental church task of evangelism. Here, the church's commitment to faith-based organizing, which advocates service by the church for the community rather than direct evangelism as a way to revitalize the congregation, weakens the appeal and fit of the evangelism causal story for members of this congregation. In addition, the technique of lay empowerment requires far fewer financial resources than some of the other solutions to the problem of congregational decline (such as the use of multimedia technology in worship).

Leaders, especially the clergy, at Good Shepherd ignored the call to see the problem of decline in terms of evangelism or to adopt the solution of evangelism after their encounter with Easum. Instead, they borrowed his assessment of postmodern culture and his contention that institutionalized religion is out of step with the emergent religiosity of young Americans, and they used it to frame their definition of the authenticity problem.[32] Good Shepherd turned to the authenticity account in part because it is the primary generic account they read or hear about from the church growth experts they favor. The church's leaders are firmly embedded in the mainline/liberal side of the problems arena, whose experts often stress the need for congregations to adapt to postmodernity and the new interest in spirituality.

Evidence of this embeddedness was often on display in the everyday life of the parish. For example, the congregation's three pastors commonly cited Alban Institute books about congregational change to justify their efforts to change the tradition. In the spring and early summer of 2001, the church's senior pastor went on sabbatical, and unlike many of his peers, he did not visit some of the country's important megachurches or take courses on church growth techniques but instead attended seminars on spirituality and worked with a spiritual director to learn about "postmodern spirituality." The church council also sponsored a series of adult education classes one summer and fall that featured a leader from the national offices of the Presbyterian Church, U.S.A., speaking about the religious implications of postmodernity and the religious culture of choice for Americans under fifty years of age.

In addition to their embeddedness in nonevangelical church growth networks, the congregation's own history and culture pushed them away from the evangelism story and toward the authenticity story. According to longtime members, Good Shepherd has always been a "civic" or "community" congregation, to use the language of congregational models.[33] It is known as a good place to raise children and to make friends. Members speak proudly of the church's history of providing community services in the areas of mental health (it opened a crisis hotline in the 1970s and still supports the organization now that it is an independent agency) and education and the help it provides a rural school in Mexico. Some members claimed the church has a "servant attitude" and pointed to a decision in 2001 by the congregation to dedicate 12 percent of its budget to "benevolence" (i.e., money that goes to the ELCA and the synod, which in turn fund a variety of church outreach and service programs).

Members often spoke about doing "outreach" in the community by making church accessible and relevant to the large unchurched population in the community, but they did not use the language of the evangelism story (i.e., no one spoke about doing evangelism or used such terms as "salvation," "conversion," or "personal relationship with Jesus"). Unlike members of Faith and Zion, Good

Shepherd's members saw the unchurched as simply that—people who did not belong to a church. Two members claimed that "90 percent of the community was unchurched but they all believed in God" (sounding the theme of "spiritual but not religious" of the authenticity causal story); they did not refer to these people as "lost souls" or sinners who needed to be saved. One member wryly noted that the congregation and Lutherans more generally were not very good at evangelism, and that was fine with him. The point of outreach was to make room for all sorts of seekers who come from "different traditions and help them on their own journey and not to force them down one path."

A congregation's embeddedness pulls it toward generic causal stories that leaders believe will help it legitimate and ultimately mobilize change. At the same time, congregational features like its history, culture, and relationship to the tradition push it away from some generic stories and help leaders shape their particular account to articulate with the interests, values, and goals of the congregation. Sometimes a congregation's connections to the problem arena reinforce preexisting theological positions and interests to alter the tradition within a congregation, as in the case of Faith and Zion. Sometimes a congregation's culture and resources help it determine which causal story to select, as in the case of Christ Lutheran.

The tradition became the target for change in most of the congregations not only because the experts identified mainline worship practices and doctrines (i.e., the tradition) as one of the barriers to growth but also because in several congregations it was a safe and easy target. In these congregations few members strongly identified with the tradition or wanted to see it preserved at the cost of losing potential members, especially among young adults. And if leaders of these congregations genuinely believe that the archive of the tradition is meaningless to potential or even current members, then changing or replacing it becomes a neat solution to what they consider to be a worrisome problem.

In general, the congregations refracted the ideas, narratives, and organizational fixes offered by church growth experts through the lens of their history, culture, and practices to construct crises of membership and meaning that served as the catalyst for change. This interplay of external information and internal congregational dynamics indicates that religious markets, religious ecologies, and the culture of American religiosity play important roles in catalyzing change, but in some unexpected ways.

MARKETS, CULTURES, AND ECOLOGIES

I have argued that leaders of these six congregations used various experts' information about and explanations of larger shifts in participation and affiliation to construct organizational crises of membership and meaning. Leaders took ideas about the rise of nondenominationalism and evangelicalism, as well as models of new worship practices and outreach strategies, from the megachurches and placed them in causal stories about the problems or potential problems their congregations faced in order to show their members why they must change their tradition or die. I have tried to show how causal stories operate as the mechanism by which external events and social forces become salient to congregations.

This practice of drawing on information or borrowing ideas from church growth experts suggests that congregations are embedded in a national market for religious goods and services. It is a market that deals in accounts of what ails mainline Protestant congregations, strategies for growth or revitalization, and claims about the religious needs and interests of the "unchurched." I call this a market because many of these church growth experts and leaders of mega-churches literally are selling products—everything from seminars about increasing market share, to educational materials, to market research on potential members—and congregations are buying.[34] This national market has far greater influence than products or competition from the local market. Surprisingly few of the congregations framed the crisis or suggested a solution that referenced other congregations in the community or the local demographic or cultural context. The congregations tended to act as if the "unchurched" in northern California had the same religious interests, lifestyles, and demographic profile as the unchurched in suburban Chicago (i.e., the location of Willow Creek's exemplar "Unchurched Harry"). Congregations assumed that the profiles of boomer and Generation X religiosity developed from national, and often anecdotal, data (as reported on in the books they read) would hold true for the boomers and X'ers in their communities.

When the congregations did try to fit problem definition and solution to the local context, they demonstrated relatively thin knowledge of their own communities. For example, clergy and members of Faith and Good Shepherd consistently claimed that the unchurched population in their suburbs was about 90 percent, yet the figure is closer to 60 percent according to county-level data in the American Religion Data Archive.[35] The experimental gospel service at Christ Lutheran in Oakland was ended after several months because of poor attendance. Although African Americans make up more than 50 percent of the population in the area, simply offering a gospel service was not enough attract their attention. African Americans in the neighborhood looking for a gospel-style worship service would have dozens of churches in the area from which to choose, all of which most likely knew how to "do church" in this style better than the organizers of the service at Christ. Ironically, more attention to what was happening in the local market rather than to models of growth from outside their context might have been more helpful since the churches with full pews on Sundays and full parking lots the other six days of the week were a couple of multiracial evangelical churches within a two-mile radius of Christ.

At the same time, these congregations, and especially the clergy, are embedded in a religious institutional sphere comprising local-clergy networks and partnerships among congregations (both Lutheran and non-Lutheran), denominational offices, church growth consultants, and parachurch organizations (such as the Willow Creek Association). Experts, entrepreneurs, and other organizational actors in this institutional sphere act as mediators of the market by framing particular religious trends as important, even threatening, and then by pushing clergy and congregations to adopt particular goods or services on the market that will enable them to adapt to these forces. For example, clergy and congregations in the Sierra Pacific Synod were encouraged to use the market research the synod purchased from a southern California company called Percept, and the synod regularly hired church growth experts to speak at one or more annual events.[36] Thus, the congregations operate, not in a free market per se, but in a mediated market in which mimetic isomorphism rather than rationality and competition drive the borrowing of ideas and practices.

In this chapter I have presented the first part of a constructivist theory of religious change that shows how the internal dynamics of meaning making turn particular external religious changes and trends into the catalysts for congregational change. We have seen how congregation leaders construct crises of meaning and membership based on their interpretation of key shifts in the American religious landscape (e.g., the decline of mainline Protestantism and ascendance of evangelical and nondenominational Protestantism). In addition, I argued that the specific causal stories congregations developed were based on their embeddedness in different religious markets and institutional spheres. Congregations tightly connected to evangelical church growth and megachurch networks were more likely to construct a story that linked the potential demise of the congregation with close adherence to the Lutheran tradition. They claimed that growth and success depended on adopting evangelicalism's emphasis on conversion and making worship accessible to and fun for non-Lutherans. Congregations more tightly connected to the denomination and/or mainline/liberal church growth networks tended to construct a causal story that emphasized authenticity and spirituality. Their accounts urged the congregation to open up the tradition to non-Lutheran and even non-Christian elements to stave off decline and ensure vitality. External forces—whether megachurch product or changes in American religiosity—provided the raw materials out of which congregational leaders constructed crises that justified their call to transform the tradition and then to mobilize support.

The central role that national religious market and entrepreneurs from the church growth industry played in congregations' construction of the catalysts for change also suggests how the Protestant culture has shifted in recent decades. In the next two chapters we will see how a religious culture that is dominated by evangelicalism and seeker spirituality shapes the strategies and processes of change in the study congregations.

Chapter 4

REFRAMING
THE TRADITION

THE ASSOCIATE PASTOR at Grace Lutheran Church in one of the Oakland suburbs began his sermon by talking about anniversaries and holidays. He listed the holidays our culture overtly marks, such as Halloween, Christmas, Veterans Day, and Thanksgiving, and then he reminded us that there are other holidays we no longer commemorate, like Arbor Day and Flag Day. Holidays help us remember our stories; they help us remember why some events are important to us. He reminded us that our stories have changed in recent years and so have the ways we remember them, and he mentioned the relatively new holiday to honor Martin Luther King Jr.'s life and work. He remarked that if you visit a Jewish cemetery you might see piles or rows of stones placed on headstones—a way of remembering the dead. He then turned to his text for the day: the story of Israel crossing the Jordan River into the Promised Land, from the fourth chapter of Joshua. At this point he moved away from the lectern and told the story from the center aisle of the sanctuary:

Israel has made it to the river Jordan and they can't cross because the people have started to murmur again as they always do. God tells Joshua to have the priests carry the Ark into the river, and as they do the river parts and the people are told to cross. Now, once they cross the dry riverbed, God instructs Joshua to have twelve elders of the tribes select a stone from the riverbed, and then place it in a circle on the soil of the Promised Land. The circle is a way of signifying that Israel is part of God's family and is part of God's salvation. This is one reason why Jews place stones on headstones in piles and in chains to remember that the dead and themselves are joined together by God's promise of salvation. Do you know why this empty chair is sitting next to the altar? During the war in Sarajevo the central marketplace was bombed, and sixteen men, women, and children were killed. After the bombing a cellist from the Sarajevo Symphony was unable to accept the murder, mayhem, and killing of the sixteen. He wanted to remember the event and he wanted the world to remember the event, so he took his cello and a folding chair on the day after the massacre and played a concert. He did this for the next sixty-eight days. He did it to celebrate the lives of the dead and not to forget them. I don't know what your bombed-out markets of your life are; what your pain is; what poison is bleeding God's salvation from you; but I want you to reclaim that salvation, to realize the Power of God's love in your life. Pick up and hold the stone you were given when you entered the church this morning. Close your eyes and think of the places where we are blinded to God's love and salvation. Then take your stone to a place in the sanctuary or gathering hall where we have experienced in the past the lifting of the burden of pain, anger, despair—the foot of the cross, the altar where we celebrate Eucharist, the baptismal font, the stained-glass windows. Place your rock there and come away transformed by the lifting of this burden.

No one moved for a minute or two and he issued the invitation again and this time the whole congregation got up. In silence, except for the occasional tap of shoes on concrete, people took a journey through the building; some walked directly to the spot where they placed their stones; others visited various sites before depositing them; many prayed before or after they placed their stones. Most placed their stones on or around the altar, some at the foot of the standing cross by the altar and at least a dozen on the baptismal font.

This ritual episode illustrates one of the strategies of change used at one of the congregations in the study and how it is tied to the Lutheran tradition. This strategy is akin to what Roof calls "retraditioning"—a way of "creating new cultural formations that provide alternative visions of spiritual and ethical life."[1] In this case, the congregation borrowed a religious practice from Jewish funeral rituals and Jewish salvation history. They took this older and non-Christian rite and created a new ritual (i.e., the placing of the stones in the church building). This new ritual was made relevant to the members of the church by the way that it was connected explicitly to current events and issues of global justice (an important concern of this congregation) as well as to individuals' personal struggles and the journey language of seeker spirituality (spirituality and seeking are other important concerns of members of Grace Lutheran). Finally, the rite was linked to three core parts of the Lutheran tradition—the cross, baptism, and the ritual of Communion—both by the minister's instructions and by members' participation in the ritual as they placed their stones around the focal points of Lutheran worship and theology.

In this chapter and the next, I turn from analyzing the catalysts of change to exploring the strategies of change and continue to develop the arguments about change set out in chapters 1 and 3. I draw on existing cultural, ecological, and market theories of religious change to explain the patterns of change and specify the organizational conditions under which congregations will use specific strategies of cultural resignification or market adaptation. In continuity with the previous chapter, I demonstrate how larger religious trends, especially the growing dominance of evangelicalism (i.e., the pietist tradition) in American Protestantism and the new spirituality, shape the strategies of change used by the congregations. I also show how the solutions presented in congregations' causal stories influence the change strategies they employ.

In this chapter I review how cultural theories understand the process of change and apply some of their concepts in my analysis of three congregations. I explore how leaders of the congregations use different strategies of resignification to push their congregations toward a liberal form of sectarianism. In the next chapter I rely on market and ecological approaches to explain the process of change among the congregations moving toward evangelicalism and nondenominationalism.

EXPLAINING THE STRATEGIES AND PROCESSES OF RELIGIOUS CHANGE

Cultural theories of religious change focus on how congregations change the religious meanings system, or culture. Often congregations or individuals assign new meanings to old symbols, rituals, or beliefs. Sargeant notes how Willow Creek leaders intentionally translate the historic and biblical language of Christianity into the therapeutic language of late-twentieth-century America.[2] In his study of baby boomers, Roof notes that religious change happens as congregations and individuals respond to larger changes in American religious culture, such as the emergence of spiritual-quest culture. One strategy of change involves the "reframing of religious language." This refers to the process whereby "religious speech or symbols are not used to convey some transcendent truth or reality as traditionally understood, but as means of *creating* truth or *provoking* confrontation with it. Rather than looking upon symbols as fixed realities in some objectivist manner, they become negotiated and situational, used to construct a set of meanings in the face of serious human dilemmas and existential concerns."[3] Both reframing and, more generally, the creation of new rituals as evinced in the example at Grace suggest that the process of change is one in which religious people actively work to redefine the symbols, values, rites, theologies, or languages of a given tradition to make them more resonant or meaningful to people for whom the tradition is outdated or unfamiliar.

Another cultural process of religious change draws on Swidler's notion of the tool kit and suggests that congregations and individuals "mine" or reach into the archive of the tradition during periods of conflict or congregational unrest.[4] In her study of congregational conflict in a Chicago suburb, Becker demonstrates how a Lutheran church emphasized certain theological themes from the tradition to justify and win support for its attempt to end its decline by becoming a multiracial community:

[The minister] drew upon and reintegrated two elements of Lutheran heritage to provide a religious understanding of tolerance and diversity. He married a commitment to social justice with the Lutheran emphasis on communalism. "Christian community" or "Community in Christ" is one of the ideals invoked most often in sermon and has become the dominant metaphor for the congregation's post-resurrection identity and mission.[5]

Cultural approaches to religious change point toward a variety of strategies whereby church leaders give new meanings to old symbols, rituals, or beliefs, create new traditions, or rediscover old ones. However, the situations of the study congregations pose new theoretical puzzles. Under what conditions will a congregation use a given cultural strategy? What criteria guide leaders' choices of strategies and processes of change? To what extent will a congregation try to protect or buffer the core elements of a tradition as they change other parts? Finally, how far can a congregation alter its tradition before it is no longer recognizable? Mining and reworking the tradition are noticeably problematic. For example, it is not obvious how a congregation could mine its tradition when some members may be unaware of what is in the archive, when others believe the tradition is not meaningful or important and thus not worth mining, and when some are drawing on elements from alternative traditions. This is the general situation faced by many of the congregations in my study, and not surprisingly, their leaders find that mining the tradition is a significant challenge. Some congregations struggle to gain consensus about whether or not to access their own archive and how to incorporate alternative traditions in the existing Lutheran tradition. In the Lutheran case, the doctrine of *adiaphora*[6] and the multiple strands of Lutheranism from which the members of each congregation came (each strand having its own understanding of what should be considered core to Lutheranism) exacerbate the difficulty of selecting, reinterpreting, and recovering parts of the tradition for contemporary use. In the remainder of the chapter, I begin to explore these theoretical puzzles by describing the strategies of change used by several congregations and by identifying the conditions and organizational criteria that guide congregations in their attempts to borrow, mine, alter, or create anew their own tradition.

THE STRATEGIES OF CHANGE AT
BAY AREA CONGREGATIONS

In this chapter I focus on three congregations that relied on the overarching strategy of reframing the tradition: Grace and Good Shepherd in the Oakland suburbs and Christ in Oakland. Roof talks about reframing as a strategy by which individuals or congregations redefine their religious language or symbol system. However, I believe this is an overly narrow definition because it does not take into account the way in which congregations try to redefine the meaning and purpose of what it means to be a Christian church. I see reframing as a master strategy that guides congregational leaders' use of more specific strategies of change that they believe will help them reframe the language, symbols, rituals, and mission of congregational life.[7] If reframing is seen in reference to Goffman's notion of framing, then it can be used in this broader manner. A tradition is like a frame insofar as it constitutes a scheme for interpreting and ordering religious events and experience.[8] A tradition helps members of a church answer the question "What's going on here?" by providing theological rationales for religious activity, a cosmology that orients individuals in the world, and ritualized activities (in the form of the Lutheran liturgy and hymnody) that guide and teach individuals how to worship God and instruct them about what to expect intellectually and emotionally from worship. Reframing, then, becomes a way of altering the taken-for-granted primary framework of the tradition of a religious group.[9] The challenge for several congregations in the study was to know how and to what extent to alter the tradition when it is not the taken-for-granted primary framework for many members of the congregation. For other congregations the challenge was to change the tradition substantially despite the opposition of powerful groups within the congregation for whom the unaltered tradition was important.

Roof notes that, in reframing, the intent is to dislodge old meanings or create new ones, and in particular, the strategy suggests that reframing advocates will take a critical and even confrontational stance against traditional religious language and symbols. At the same time it is a strategy by which religious leaders can help people find a new language (or provide one for them) with which they can make sense of their religious experiences. Given the larger shift in American Protestantism away from doctrine and toward experience, and the lack of familiarity or even salience that religious doctrine has for many Christians (including Lutherans), reframing becomes a way to develop a new language for articulating the religious truths contained in doctrine without using the religious jargon.[10]

One strategy for reframing is *translation,* whereby congregational leaders translate core theological concepts from the Lutheran tradition (or from one of several other traditions such as the pietistic or revival tradition of American Protestantism, the ancient church, or Buddhism) into a language that is more contemporary and understandable.[11] Translating the term "sin" into the idiom of therapeutic psychology by using such terms as "alienation" or "dysfunction" is an example of this type of reframing. A second strategy is *reemphasis,* whereby church leaders shift the theological, symbolic, or ritualistic emphasis away from certain elements of the tradition in favor of other elements. This was seen at Good Shepherd when the pastors no longer emphasized the cross and resurrection in their sermons and instead spoke more often about the life or model of Jesus, suggesting a shift in emphasis from the Lutheran doctrine of justification to the Lutheran doctrine of sanctification.

Three other strategies of change also helped some of the congregations reframe the tradition under which they lived. *Contextualization* is the attempt to adapt the tradition to more closely fit the demographic and sociocultural context of the local religious setting. One version of this strategy is seen in the congregations that tried to incorporate religious practices, symbols, or ideas from the non-Lutheran traditions of new or prospective members or from the ethnic populations the church is serving or trying to serve. A second version is to emphasize certain theological ideas, ethical principles, or ritual practices that will appeal to the interests and needs of specific populations, such as gay or lesbian persons. Contextualization was the favored reframing strategy of the Oakland congregations. Contextualization serves to reframe a tradition by shifting the emphasis away from certain elements of the tradition, such as the intellectual and nonemotive style of worship that has characterized much of American Lutheranism, and stressing other elements, such as the pietistic or emotional strand of Lutheran worship by adding gospel music or the call-and-response style of preaching. The strategies of reemphasis and contextualization are similar but technically different. The strategy of reemphasis simply means that the congregation ignores some elements of the tradition and highlights, uses, talks about other elements more. Contextualization means that the congregation intentionally tries to alter the tradition to fit the religious interests, needs, or expectations of a particular population, such as African Americans.

Retraditioning is another strategy that congregations used to create new religious practices, especially rituals, by incorporating parts of other religious traditions into the life of a congregation. Retraditioning tended to be used periodically at a few congregations as the means to expand the ritualistic repertoire of the congregations and sometimes to shed new light on certain features of the Lutheran tradition but not to remake the tradition or replace it with a totally new or different tradition. The third strategy is what Roof calls *reconnecting*. Congregation leaders turn to this strategy to help members connect with lost, forgotten, or unknown elements of the tradition.[12] Reconnecting commonly was used in combination with one of the other strategies when church leaders were pushing for more radical departures from the Lutheran tradition. It was used to remind members of the deficiencies of the tradition (as in the case of churches that lamented Lutheranism's historic inability to win converts as they tried to adopt the evangelism solution to the problem of growth) or to signal continuities with the tradition (as in the case of churches that spoke about Luther's notion of being "little Christ's" to one's neighbor to defend their attempt to shift the emphasis toward Lutheran ethics and away from belief or doctrine). This strategy most commonly took the form of appeals or reminders about their church's connection to Lutheranism as leaders tried to defend or gain support for proposed changes. For example, most of the congregations that were incorporating contemporary praise music or rock and roll into worship justified it by claiming they were simply following Luther's example of using the popular music of his day (i.e., German drinking songs) to share the message of Christianity.

Reframing at Grace Lutheran Church

At Grace Lutheran Church reframing was employed to help members find a language of their own by which they could make sense of their religious experiences or to help them translate older, and perhaps less meaningful, terms into contemporary language. It was also used to redefine what it means to be Christian in ways that pushed members and the church toward a countercultural position vis-à-vis the larger community in which it resides.

Grace is a church that is willing to remake the Lutheran tradition for three interrelated reasons. First, it is a home for many former Lutherans, Episcopalians, and Roman Catholics who had been rejected by or had rejected the churches of their childhood. As such, the Lutheran tradition was a fuzzy memory for some and relatively unfamiliar for others. At the same time, many of these former churchgoers had fond memories of certain parts of the liturgical traditions shared by all three groups (such as chanted liturgy and the sacrament of Communion). Second, its leaders and many of its members place a particular reading of the gospel that stresses liberation above the keeping of tradition. Third, the church has long-standing commitments to promoting ecumenism and interfaith partnerships, working for social justice, and fostering spiritual practices that help individuals experience the sacred. These commitments have helped the congregation cultivate an ethos in which compassion, inclusivity, experimentation, and change are given such importance that they compel the congregation to open up the tradition or mine their own tradition for those elements that will further these values.

Tom Irons, the senior pastor, spoke about the tradition and the congregation's connection to and willingness to bend it during one of our interviews:

> Well, one of the core pieces of my faith is from Galatians, "For freedom Christ has set us free." And if our faith has nothing to do with the liberation of people where they are, I think it is worthless. . . . My contention is that the only tradition we have is the living Christ. Nothing else matters. Now I appreciate and value the wisdom accrued over the ages in some of our teachings, but those are tools now to be utilized to bring illumination and hope and encouragement and transformation to the people who are alive now.

The pastor refers implicitly to Luther's notion of the freedom of the Christian and the more general belief that the ministry of Jesus was to bring freedom or liberation, and he makes these, rather than the particular elements of the Lutheran tradition, the standard that guides the congregation. Later in the interview we were talking about worship and he noted that "the [Lutheran] liturgy has several component parts which can be rearranged any way you want, but it does provide a powerful flow. I appreciate it deeply and I think that the rhythm has worked itself into the community life here and it provides some sense of order for us. There's no need to get rid of it for some other modern form, but each element can be transposed in any direction."

Members spoke with equal passion about the power of the Lutheran liturgy to provide them with a sense of meaning and connection to the sacred and one another, and the way in which worship, which is different every Sunday, opens them up to see the Christian life and Christian community in new ways. For example, one member, a scientist, said that "the liturgy has an order to it that seems to make your soul echo within this framework. It's like the chants and hymns reach down and just resonate with your whole being." Other members spoke about how new things in worship (such as the use of drama and art or re-written creeds and liturgies) and the consistent sermons about "real forgiveness, real grace, real mercy, and real justice" made them think and want to participate. Several members shared stories with me of growing up Lutheran or Catholic and how the liturgy had become rote for them, but at Grace, you cannot sit back and "mouth the words because the words of the creed or confession or Lord's Prayer might be different from the *LBW* [*Lutheran Book of Worship*] or the way we did it last week." One woman who grew up in a Lutheran church but considered her-self basically nondenominational as an adult said that she found that the form of the liturgy gives her a sense of order and stability, while much of the altered content of the liturgy, along with the sermons, "challenges me to think outside myself; challenges me to be accepting of other people as they are."

This commitment to liturgical worship is in itself countercultural. Few Prot-estant denominations follow a codified liturgy, and those that do are increas-ingly moving toward nonliturgical worship services modeled after evangelical and nondenominational seeker churches. Moreover, "American society is a non-liturgical society because," as Wolfe notes, "its pace of life [is] too fast, its com-mitments to individualism too powerful, its treatment of authority too irrever-ent, and its cravings for innovation too intense to tolerate religious practices that call on believers to repeat the same words or songs with little room for creative expression."[13] Grace takes a stand against much of American culture by adher-ing to the historic liturgy but also finds itself following the cultural pressure to innovate.

Over and over again, members and clergy spoke about a sense of continuity or connection to the tradition and a freedom to innovate, much like a jazz musician might play a "jazz standard." Members spoke passionately about the surprises in worship and how no matter what happened they were always able to "connect" with God or members of the community. The former president of the congrega-tion claimed that worship at Grace "honors all that which is holy in life. One rea-son we experiment so much is that we are looking for ways to honor the diverse ways we experience the holy—sometimes it means incorporating Bahai or Bud-dhist things; other times it means saying the Lord's Prayer according to the old Lutheran Church Missouri Synod words because that really connects for some people." One outcome of this willingness to experiment is that change has become normative for members of the congregation. Thus, when worship leaders or teach-ers play with the conventions of Lutheran worship, add new traditions from other religions, or reframe Lutheran theology in the more contemporary language of psychotherapy and spirituality, it is seen as a normal part of life at Grace.[14] More-over, as several interviewees claimed, it was the constant newness in the content and structure of worship that often helped them to see their faith in new ways.

Worship at Grace often followed the Lutheran liturgical order and relied on several important Lutheran theological concepts such as God's grace, but inevitably the service and the teachings were modified in ways that forced members to listen and that challenged their preconceptions. The goal of worship according to the pastors and many members was to engage people in the story of liberation in the gospel so that they and the community as a whole are transformed. Worship thus became a venue for reframing, retraditioning, and reconnecting. On a given Sunday, feminine terms for God might be substituted in the prayers, a circle dance might be performed to celebrate the sacrament of Communion, or the creed might be spoken directly to the person sitting next to oneself in the pew to make the statement of faith more than a ritual of rote recitation. These changes to the liturgy compelled people to listen and participate in new ways and thus kept worship fresh.

At Grace, retraditioning often serves to awaken the congregation to new insights into the nature of God and their own religious identities. For example, one Sunday in Lent the pastor gave a sermon on Jesus' teaching about loving one's enemies. He pointed out that forgiving and loving our enemies goes against the way we commonly think about evil in our country: namely, that evil is an irreversible force that must be addressed only by eradicating it. "That is false; a lie. This is not God's way. The power of God's love is that it can change evil. But the problem with love is that it is a daily thing; it has no lasting power. And so we start each day from scratch and must love the ever-present enemy." After the sermon the congregation was instructed to stand in a circle and invited to speak aloud the name of a person they needed to forgive and offer a blessing for that person. This new ritual turned the abstract concept of loving one's enemy into a lived reality.

Another example illustrates the power of retraditioning to open up church members to hear the radical claims of the Christian witness. The Lutheran order of service usually begins with a processional hymn, followed by the pastor's greeting to the congregation, and then the Prayer of the Day. One Sunday after the congregation had responded to the pastor's greeting of "The Lord be with you" by saying in unison, "And also with you," the pastor suddenly broke from the order and announced, "The proper response is, 'But he didn't need to.'" We then began the liturgy again with the pastor reciting something God had done that day and the congregation responding, "But he didn't need to": "God gave us sleep," "but he didn't need to." "God woke us to the day," "but he didn't need to." "God kept the laws of gravity at work overnight," "but he didn't need to." "God gave us scripture," "but he didn't need to." "God gave us Communion," "but he didn't need to." Each call and response increased in volume, speed, and passion until the sanctuary echoed with our shouts. This little bit of ritualistic innovation—retraditioning of a sort—prevented the congregation from simply parroting back the written responses in the hymnal, forced them to listen, and reminded them of the central theological message about God's grace that was always present at worship.

The primary work of reframing was often employed during teaching moments in small groups, sermons, or newsletter articles. My fieldwork at Grace coincided with the seasons of Lent and Easter in 2001, during which the pastor reframed some of the theological and liturgical themes of these two yoked seasons of the Christian calendar. This reframing work began at the worship service on Ash Wednesday. For Christians in the liturgical traditions (Roman Catholic, Episcopal, and Lutheran), Lent is typically understood as a forty-day period of sacrifice in which individuals often give up some important activity or favorite food as a way of preparing for the death of Jesus on Good Friday and emulating his sacrifice. In his sermon, the senior pastor reminded the congregation that Lent is a time for prayer and fasting, but he also noted that we have a hard time doing them: "We don't like to be alone with God. We can sit for hours at a boring party with our friends or stuffing ourselves with dessert but we can't sit for a few minutes to be alone with God. Perhaps this is the year when you learn to pray." So far, the sermon was fairly standard fare for Lutherans, nothing out of the ordinary. But then the pastor advocated a shift in the way Christians could and should think about Lent and the sacrificial spiritual practices that regulate the season:

> Lent is about asking what is really important. These religious practices are supposed to help us focus on this question. Sacrifice is not about giving things up—it's about becoming sacred—you and I becoming sacred before God. So give up guilt. Give up worthlessness. You are not worthless; you are the beloved of God. Give up self-centeredness. These are the things to give up, not chocolate. Eat chocolate if you need it. Lent is about life and becoming fully human.

Guilt and human worthlessness in relation to the righteousness of God have been central parts of Lutheran theology and perennial sermon topics during Lent. There are many jokes about Lutherans and guilt (and Catholics and guilt) within the tradition, which the pastor was claiming were not funny at all. The pastor turned a Lutheran way of understanding human nature and Christianity upside down here by claiming that Lent is about life, not about death, and that the things we give up in Lent should be those things that diminish life or lead to death.

After a simple Lenten meal, twenty of us gathered in a circle to answer the question, "What is alienation?" After some time for reflection, members shared personal stories about alienation and reconciliation; others simply offered one-word definitions of the concept. Many of the stories framed alienation in terms of broken or dysfunctional family relationships and the struggle to overcome bitterness, loss, despair, or anger resulting from those relationships. Throughout the reflection and sharing period, Pastor Irons sat quietly listening to his congregants. Then he offered a short summary and commentary on people's stories:

> In my years of study I am persuaded that "sin" is an important concept but that sin doesn't work well. It isn't meaningful to people today. When you

say "sin," no one is quite sure what it refers to. But alienation—separation, broken relationships—we get alienation. We all experience alienation. All humans are alienated. At best you might be in recovery [this statement received a few laughs]. But alienation is not a problem that we can solve. It is a condition—part of what it means to be human.

Here the pastor has taken a key theological term from the Lutheran archive—sin—translated it into the more familiar idiom of popular psychology, and allowed members to define it in their own language. At the same time he retained the Lutheran understanding of sin as a condition.

Although I heard therapeutic language at Grace, I more commonly heard the language of contemporary spirituality: being on a journey, practicing meditation, studying Zen Buddhism, walking the labyrinth (the church had a large labyrinth painted outside the sanctuary and occasionally included a labyrinth walk during worship), or turning head knowledge into heart wisdom. At the start of the Lenten season, the senior pastor's article in the monthly newsletter urged members to use the three wisdom tools of listening, contemplation/reflection, and prayer/meditation "to deepen our understanding of God" and to "be absorbed into the liberating truth of God's infinite compassion for each of us and all of life." This sounds more like the language of medieval mysticism than the historic language of Lutheranism. Yet this idiom is not completely divorced from the Lutheran tradition, as suggested in the following two examples in which members connected their understanding of spirituality with Luther's teachings or theology. One member noted:

Luther talked about how everything in the world can be put to a spiritual purpose. The key is like Joe Sittler said [Sittler was a Lutheran theologian]: all of creation is connected in a spiritual ecology. The deepest human longing is to be accepted as a child of God; the challenge of spirituality is to see others and ourselves as children of God.

When I asked him how Grace helps cultivate this notion of spirituality, he remarked that he always hears about "God's all-encompassing love" in sermons and experiences it "during Communion when you look into the eyes of the person giving you the bread or wine and you realize that this person is the means of grace for you and you are connected to them. Words can't really describe the experience. This is the church. Communion is the contemplation of each other's mystery and reveling in it and lifting it up when other people can't see it."

The language of spirituality and practices of contemporary American spirituality also are invoked directly in sermons and worship services. Sermons were peppered with journey language, and the pastor always rang a Tibetan singing bowl to signal a period of meditation at the end of Communion every Sunday. In the following example, the senior pastor reframed how his congregation should think about suffering and the spiritual life by contrasting mystical and therapeutic versions of spirituality with the ways in which middle-class suburbanites tend to respond to suffering. In this instance, reframing is not about shifting the emphasis within the tradition but about finding a new way of articulating and experiencing the Christian life:

> There is much suffering in our world—economic, physical, mental, emotional. The experience of brokenness, of suffering, is aloneness, being unloved, abused, dismissed. And we think to ourselves, "We shouldn't feel this way; we should be happy." Isn't that why we moved to this suburb? And we usually look to escape our suffering. But the first, true step toward dealing with suffering is to enter into it. But we really want to avoid the pain, the anguish, the fear. So we try to get everything under control. We clear our desk, put up a missile shield, pray to God and to Alan Greenspan that everything will be under control. [*In a very loud voice*] But it is all ludicrous. [*In a stage whisper*] The secret of spiritual life is that everything is our life. Integrating, incorporating, dealing with suffering is part of our journey to becoming fully human. Faith takes on our depression and turns it into cleansing. Faith takes our suffering and makes us love ourselves and even our enemies.

The shift to the language of spirituality also is evident in a statement of faith the congregation issued in 2003. The statement was grounded in the Lutheran doctrine of God's unconditional love for humanity as expressed in the death and resurrection of Jesus. However, the language in which the doctrine is articulated bears the marks of contemporary spirituality and spiritual seeking; it stresses experience over intellectual assent, community and relationships over church and membership. It does not rely on the historic Lutheran idioms of sin, grace, atonement, or justification, nor does it refer to judgment and the demands of personal morality that many members of Grace associate with organized religion. It is even written in the form of a poem, an unconventional genre for a religious creed:

WHAT WE BELIEVE — THE TRUTH WILL SET YOU FREE!

The Gospel is God's unconditional promise of fulfillment
Made human in the experience of Jesus' death and resurrection.
The Gospel involves no ifs, ands, or buts.
It does not say
If you repent, or *if* you believe—
If you do your best to live a good life, or *if* you fight on the right side of issues,
Or *if* you behave as a moral person . . . then God will fulfill you.
You don't have to be good to experience the love of God.
Rather, the Gospel says,
"Because the Crucified lives as compassionate Lord, our present reality is blessed."
Any talk of Jesus and God and human life

That does not heal and transform our lives, relationships, community and creation,
Makes the Gospel a lie and irrelevant to the hearts of hearers.
Embodying the love of Christ releases wisdom and peace and joy.
Because Jesus the Christ is alive, your ultimate destiny
Is absolutely and unconditionally good!

The statement of faith summarizes how Grace reframes the tradition in the language of spirituality and shifts the emphasis in the tradition from intellect, doctrine, and church to emotions, experience, and community. More generally, the reframing work at Grace draws on (or reconnects with) the liturgical and theological parts of the Lutheran tradition and gives it new relevancy, salience, and meaning by translating the tradition into the language and practices of the religious culture of seeking. The reframing encourages members to adopt religious beliefs and a Christian identity that are countercultural, whether that means trying to love one's enemies, welcoming and publicly advocating gay and lesbian persons, or helping individuals escape the pressures for control and security that dominate the professional careers and suburban lives of the church's members. The congregation's culture of experimentation and its membership of people with relatively loose ties to any one tradition made it possible to use re-traditioning. A comment from one of the individuals who was going through the process of the catechumenate (an early church tradition of initiation into the way and beliefs of Christianity that Grace had claimed as its own new tradition in 2001) suggests the way in which reframing is reshaping the congregation and the tradition at Grace:

The catechumenate has been an important part of my journey towards self-enlightenment and knowledge. We read a book about simplicity and the Bible, and both have helped me understand what is essential in life. God gives us hands to work and hearts to love freely; we didn't do anything to earn it. The church is teaching me this lesson; that's why I decided to re-up. But I didn't want to just join a church; I wanted to join the movement, Christianity, again.

Reframing at Good Shepherd Lutheran Church

The reframing work at Good Shepherd, a congregation just a few miles from Grace Lutheran, also emphasized changes in the religious language and practices of Lutheranism. The clergy at the church were intent on largely replacing not only Lutheran idioms but also Lutheran theology in order to change members' understanding of the nature and purpose of the church and Christianity and to provide members with a new language to make sense of postmodern, posttraditional culture. In particular, the clergy were using different religious terms to challenge the Lutheran doctrine of atonement, Lutheran ecclesiology, and a Lutheran way of talking about fundamental religious experiences. They also were challenging the de facto compartmentalization of church and faith in

American society that defines religion as a private affair and keeps it separate from other spheres of daily life and the prevailing consumerist ethos that treats religion like any other commodity in the marketplace.

One of the noticeable changes in the religious language at Good Shepherd was the absence of the Lutheran language of human sin, the cross, and atonement. The cross is the central symbol in Lutheranism as a sign of God's victory over sin (in the death of God's son, Jesus) and God's unconditional acceptance of sinful human beings. The cross is a central part of the Lutheran doctrine of atonement as well. This doctrine is predicated on the theological claim that all humans were created good but as heirs to the original disobedience of the first humans (Adam and Eve) have become sinful by nature—sin being the separation and alienation between God and humanity. The only way this breach in the divine-human relationship could be repaired was through a scapegoat who would be sacrificed for the sake of all of humanity. This scapegoat, according to Lutheran theology, is God's son, Jesus Christ, who was crucified on a cross.[15]

This doctrine has been a linchpin of Lutheran theology since the Reformation, but at Good Shepherd, the clergy had stopped using this language and references to it. The senior pastor, Dave Richards, noted in one interview: "We don't use that cross language anymore. Or hardly at all anymore. Jesus died on a cross for you. I mean, I would never say that anymore. So some older members are upset by this. They're like, where's the cross? I mean, we need to have the cross. And I think, subtly, they're missing not only the physical cross, but they're missing their language."[16] Andrew Olson, the pastor for lay development and mission outreach, noted in our interview that people had written letters to the pastors complaining that they no longer heard references to the cross, sin, or Christ in sermons and that they "miss the atonement language."

The absence of atonement language was most evident during the ritual of Communion. The rite includes a recitation of salvation history (i.e., a narrative of God's actions to save humanity at different times that culminates in the sacrifice of Jesus on the cross) and the words that Jesus allegedly used during his last supper, the event that serves as the model for the rite, including "This cup is the new covenant in my blood, shed for you and for all people for the forgiveness of sins," "body of Christ," and "blood of Christ." These words are spoken when the bread and wine are given to the members of a congregation. The liturgy also has several places in which Jesus is referred to as the "Lamb of God" who is sacrificed to save humanity (the phrase references the ancient Jewish custom of sacrificing a lamb to appease a God angry with the disobedience of Israel), and it is customary to sing the "Agnus Dei" (i.e., "Lamb of God") during Communion. However, the pastors at Good Shepherd omit the salvation history and references to Jesus as the lamb of God during the rite and substitute the words "bread of life" and "cup of blessing" for the terms "body" and "blood," suggesting a shift away from the language of animal slaughter that is referenced by the traditional terms but that is alien to our time and place. For some members the rite has been stripped of its familiar words and no longer signifies God's redeeming action.

Although the senior pastor did not offer a rationale for this change, his colleague suggested that an important reason for this reframing was that the language does not make sense to non-Lutherans and thus keeps the church closed to visitors or outsiders. During the interview with the new pastor of worship and music, I asked him to explain why he radically changed the first worship services he led. In his response he made the connection between redefining the meaning of church and changing the religious language of Lutheranism: "I took the old service and just changed some of the words so they were not so male normative. And then I took some of the bloody lamb imagery out because it only connects with people in the club." Thus, changing the doctrinal language not only updated or modernized the way in which the congregation communicated but also, he hoped, served as a recruitment tool. The unspoken assumption is that postdenominational and post-Christian Californians will not be interested in learning about or participating in Christianity if the language they hear in church is not familiar or positive. This is similar to the shift made by seeker and nondenominational churches in which the negative aspects of Christianity (sin, judgment, and demands for a radically changed life) are downplayed.[17] However, the goal of Good Shepherd's leaders is not to replace doctrinal language with the therapeutic language of self-fulfillment as at Willow Creek and other seeker churches but to offer a language that helps people understand what counts as an experience of the sacred and what will make their lives meaningful and connected to a community and a purpose that is greater than the individual.

All three pastors believed that abandoning Lutheranism's atonement language was necessary to shift attention toward what it means to live an authentic Christian life and away from how to be a member of a church. This shift to emphasize authenticity over membership and tradition was at the heart of the congregation's causal story. Pastor Richards ruefully acknowledged that for years all the church has done "is teach the laity how to do church. We haven't taught them how to live their Christian faith in their life. We need to be thinking about how do we transform ourselves so that church can bring meaning to people's daily lives and their life of faith in a very complex world." He and the other pastors are convinced that their members and, more generally, people in their twenties, thirties, and forties are not at all interested in serving or even joining the institutionalized church (which for them means a religious organization dedicated to self-reproduction).

They attempted to accomplish this reframing agenda both linguistically and ritually. The changes in the rite of Communion illustrate a modest effort at reframing, but a more radical attempt came about as the clergy and worship leaders inserted concepts and terms from Buddhism into the worship life of the congregation. In particular, the pastor of worship and music often spoke in the language of Buddhism—being mindful and compassionate and having a different concept of time. Being mindful, being present, and the stress on compassion are basic Buddhist teachings.[18]

One of the earliest changes to the liturgy, an attempt at retraditioning, came when Pastor Thompson, the new minister for worship, substituted a service he created for the church's usual liturgy. The new service, called the "Blessing of Life" service, bore little resemblance to the structure or content of the Lutheran service the church usually followed, although ties to the tradition could be seen in a close reading of the service. For example, liturgical scholars generally agree that Lutheran worship is organized in four parts: gathering, the Word (i.e., reading of the Bible and the sermon), the meal (i.e., celebration of the Lord's Supper), and the sending of believers into the world. They also generally agree that worship is about God and not about human beings, that God is made present to humans in the reading of scripture and in the bread and wine of the Lord's Supper, and that laypeople should be full participants.[19] This structure and these theological principles were present in the "Blessing of Life" service, but unless participants were liturgical virtuosi, they would have trouble identifying the service as Lutheran. While many members appeared lost and confused during the service, and some reported being disturbed by the change in the structure of the liturgy, they were more upset by the shift in the theological content of the service.[20] For example, in the standard Lutheran confession of sin, each participant publicly states, "We are in bondage to sin and cannot free ourselves." But in the alternative confession (called "release"), each participant acknowledged, "I separated myself from God's designs; my actions, words, and ways of living were not of love." In the standard absolution, the minister pronounces that "Almighty God, in his mercy, has given his Son to die for us and, for his sake, forgives us all our sins." In the new version, there is no absolution at all. Instead, the participants read a declaration in unison of how they will now try to live, and this is where the language of Buddhism appears:

> I encounter the Triune God and pay attention to all the ways God is present in my life. I notice and have gratitude to God for all of life's expressions. I accept God. I listen to God. I live God. The essence of God is who I am. All times, all places, all objects reveal God's complete Love. Realizing this, we give care with compassionate hearts and minds to all living things—to people, to animals, to the whole of nature. . . . I dedicate my life to assist all of life to know joy. I dedicate my life to awareness, that my ways of living will transcend all delusions and socialized conventions which hinder truth. I dedicate my life to follow my One True Life's path.

The liturgy included a variety of terms from Buddhism and from a more generalized Christian spirituality, such as understanding, seeking one another's highest good, truthful words, truthful behaviors, virtuous livelihood, balance and concentration, constant mindfulness, meditation and union with God. The service was not well received, with many members complaining to the pastors and lay leaders that Unitarian or New Age ideas had replaced Lutheran theology.

The service was relegated to an experimental third service for the remainder of the year. In her field notes of one such service, a research assistant (a PhD student in the area of spirituality and world religions) noted:

> The Blessing of Life service is Judeo-Christianity meets Buddhism. The words have to do with mindfulness and may all beings be happy. It is part of the Metta Sutra. I've heard Pastor Mark [Thompson] lead this service several times and he gives the same spiel each time. He talks about the need to change the hierarchical structures of the church and change our worldview. . . . I realize that what Mark is saying is new to most of the people at Good Shepherd but it is fairly standard in Buddhist circles. It is letting go of original sin, leveling of roles between laity and clergy, practicing compassion, embracing all sentient beings.

Her assessment was corroborated by clergy and the lay leaders whom I interviewed in terms of the goal of changing members' religious worldviews and the meaning of church. The leaders' reframing drew on their authenticity solution, in which the authentic Christian life was defined in terms of following the "way of Jesus" or the "way of love" and the authentic Christian community was one that empowered people to follow this path. Again, the reframing relied on the language of Buddhism and seeker spirituality because the church's leaders believed it would allow them to connect with young adults more easily than the historic language of Lutheranism. This reframing is evident in an article Pastor Thompson wrote shortly before he introduced the Blessing of Life service:

> If we are mindful (conscious of and intentional) about deepening our relationship with the Sacred, all things look differently. The stresses we experience are put into perspective. . . . Our desires and expectations become less rigid and imploded when we bring to life a life of compassion and love. That was the way of Christ. How we view the world and our role in it is an important ongoing spiritual exercise.

In addition to this challenge to Lutheran theological and liturgical language, the clergy, in particular, also challenged a conventional understanding of the purpose of the church. They criticized a notion of the church as an organization one joins or leaves on the basis of how valuable the goods and services provided are for the individual. They also attacked a membership-driven understanding of church commonly pressed by church growth experts, denominational officials, and people who were part of Good Shepherd in the booming membership years of the 1940s and 1950s. In short, the clergy were challenging the individualistic, pragmatic, and consumerist orientation to religion that characterizes much of post-1965 American Protestantism.

The clergy pressed for new definitions of church and the Christian faith in a variety of public meetings and newsletter articles. The pastor of worship and music was one of the leading voices in this reframing effort. Thompson's first column was entitled "What It Is to Be Church," and while he used it to look at the historical development of the Christian church, he also used it to stress that church is fundamentally not about membership or organization but about being and experience. He wrote, "Jesus did not found a church nor a religion—his life was simply about 'God-with-us-and-for-us.' . . . Foundationally church is rooted in experience—the experience of God's way of being in the world (Jesus' life)." According to the pastors and several members, worship, education, and fellowship at Good Shepherd were intended to help people experience God and live lives that emulated the life of Jesus. Repeatedly, the senior pastor argued that his church, especially the church council, who were concerned with a downturn in growth, should think in terms of discipleship and not membership. "The church should be a breeding ground for disciples—people who connect their faith with their living—not a club," he argued at one council meeting.

The pastors used a series of dinner meetings in late 2001 and early 2002 to articulate and win support for their reframing. At the first meeting, Pastor Thompson opened the evening discussion of the topic "What Is Church All About?" by shifting the terms from church to community, from membership to experience, from belief to action, and from self to God. In one way he reconnected to the tradition insofar as Lutherans believe God should be the focus of worship and all activities of the church, but he also pressed the congregation to adopt a somewhat countercultural or at least alternative vision of church, defined implicitly against consumerist and membership models—church as a community following Jesus and not American culture, centered on God and not on the self:

> The church is the community of people faithful to the way of God in the world. The church is a community that practices loving one another, being inclusive rather than exclusive, seeking the best for others. If we don't do these things, then we are not church. When I was younger I used to think about church in terms of what I got out of it and usually I didn't like it because I didn't get a lot out of it. I learned from a professor of mine that, essentially, we are not supposed to get anything out of it at all. Church is about worship, which has more to do with gratitude and humility and noticing the ways in which God loves us deeply. Church is where we come to give thanks to God for all the things God has done for us. It's not about what I get out of it but what I bring to it. We live in a culture that constantly reminds us that life is about getting what we want when we want it; and surely getting one's needs met is important, but it is equally important to think about what we really truly need for an authentic life.

At a second dinner meeting, at which the members were trying to figure out what the term "missional church" meant (this term comes from the title of a book all pastors in the synod were suppose to read and teach in 2000), Pastor Richards suggested that being missional is to run counter to how many people in our society think about church: "The church is not about providing a bunch of religious products which we consume—you come to church and get Communion, an inspiring worship, some teaching, a little fellowship—instead, the church should empower people to live lives of faith together." He followed up this discussion with a newsletter article in which he urged the congregation to "say goodbye" to a perspective that treats church as "a provider of religious goods." He confessed how he can sit and consume worship much like he consumes a restaurant meal and noted, "Thinking that the church is there to provide religious services that meet my particular needs is a pretty easy mentality to fall into since the entire consumer culture functions in just such a way." He suggested that we should not come to church "just to consume, but to open our lives to the way of Jesus, and to let the very spirit of the living Christ move through each of us to others in the community." Doing this, he concludes, will help each person find the courage to let following the way of Jesus seep into his or her being and everyday life and thus "participate in God's cosmic and eternal love." And for the clergy and some of the lay leaders of the congregation, this is ultimately the purpose of the Christian community.

While much of this reframing work is done to combat a larger Protestant or American understanding of church, it also subtly shifts the Lutheran understanding of church away from worship toward ethics. Lutherans historically understood church to occur when people gathered to hear the Bible (especially the gospel message of Christ crucified and resurrected) and participate in the rite of Holy Communion.[21] The ministers of Good Shepherd were suggesting that church is more than simply hearing the Word and receiving the sacraments; rather, it is a community that actively and intentionally lives out the way of Jesus by loving and serving others. The pastors often reminded members of the central role of the gospel and the sacraments but pushed the congregation to think of church in a more activist manner. For example, in an essay about worship, one pastor alluded to the important role of worship for a Lutheran understanding of the purpose of church but then redefined worship in a more activist mode: "Worship is primarily defined as attitudes and behaviors which bring to life humanity's attention to God. Attitudes and behaviors which clarify the living Christ—the Light of the World, our light—the Light of God with us and in us. That seems to signify worship as a way of living, a way of being in the world."

In short, reframing at Good Shepherd is oriented toward redefining what it means to participate in or belong to a church. It challenges common ways of thinking about church as a voluntary organization, as designed to meet individual religious or spiritual needs, or as an activity, set of beliefs, and relationships that are compartmentalized and kept apart from daily life. Instead, church is redefined as a community of people committed to following the path or way of Jesus and God, which will lead to an authentic life. This strategy relies on the language of spirituality while at the same time launching a critique against the individualistic nature of much of contemporary spirituality. The clergy (with the support of lay leaders) abandoned some of the theological language and ritual elements of Lutheran worship and did little to explicitly reconnect with the tradition. At the same time, they added new terms and practices from non-Lutheran sources. They adopted these strategies, in part, because they believed younger members and the population at large had no familiarity with and no interest in cultivating a distinctly Lutheran identity and, in part, because of their commitment to creating a new way of being the church that would meet seekers' demand for an authentic religious faith.

Reframing at Christ Lutheran Church

Christ Lutheran Church, in Oakland, relied more heavily on the strategy of contextualization than did Grace and Good Shepherd because the congregation's leaders were trying to make the congregation's demographics and culture match the diverse population in the surrounding neighborhoods. Contextualization took the form of opening up the tradition to include elements from the religious cultures of nonwhite racial and ethnic groups and, as such, did not so much change Lutheranism as expand it. At the same time, in order to meet the transformational goals of multiculturalism and to overcome years of decline, congregational leaders tried to reframe the tradition by reinterpreting two core theological commitments within Lutheranism—the priesthood of all believers and service to one's neighbor.

Recall that Christ Lutheran was a new congregation in 2001, the product of a merger of two small and aging congregations in Oakland.[22] Its leaders wanted to increase the membership and increase the level of participation among members. The contextualization strategy was intended to make the congregation a welcoming place largely for nonwhite groups who lived in the neighborhood but had no historic connection to Lutheranism. This meant that the church began to add music and ritual elements from a variety of cultures, in particular the theology and worship styles from the African American tradition since its pastor was African American as were roughly 25 percent of the members. An early attempt at contextualization was the creation of a Sunday evening gospel service in 2000, but it failed to draw more than ten or twelve participants (nearly always members) and was canceled after a few months. However, a new music director arrived shortly after Pastor Barbara Nelson took over as the congregation's sole pastor, and she quickly added gospel music and spirituals to the choir's repertoire. During the next year she invited guest musicians, including African drummers and Jamaican steel drummers, and many services included one song from one of the ethnic hymnals published by the ELCA. The congregation commonly used the ELCA worship book called *This Far by Faith*, in which the hymns and liturgies draw on historic rhythms and music of the black churches. The members I interviewed liked the addition of newer and often more upbeat music and were aware of how it connected to the congregation's goal of becoming multicultural, but they also missed the old familiar hymns and more sedate style of worship, with which they were comfortable.

At the same time as new music styles were added to worship, Pastor Nelson also began incorporating new worship styles and a theology of liberation into worship services. Field notes of worship from 2002 chart an increase in both the number of times Pastor Nelson tried to initiate a call-and-response style of preaching and a more expressive worship style (e.g., clapping and bodily movement) and in the number of members following her lead. Early in this innovation, I interviewed an African American man who had joined the church after Pastor Nelson took over because of her commitment (and by extension the congregation's) to racial reconciliation and multiculturalism. He noted that despite the congregation's good intentions, it still had work to do before reaching this goal:

> One major evolution I've seen take place is the service. You know, it's getting a lot less stuffy. These older white folk tend to—this is a stereotype, I know—but they tend to be very traditional Lutherans. And the liturgy, it's got to be just a certain way. And if it's not according to the book, then they complain. We've had a Jamaican steel drummer come, and Melanie [the music director] is fabulous. I mean, just great music, and she will bring in South African music. They'll do songs that maybe have Asian roots and it's just an eclectic mix of music. And the pastor, she isn't afraid to say to the congregation, "Can I get an amen?" And people look at her like, "What? We don't do that."

Later that spring Pastor Nelson was preaching about the work of the original disciples as witnesses to God's love after Jesus had died; she focused on what it means to be a witness to the reign of Jesus in Oakland. Toward the end of the sermon she discussed the phrase "can I get a witness?" in the black church. She noted how "in the black church when the pastor asks for an amen or a hallelujah, or my favorite, 'can I get a witness?' the pastor is really asking the people, 'Have you had this experience, and if so, will you tell us about it?'" She paused and then asked, "Can I get a witness?" Surprisingly, a seventy-year-old white woman stood and told her story about experiencing pain in her heart as she walked the road to Emmaus on a trip to the Middle East. She explained how two strangers applied acupressure and healed her, and then claimed that the Holy Spirit had been working through them. A few Sundays later after a Saturday of canvassing the neighborhood to learn from residents what they believed were the problems facing the neighborhood, Pastor Nelson again asked for a witness. Three members jumped up and relayed their stories about meeting their neighbors and spoke about their convictions that this process would eventually bring people to the church.

The reframing work, more narrowly defined, centered on redefining the Lutheran notion of the "priesthood of all believers" and the Lutheran ethic that stresses service to neighbor done as a response to God's love and translating it into language from the church growth movement. Christ Lutheran is an aging congregation where most members do little but attend Sunday morning worship and the occasional congregational meeting or meal. The pastors and council believed that transforming the church into a multicultural congregation committed to serving the community and, in particular, working to end injustice related to race, class, and sexual orientation would require greater participation and engagement by members.

However, rather than explaining the priesthood of all believers and its implications (the doctrine denies that there is a substantive spiritual difference between lay and ordained persons and thus encourages all believers to be active participants in the ministries of the church and to bring their faith to bear on all aspects of daily life), the congregation's leaders urged members to make Christ Lutheran a "permission-giving congregation." The church's leaders had picked up this idea at a conference led by church growth experts William Easum and Thomas Bandy. A permission-giving congregation, they learned at the conference, is one in which members are helped to identify their unique gifts for ministry and in which decision-making structures are minimized to allow lay members to start up new programs or ministries that will capitalize on their gifts without having to obtain formal permission from the pastor or council.

Throughout the merger process the pastors and council members at public meetings and in newsletter articles introduced the idea of the permission-giving congregation and urged members to "take ownership" of the congregation's ministries. The church's leaders saw the merger process as a time to dream and develop new visions for what the church could do and be. At several council and congregational meetings I attended, the pastors led brainstorming sessions at which members listed ideas for recruiting younger members, serving the community, and new programs for existing members. In the spring of 2002, Pastor Nelson devoted several sermons to providing a theological rationale for becoming a permission-giving congregation. For example, in one sermon she used the story of "Doubting Thomas" (in which Jesus appears before the disciples after his resurrection and Thomas demands to touch Jesus' wounds before he will believe) as an entryway into a broader discussion of how faith communities learn new ways to live together when the old ways die or no longer work. She first engaged in some exegetical work, noting how God sent the Holy Spirit to help the disciples continue Jesus' "widow's ministry" (i.e., taking care of the widows, orphans, and more generally the poorest members of society). She then showed how the post-Easter stories apply to Christ Lutheran:

> Your idea of who your pastor is or should be is dead. The idea that the pastor leads worship, preaches, visits and cares for members is dead. This is the old way of being church where the pastor does the ministry, but the old ways no longer work. Christ Lutheran is becoming a permission-giving congregation where you are given permission to do ministry. Now just as the disciples' world had fallen apart when Jesus was killed, he returned with the gift of the Holy Spirit to help them find new ways to do the widow ministry; so too does the Holy Spirit come to us today. The old way is dying but that's not the last word. God is with us, and don't doubt it. The Spirit will provide a way for all of us to understand the new ways.

Two weeks later she took a line from an old Lutheran hymn that calls Jesus the "shepherd of souls." She began by explaining what it means for us that Jesus is the shepherd of souls: "Jesus is the shepherd of our souls who heals us. He encourages us to follow him and engage in shepherd ministry. This ministry is vital today in a world of people who are spiritually hungry. Modern life takes more from our souls than feeds them." She then told two stories about congregations that looked a lot like Christ Lutheran—an aging membership, following years of stagnation but now on the cusp of transformation. The first account was about a couple who had lost their only child to AIDS; while they remained in the church, they were angry at God for the loss of their son and bitter about losing their retirement monies, which they had spent to care for him. However, members encouraged them to attend a Bible study during Lent one year, and the Word opened their hearts for healing. Pastor Nelson noted how the Word and the sacraments (i.e., baptism and the Lord's Supper) are the means by which Jesus restores us and heals us. In this first story, the pastor upheld the emphasis on Word and sacrament within Lutheranism, as if to signal to her audience that she was not challenging some of the core values of Lutheran theology. Then she related the second story. She described a congregation similar to Christ Lutheran but one that had developed a range of ecumenical ministries despite its small size and aging membership. She then concluded with a call to action in which she challenged the congregation to take a more active role in the congregation's ministries. While the underlying meaning remained thoroughly Lutheran (i.e., she emphasized the Lutheran theological commitment to serve others because it is the proper response to God's saving activity through scripture and the sacraments of baptism and Holy Communion), she used a new term, "shepherd ministry," to describe a more activist congregational identity:

> This congregation does shepherd ministry; it's not done just by the pastor. Shepherd ministry is a ministry of care. When we are baptized, we become associate shepherds, and in our baptismal covenant, we promise to continue learning from the Word, to love god and neighbor, to be renewed by the sacrament of Communion. Loving our neighbor is where we become shepherds of souls.

Occasionally, both pastors tried to reconnect directly to the Lutheran tradition, as in the example above, while also reframing Lutheran ethics and ecclesiology in newer terms such as "permission giving" and "shepherd ministry." In addition, they often turned to the language of rights and justice used by the religious Left, and it seemed to trump the use of explicit Lutheran idioms. Both pastors held strong commitments to justice issues, especially racial and economic equality, and defined the congregation's new identity and vision in justice language. In 2000, Pastor Will Hoch peppered his sermons and newsletter articles with discussions of Jubilee 2000 (a national program whereby religious organizations lobbied developed nations to forgive the debt of developing nations) and the biblical claims for human liberation. For example, in one sermon, he began his discussion of what he called "God's Sabbath economy" by relating it to the Lutheran rite of confession and absolution and ended his discussion with a reference to the resurrection—classic Lutheran themes—yet throughout he used the language of liberation theology:

> My favorite part of the service is the words of absolution. They follow the confession and are not fantasy. St. Paul said, "I did not receive the spirit of slavery, but the spirit of adoption." We are clothed in the power of the Holy Spirit, who gives us the power for transformation of life that brings hope. God will still make all things new as we are redeemed and set free from bondage. . . . Let go of your bondage and be filled with grace. God's blessing comes in the shape of power—a power that changes victims into victors and denounces racism, classism. This is Jubilee Sunday, where those who have been oppressed are to be set free from their debts. It is part of our heritage that in God's family we have already won the victory. God has promised us the jubilee, the liberation from bondage when Jesus died.

The paired terms of "confession" and "absolution," "bondage" and "freedom," "grace" and "resurrection" come from the heart of Lutheranism and might be recognized by those closely listening. However, the emphasis in the sermon (and in the newsletter articles on jubilee) was to align the congregation with the more ancient Jewish tradition of jubilee and the liberatory aspects of the ministry of Jesus. In effect, Pastor Hoch was arguing that this new congregation would be modeled after Jesus and scripture rather than the denomination. During an interview, Pastor Hoch spoke passionately about his increasing commitment to God's Sabbath economy and his weakening commitment to the Lutheran church. Our interview took place after a team from the national church offices had evaluated all of the urban parishes in Greater Oakland. He described his ministry and the direction of the church when I asked him to comment on the visit:

> See, the urban team is looking for evangelism strategies—the old door-to-door [strategy of asking the question] "If you die tonight, do you know where you're going to spend eternity?" That's a simplification, but that's what they're about. That's not my theology. I say the sooner that kind of evangelism dies in the church the better. We have to realize it's about making disciples, not about making converts. I'm so much there, Steve, that I don't know whether I'd be ordained in the Lutheran church if I had to do it today. I know I'm left of center! I'm left of left! I believe in a Sabbath economy where it calls for enough, not for an accumulation of, stuff. And the very same people who bitch and moan about the sermon, "He's giving us all that Old Testament crap," well that's what they don't want to hear. They don't want to hear "remember you were slaves." They don't want to hear that they're enslaved to modern culture. I'm not willing to play at

religiosity. I want to make a difference. I'm not here to be a chaplain. I did not come here to preserve the status quo. I came here to change things. And I am willing to risk losing members—all those who are opposed to a racially, culturally, and sexually inclusive congregation.

As at suburban Grace and Good Shepherd, there was an intentional effort to make Christ Lutheran countercultural, and as I argue in the concluding section, it was an effort to push the congregation from church to sect, albeit a liberal version of sectarianism. While the reconnecting work appears to be a strategy to reassure members that the congregation is still Lutheran and to show how the new church remains tied to the historic theological commitments of Lutheranism, it tends to be overshadowed by the reframing of the church's identity and mission in the languages of church growth and liberation. In interviews, coffee hour conversations, and public meetings, members consistently voiced their confusion or suspicion about the new language the pastors were using.

Despite their concerns, those members who stayed through the merger at Christ Lutheran were willing to go along with most of the changes, in part because they recognized that as their numbers continued to dwindle something had to be done; in part because they willingly hired a pastor who was committed to changing and adding to the tradition in order to attract a younger and more diverse population; and in part because the long-standing bonds of family and friendship that knitted members together overrode the losses they experienced when the liturgy, music, or theological language changed.

THE CONDITIONS FOR CHANGE

The three case studies highlight a number of organizational and cultural conditions that encourage the selection and implementation of specific strategies of change. Perhaps the most important condition that facilitates or constrains change is the receptivity of the current membership to change. For example, congregations will turn to reconnecting when there is a significant pool of members for whom the Lutheran tradition is important and meaningful. Under this condition the strategy becomes a way of signaling continuity with the tradition to these members and hopefully of winning their support for the proposed changes. Christ Lutheran is a good example of this. More cynically, reconnecting may occur when leaders believe they need to legitimize more radical efforts to change the tradition and hence mollify a powerful group of members who are very committed to the tradition. The leaders at Good Shepherd used this mode of reconnecting by reminding members that Luther himself relied on popular music and the vernacular rather than churchly language when he tried to reform the Catholic church. Reconnecting may also be employed (as in the case of Grace Lutheran) when newer members are coming from other liturgical traditions or have been away from Lutheranism for many years, and thus reconnecting is a way of helping both groups become familiar with the tradition.

Reframing, in its narrow definition, will be a preferred strategy when congregations have members or a prospective pool of members for whom the tradition is foreign or when there is low interest and commitment among members for preserving the tradition. Reframing will take on a more radical tone, as in the case of Good Shepherd, when the congregation's leaders believe that the only way to make religion relevant and meaningful is to abandon or aggressively criticize the allegedly archaic language of the tradition because it is both outdated and empty of meaning for new and prospective members. This was evident in Good Shepherd's abandonment of atonement language and its adoption of Buddhist language.

A second condition that shapes the selection and use of change strategies is the culture of the congregation and, more specifically, the relationship of the congregation to the tradition. There will be a greater willingness to reframe the tradition when the congregation is less tied to preserving it and when the congregation's identity is less firmly rooted in Lutheranism and more strongly grounded in a generic Christian identity. Of course, part of the reframing effort is to convince members that the tradition does not need to be preserved intact and to adopt a religious identity that transcends the tradition. Thus, the reframing can reinforce the preexisting loose ties to the tradition, as in the cases of Grace and Good Shepherd. Conversely, when a congregation is more tightly wedded to its tradition, as in the case of Christ Lutheran, reframing can be more difficult, and leaders may need to work more diligently at reconnecting to show members that the proposed changes will help preserve or at least not significantly alter the core of the tradition.

At the same time the tradition itself sets the parameters for change by providing a core set of beliefs and practices that serve as a benchmark for identity. For example, at Good Shepherd the senior pastor remarked in one interview that the only thing that would keep the congregation Lutheran "was its commitment to grace," while at Grace Lutheran, the consistent reliance on liturgical form, a radical theology of grace, and the sacrament of Communion were the pieces of the tradition that were used to define the church as Lutheran.[23] In all three cases, the congregations' leaders believed they were buffering the core of the tradition, but as will be evident in chapter 6, exactly what constitutes the core of the tradition and who is authorized to define or change it were contested issues. Retraditioning was the preferred strategy to make the core more relevant and meaningful and thus protect it. It worked best at Grace and Christ.

When change is defined as legitimate and thus considered normative by the congregation, it is easier to use retraditioning and reframing, as illustrated by the spirit of experimentation at Grace Lutheran. Good Shepherd's leaders were intentionally trying to make change normative as the clergy, especially, tried out new theological terms, new music, and new definitions of church on a regular basis. The clergy all reported that they were regularly changing practices at the church in order to break down members' old categories and expectations and to force them to think about the congregation and the Christian faith in new ways. However, congregational culture among older members and those for whom the historic worship and theological traditions were important was not particularly open to change. Leaders seeking change also attempted to tap into preexisting beliefs and values and align them with proposed changes. The clergy and lay leaders at Christ Lutheran in Oakland and Grace Lutheran in the suburbs turned to the language of liberation theology and the political Left in part because it was congruent with long-standing religious and political commitments of both churches and many individual members.[24]

A third condition that shapes how congregations change is the broader cultural context in which congregations are embedded. In particular, congregations are embedded within a system of public and shared codes, schemas that provide categories, commonsense understandings, interpretive frameworks, and rules that organize action.[25] For example, codes may define the criteria by which individuals rank order people or objects, as in the gift-giving code that operated in Caplow's study of "Middletown," in which more-valued persons and those with whom one was intimate were given more expensive gifts. Everyone in Middletown is aware of the code and aware of the social implications that will follow if they do not follow the code. Thus, the code sets expectations for behavior and sanctions for violating the code.[26]

The three congregations featured in this chapter were embedded within several larger religious codes that shaped the ways in which they were trying to reframe the Lutheran tradition. Grace and Good Shepherd relied on the general language of spirituality and the personal quest for spiritual fulfillment, religious meaning, or authenticity, which is one of the dominant discourses in American Protestantism. By incorporating the language of spirituality into their congregation's tradition, these two churches also were adopting the code of "spiritual but not religious," which defines church or organized religion as bad. In doing so, congregational leaders believed they needed to make their congregations less churchlike and thus distanced themselves from a strong denominational identity and from much of the explicit theological language of Lutheranism.

All three congregations were also embedded in the language of religious choice and consumption that has organized much of religious life in the United States since the mid-1960s. This language has shaped affiliation and membership and now legitimates the phenomenon of religious switching that has been institutionalized in American Protestantism. It has also shaped the programs of many congregations in terms of offering multiple worship services, often in different styles, and multiple opportunities for small-group participation. A number of commentators have noted the not-so-subtle influence of consumerism on American religion. They show how the values of unlimited choice, convenience, and service to the buyer have been adopted and institutionalized in the programs, worship services, and even architecture of many congregations in the United States.[27]

Each of the congregations has an ambiguous relationship to the language of religious consumption and the values of choice and individualism. On the one hand, they explicitly challenged their members not to treat faith or participation in the congregation like any other consumer good. This was most clearly articulated in the reframing strategy at Good Shepherd. All three congregations also attacked consumption itself as part of their larger effort to emphasize and augment the service and justice aspects of the Lutheran tradition. On the other hand, Christ and Good Shepherd offered multiple worship services in differently styles and in the language of spirituality that all stressed the individual's pursuit of growth or fulfillment. Consumption and religious choice shaped the congregations' reframing insofar as they are seen as the cultural forces the tradition must overcome to offer people authentic religion. In other words, leaders at these churches redefined the tradition to show how it stands in opposition to the individualistic and corrupting influences of choice and consumption. At the same time, by encouraging members to think of their own religious journeys in individualistic ways, congregational leaders subtly signaled that choice and a consumerist orientation are legitimate.

FROM CHURCH TO LIBERAL SECT

The three congregations featured in this chapter shared similar strategies of change, and each used these strategies to place the congregations in higher tension with the surrounding sociocultural environment and thus push the congregation toward a sectarian identity.[28] These congregations do not look like classic sects, because they do not espouse an otherworldly theology, do not serve an impoverished or dispossessed population, do not define membership in terms of exclusivity and high demand, and do not seek to keep members from the morally corrupting influence of society. Yet they share some of the key characteristics of sects. Each congregation has taken a clear theological and ethical position that challenges some of the systemic corruptions of American society (discrimination by race, ethnicity, class, gender, and sexual orientation) as well as the systemic pressures that encourage members to ground their identities in distinctly this-worldly concerns like career, wealth, and consumption. In this way they are trying to increase the tension between the church members and their sociocultural setting.

Each congregation also has tried to define itself as a community of faith rather than a "church" and has been willing to break with or redefine the denominational tradition in order to do this. The leaders at each of the congregations were pushing their members to engage in conversation about the nature and purpose of the church and to adopt a more biblically centered, Christ-centered perspective that more closely dovetailed with the early church's ecclesial understanding rather than a denominational and hence accommodationist understanding. Much like Miller's postmodern primitives, these congregations are trying to return to a model of the ancient church, but unlike Miller's new paradigm congregations, they are making the move in order to promote the liberatory aspects of Christianity.[29]

However, none of the three churches actually became a sect. Although the clergy and lay leaders pushed each congregation toward a more sectarian identity, they encountered resistance and indifference from rank-and-file members. Part of the difficulty is that sects make high demands on members and attach sanctions to those demands, but these three congregations did not make membership contingent on meeting any particular demands on participation, financial giving, or following of behavioral codes. Instead, they tried to help members embrace a more radical understanding of Christianity in which their faith would inform and shape every aspect of their daily lives. This is an attempt to create a high-demand religion, but it was undermined by three organizational features of these congregations. First, the congregations did not create or institutionalize any enforceable sanctions to ensure that members complied with the high demands; the leaders merely hoped that members would internalize the demands and thus voluntarily comply. Second, each congregation had a culture of low participation among the majority of members that was difficult and slow to change (many of the leaders of these churches spoke about the "80/20 rule," in which 80 percent of the congregation's work is done by 20 percent of the members). Third, each congregation defined outreach and the mission of the congregation in terms of sending members out into the world to serve rather than in terms of calling the unchurched into the church to be saved. The lack of enforceable demands, the inability to completely change a culture of minimal participation, and the service orientation tended to short-circuit the move toward sectarianism.

Nonetheless, this move toward sectarianism is a surprising finding because church-sect theory generally argues that sects tend to be more conservative theologically and biblically. Moreover, when churches move toward more sectarian identities, they are usually responding to competitive pressures from more conservative and successful congregations, and as Chaves notes, the historic pattern has been for churches to adopt less ceremonial and more enthusiastic worship traditions.[30] At the same time, this move supports the theoretical claim that revitalization often is fueled by a return to orthodoxy and sectarianism, even if it is a return to a liberal form of orthodoxy.

Chapter 5

IN THE IMAGE
OF EVANGELICALISM

THIS WAS NOT the Lutheranism in which I was raised. Rock-and-roll music greeted me when I entered the sanctuary at Faith Lutheran Church. A six-piece band with three singers was belting out an up-tempo song about Jesus. I read the announcements on a giant video screen that was high up on the front wall of the church and watched the young families and empty-nest couples come in, greet friends, and find their seats. The band finished with a five-minute instrumental jam session, and as the lead guitarist brought down his guitar on the final beat, the congregation erupted in applause.

The service continued with the "Greeting" and "Confession" from the traditional liturgy but then the service departed from the standard form.[1] Instead of the customary "Kyrie" and "Hymn of Praise," the Faith Lutheran Players provided a short play entitled *The Home Run*. Two men sit at a small table in front of microphones, and then three men with gold wings, apparently angels, and baseball hats enter holding signs that read "Go God," "I [heart] Jesus," and "John 3:16." They sit down on a portable riser and commence to talk about the poor play of their team during the game. In the background, "Take Me Out to the Ballgame" is playing. The bottom of the seventh inning begins when "Ivan Inconsistent" comes to bat. The team expected him to be a great hitter, but despite his regular church attendance he never tells anyone about the Lord. The play-by-play commentator describes the scene in which Ivan is standing by the water cooler when a coworker comes up and asks a question. The announcer speculates that "maybe this time he'll invite her to church. "A great pitch to hit" yells the color commentator but Ivan fouls it off when he starts to talk about his dog. His coworker asks again, and the angels plead for Ivan to "tell her about the Lord, tell her something," but Ivan mumbles that he has to get back to work. "Another strikeout," laments the play-by-play announcer. The second batter, Constant Carrie, hits the ball and then beats the throw by the Jehovah's Witness. The color man notes that she had her Bible with her and stole that soul away from the Jehovah's Witness. Next up was Simple Sarah, who gives in to temptation and bunts weakly into the second out. With a runner on base, up comes Powerful Peter, the team's best hitter. The angels get excited and start yelling for Peter to win someone for the Lord. Peter steps up to the plate and hits a deep fly ball. "It goes over the devil's head, it's going, going, gone, a home run. Peter has led someone to accept Jesus as his personal lord and savior. God's team wins another one."

The service resumed with a scripture reading (but not the reading of the Gospel text from *The Common Worship Lectionary* as would be normal), and then one of the associate ministers preached a sermon called "Plugged into Healing."[2] A common feature of Lutheran preaching is that it explains the meaning of a text from one of the four Gospels, often drawing connections between it and at least one of the other texts appointed for the day in *The Common Worship Lectionary*.[3] This sermon, instead, used church growth expert Leonard Sweet's book *The Jesus Prescription for a Healthy Life* as its text. The main theme of the sermon was how people make themselves sick by holding in their emotions, working too many hours, and pretending that all is well in their lives. He discussed Sweet's Ten Commandments of Stress, which seemed to tout insights about stress, health, and prayer from medicine and psychology. He concluded with a discussion of prayer's role in healing: "Prayer is the way in which we tap into the divine healer and restore our relationship. I believe this is what Jesus was about. Christ was into restoring some kind of connection and right relationship with the center core of God in life. The gospel is about that kind of restoration of relationship. Did you know that the word "savior" in Greek means not only "savior" but also "healer"? When we accept Christ as our savior, it means we are healed; we are restored to oneness with God."

I left the service that Sunday morning unsure if what I had witnessed was Lutheran or some other form of Protestantism. Certain pieces of the Lutheran worship tradition were present (the "Confession" and rite of Holy Communion), but much of the order and elements of the tradition were absent and had been replaced by elements from evangelical-like worship: rock-and-roll "praise music," a drama about converting souls for Jesus, and a theological message that stressed the individual's decision to accept or not to accept Jesus as personal savior. Even the sermon seemed out of place in a Lutheran church with its reliance on popular psychology and its relative inattention to both the Bible and the primary task of explaining how some biblical text illustrates God's saving work in Jesus Christ (the latter is a cornerstone of Lutheran preaching).

After months of fieldwork and interviews and reviewing the literatures on evangelicalism, seeker churches, and worship traditions in American Protestantism, I became convinced that I was seeing a new type of Lutheranism, a hybrid of sorts. It was heavily influenced by American evangelicalism and the therapeutic and pragmatic culture of American society. It retained certain theological and liturgical features of the Lutheran tradition, but those elements had been subtly and not so subtly changed in the borrowing process.

The attempt to adapt Lutheranism to the revivalistic or pietistic tradition has a long history. In the nineteenth century Baptists and Methodists provided the model for Lutherans seeking to Americanize the tradition. Today, independent evangelical or Baptist churches, the heirs of the revival tradition, often provide the model of how to be a growing, relevant, successful church. Yet this model, which follows the revival worship tradition with its emphasis on the individual's salvation, orthodox theology, and a literalist biblical hermeneutic, does not fit neatly within the Lutheran theological and worship tradition. The first two congregations that I will discuss in this chapter are blending Lutheranism with the revival tradition and evangelicalism because they see this as key to congregational growth and to fulfillment of the New Testament commandment "to make disciples of all nations."

However, they did not adopt the ideas, values, and practices of these alternative traditions wholesale or uncritically. They engaged in what I call "selective isomorphism"—borrowing elements from non-Lutheran traditions that could easily be incorporated into their services and that dovetailed with their own understanding of what is essential and what is nonessential within Lutheranism (e.g., they justified making rock-and-roll music a central part of the worship services by citing Luther's own use of the music of his day, but they kept the sacrament of Holy Communion as a regular part of worship).[4] The process of change at these congregations resembles the kind of adaptations that market and ecological theories emphasize, in which churches adopt the rituals, forms of worship, or theology of successful newcomers or define themselves against new players in the market by cultivating specialized identities to serve a small market niche.[5]

Two recent studies provide insight into the process of adaptation. Finke argues that the process of change among vital religious organizations is one in which the leaders preserve the core teachings while introducing innovations that reinforce these teachings and do not threaten the core. His empirical illustrations suggest that religious groups buffer the core theological teachings but freely borrow and then adapt ritual practices, recruitment and retention strategies, and technology from other successful groups in order to increase market share.[6] Similarly, Chaves, arguing from an ecological perspective, suggests that the process of change is marked by innovation and continuity. Clergy or lay leaders who introduce new worship practices need to ensure that the new practices will both allow the church to occupy a new religious space in the market and signal continuity with the historic worship tradition: "They must both establish themselves as 'real' religion and differentiate themselves from other religious options. Continuity in worship practices declares, 'We are religion of a legitimate sort.' Innovation declares, 'We are religion unlike—and better than—others that you know.'"[7]

Although I draw on Finke's and Chaves's insights into the process of change, my concern is to identify the conditions that facilitate or constrain the kind of adaptation they discuss and to more fully understand how such adaptation works. My case studies raise several questions that market and ecological theories do not fully address. Do congregations simply adopt the same practices, programs, or ideas of successful churches uncritically or are they filtered through the lens of their own tradition? How does the process work when there is little consensus about what constitutes the core of the tradition? How did the practice of borrowing from outside the Lutheran tradition lead these congregations to alter the tradition's core either intentionally or unintentionally?

I answer these questions in the rest of the chapter largely through extended case studies of two congregations: Faith Lutheran and Zion Lutheran. Faith Lutheran is in the Oakland suburbs and is the most evangelical of all the churches in the study. It has jettisoned much of the tradition that its leaders consider outside the core, and little remains to mark the congregation as distinctly Lutheran. The church's leaders believe that they have been able to adopt the forms of non-Lutheran worship without sacrificing the Lutheran theological content, but as I argue below, the form/content distinction broke down when the borrowed forms of worship, theology, education, and biblical interpretation were adopted. Zion Lutheran, in the heart of Silicon Valley, followed a similar path of change, although it has kept much more of the tradition, especially in worship, than Faith. Both congregations relied on a different set of change strategies than those used by the congregations reported on in chapter 4. Their efforts to alter the tradition were driven by their "evangelism" causal stories, the influence of church growth experts, and the organizational models of the megachurch. They relied on the strategy of hybridization, in which they blended elements from evangelicalism with Lutheranism to create a new form of Lutheranism.

In the remainder of the chapter, I explore how Faith and Zion used hybridization to refashion the worship and theological traditions of Lutheranism; how the adoption of non-Lutheran forms of worship, educational models, and decision making pushed these congregations toward evangelicalism in some unexpected ways; and how the cultures of individualism, pragmatism, and consumption that underlie much of evangelicalism also have reshaped Lutheranism in these two congregations. At the end of the chapter I discuss how two other Silicon Valley congregations, St. Peter's and Resurrection, were trying to preserve the Lutheran tradition even as they borrowed from the evangelical church growth and megachurch literatures. These two congregations used hybridization in a much more limited way to solve pressing organizational problems rather than to "evangelicalize" Lutheranism.

BLENDING ANTITHETICAL WORSHIP TRADITIONS

The congregations trying to blend the popular American evangelical, or "frontier," tradition with the Lutheran tradition faced a difficult challenge because the traditions are significantly different.[8] They carry distinctive understandings of the purpose of worship, and those different understandings shape how worship is organized, what ritual practices, values, and beliefs are emphasized, and what role participants play in the service. Table 2 highlights some of the main points of difference between the two worship traditions. Although Lutheran worship in the United States has been quite varied over the past two hundred years, it has gradually coalesced around a common set of ritual practices and theological

Table 2. The Evangelical and the Lutheran Worship Traditions

Features of Worship	Evangelical Tradition	Lutheran Tradition
Purpose	• Conversion/commitment of the individual	• Gathering of community around God's gifts of Word (the Bible and saving message of Christ Crucified and Resurrected) and sacraments
Structure	• Three parts: preliminaries, sermon, altar call	• Four parts: Greeting/Gathering, Word (Bible reading/ prayer, hymn), Holy Communion, Sending (follows the Common Rite)
Emphases	• Individual decision and individual choice • Experience and emotion • Pragmatism: use whatever means necessary to bring about conversion	• Corporate participation in the liturgy • Sacraments of baptism and Holy Communion • Confessional • Appeal to intellect and doctrine
Key practices	• Contemporary music (rock and roll, country, jazz) • Multimedia presentations • Drama • Tailored to homogeneous, target populations	• Participatory liturgy • Centered on sermon and Holy Communion
Nature of preaching	• Application • Topical • Stress on personal benefits of being Christian • Moralistic: Bible as guidebook	• Exegetical • Follows lectionary • Proclaims God's activity in the cross and resurrection and God's promises in the sacraments
Role of participants	• Passive observers • Make decision to believe or strengthen commitment	• Active participants (liturgy = "Work of the People") • Response to God's Word and promises

emphases that operate as the de facto core of the worship tradition.[9] Worship is understood as the gathering of a community around God's gifts of Word (i.e., scripture and the story of God's saving activity in the life, death, and resurrection of Jesus Christ as recounted in hymns, prayers, canticles, and creeds) and sacraments (i.e., the rites of Holy Communion and baptism, in which God provides the visible means of God's love, acceptance, and forgiveness for human beings). Worship is the occasion for the community to respond to God's love and grace through "praise, surrender and thanksgiving."[10] In this sense, then, worship is corporate, communal, and centered on God.

Worship in the Lutheran tradition is grounded in and organized around the earliest practices of the ancient church (back to the second century) that follow the witness of the New Testament. These ancient practices or ways of worship are known as the "Common Rite," and Lutherans trace their liturgical roots to the medieval German masses of the Reformation. The Common Rite is organized in four parts (gathering; reading and learning about the sacred stories and proclamation of the gospel; Holy Communion; and sending the community into the world to serve). Lutherans enshrined the Common Rite's central focus on scripture and the sacrament of Holy Communion in the Augsburg Confession's definition of church and worship.[11] This organizational structure and theological orientation were given additional legitimacy in the 1978 *Lutheran Book of Worship* (*LBW*), which declared, "Every [Lutheran] service, whether elaborate or spare, sung or said, should be within the framework of the common rite of the Church, so that the integrity of the rite is always respected and maintained."[12] The "essential elements" that are included in the various Sunday services in the hymnal should all come from the Common Rite.[13] Thus, Lutheran worship is ecumenical and confessional.

Finally, worship in the Lutheran tradition emphasizes process rather than outcomes. It understands worship as a fundamental means of initiating the new believer or newcomer into the community of faith. The sacraments of baptism and Communion serve as rites of passage and offer new identities and instruction in the doctrines and behavioral codes that govern the Christian life. White notes that worship in the liturgical traditions (i.e., Roman Catholic, Episcopal, and Lutheran) is the church's primary means of making and nurturing Christians because "the Christian faith is reiterated in the systematic reading of God's word and reinforced in hymn singing, prayer, and preaching. . . . Becoming a Christian, in large measure, is learning to worship as a Christian."[14]

Conversely, the purpose of worship in the evangelical tradition is to bring about the conversion of the individual. White argues that worship in this tradition is grounded in nineteenth-century revivalism and the frontier tradition, which lead to baptism rather than moving on from baptism as in the liturgical traditions.[15] He also notes that, unlike Lutheranism or Catholicism, in which worship is located in a community, the church is largely ignored in the frontier tradition or at best seen as providing the context for individuals' conversion: "Revivalism sought to bring individuals to faith; it virtually ignored the Church as a community of faith. The central concern of revivalism is with producing an individual relationship with God. The Church largely existed as a catalyst to make this reaction take place. . . . The model of the Church was proclamation, not life together."[16] Thus, worship in the evangelical tradition is individualistic and evangelistic, as opposed to corporate and sacramental.

The overarching goal of the individual's conversion organizes all other elements of worship in the evangelical tradition. For example, the service typically is divided into three sections: the preliminaries usually include upbeat music, a pastoral prayer, and a scripture reading, which prepare individuals to hear the message of salvation; a sermon, which endeavors to show how Christianity is relevant and important for individuals and has the goal of encouraging individuals to make a decision to become a believer; and an altar call, during which individuals make their decision public by gathering at the altar rail for prayer. In the contemporary tradition, the public altar call has been replaced by stepwise programs that help the individual move from visitor, to convert, to church member.[17] Similarly, preaching in this tradition tends to emphasize the practical applicability of the Bible and the personal benefits of the Christian life as a way to "sell" Christianity. This tends to recast Christianity into individualistic and therapeutic terms, reducing the faith to a set of principles that will make the individual happy or fulfilled.[18]

Another way in which the goal of conversion shapes evangelical worship is its utilitarian or pragmatic nature. Charles Finney, the great nineteenth-century revivalist and key architect of the tradition, claimed that conversion was a matter of technique, and he was willing to use whatever methods or measures were necessary to produce a harvest of souls. And the methods he found that worked best tapped into people's emotions to produce an experience of recognizing God's forgiveness and love and then the benefits of being a Christian. Finney argued that following inherited liturgical forms or practices was not important if they did not produce converts, and thus liturgical forms should be abandoned if they did not work. This utilitarian perspective remains alive in the contemporary evangelical tradition. Evangelical worship tends to be technique driven, as evinced in the advice offered by church growth experts or in the models of the megachurches that urge congregations to adopt rock-and-roll music, multimedia presentations, and marketing to target populations to promote numerical growth. More generally, worship is organized to appeal to emotions and the perceived religious needs and interests of the alleged "unchurched." Church leaders report great willingness to experiment with musical genres, preaching styles, architecture, and technology to find the best combination that will produce a happy, upbeat, exciting experience such that visitors will want to return.[19] In other words, worship in the evangelical tradition appeals to emotion and experience rather than intellect and doctrine and will experiment extensively with any technique or technology to create an environment conducive to conversion.

Evangelicalizing Lutheranism

Advocates of the Americanization of Lutheranism (i.e., adopting the frontier tradition) among nineteenth-century Lutherans often framed the debate and thus the future of the church as a matter of the choice between "orthodoxy and empty pews or compromise and full pews."[20] Leaders at Faith and Zion spoke about worship in similar either/or terms as they described and defended their work to change the Lutheran worship tradition. Their causal stories, as described in chapter 3, framed the problem facing their congregations in these dichotomous terms: if their congregations were to grow, then they would have to abandon at least some parts of liturgical Lutheranism because it does not attract non-Lutherans and the supply of "cradle Lutherans" from the Midwest had dried up. Thus, these two congregations believed that combining pieces of the evangelical tradition with the best parts of the Lutheran tradition was the best strategy to ensure that the pews would remain full into the future. They attempted to preserve the core of the tradition while updating the Lutheran worship with the "forms" or techniques of evangelical worship, but in so doing, they pushed the tradition more solidly into the evangelical camp. This happened, I argue, because evangelical forms of worship, education, and decision-making structures actually carry theological meanings about the nature of God and the Christian life, the purpose of church, and the grounding of religious authority that force the congregations to remake Lutheranism in the image of evangelicalism.

Faith and Zion primarily relied on the strategy of selective isomorphism to blend the two traditions. This strategy is a form of mimetic isomorphism insofar as these congregations copied the organizational practices, ideologies, and structures from successful evangelical congregations. However, it differs insofar as the goal of the borrowing process is not simply to copy the model but to integrate particular elements from the successful congregation into the tradition in ways that revitalize the tradition or create a new tradition. In particular, specific elements of the Lutheran tradition—the theological commitment to *sola gratia*, "Word and sacrament ministry," and the reforming impulse of the Protestant Reformation—were buffered from wholesale change and used to guide how elements from non-Lutheran traditions were selected and integrated into the Lutheran tradition. This process of innovation was evident in how both congregations restructured worship by grafting the forms of evangelical worship (e.g., order, music, preaching styles) onto the Lutheran worship tradition. The result was a "contemporary" or "blended" worship service in which some practices of the evangelical tradition (such as "praise music" led by a rock band) were incorporated into a service that generally followed the Lutheran ordo (order of service).

Many of the leaders and members of both congregations claimed that this process did not alter the tradition fundamentally. Indeed, some argued that they were merely being true to Luther's reforming impulse and using the cultural forms of the day to communicate the gospel in relevant and hence effective ways. Others argued that they had simply changed the music or tinkered with some of the elements of the service, but that the updated service was still liturgical and still committed to the principle of Word and sacrament. For example, the worship coordinator and leader of the "praise band" at Faith Lutheran spoke about the worship war that engulfed the congregation five years before the study began when a former pastor hired a Pentecostal woman to lead worship at a new "seeker service." She noted that the war was short lived in part because members came to see that worship had not really changed: "When it comes down to the basics of worship, the contemporary service is Lutheran. The music is different, and the fact that we have drums and don't have an organ. But the rest of the worship is really the same. We still do Word and sacrament and read our lessons—that hasn't really changed." Similarly, several members of Zion Lutheran claimed that their contemporary service was still liturgical or followed the Lutheran order of service despite the substitution of evangelical music for hymns from the *LBW*. One of the members involved in the development of this service noted that "the contemporary service isn't that different from the traditional one. The litany will be different. The music will be different. We won't have anything like the chanted litany from the old book [i.e., the *LBW*]. But it still has the basic structure of Lutheran worship and it performs the same function."

Although a handful of members at both congregations lamented the marginalization of "traditional worship" (it was placed at the earliest and least attended service at both churches), most did not consider their worship less Lutheran or out of step with essential features of the tradition. This common response may be a result of the careful way in which leaders of the congregations blended the evangelical and Lutheran worship traditions. It also may be a result of the relatively thin understanding of the tradition that many members possessed.

Yet the addition of elements from the evangelical tradition was pushing these congregations away from Lutheran worship practices toward something that looked more similar to what one would find at Willow Creek Community Church or any number of nondenominational, evangelical churches in the United States. The most obvious and far-reaching changes to worship at Faith and Zion were seen in their adoption of the music of evangelicalism. At first glance, the addition of light rock music and a band and the substitution of praise music for classic sacred music and hymns might not appear radical, but this shift changed the structure, emphasis, and theological content of worship at these two congregations so that they more closely resembled the individualistic, experiential, and pragmatic features of evangelicalism.

Worship in the evangelical tradition is organized to create a rich emotional experience for individuals that will open them up to commit or recommit themselves to a personal relationship with Jesus. Much of the music currently used in the tradition, especially at the megachurches that serve as the model for Faith and Zion, is called "praise music"—up-tempo, singable songs with a simple theological message that mimic "Top 40" pop rock. Sargeant notes that this music tends to focus on the individual rather than on God, in contrast to much of classic sacred church music, and emphasizes emotions over intellect, experience over doctrine, and the personal benefits of belief.[21] Leaders of various megachurches and experts from the church growth industry consistently urge congregations to use rock-and-roll-based praise music for several pragmatic reasons: first, it is the style of music most familiar to baby boomers and younger generations and thus makes worship more accessible; second, it conveys a sense that the church is open to outsiders because it does not rely on the parochial music, language, or rituals of the tradition that often are alien to the unchurched or formerly churched; third, it signals a strong ethos of informality and anti-institutionalism that resonates with people under the age of fifty-five.[22]

Zion Lutheran in Silicon Valley first added a contemporary service that featured praise music and a band in the late 1980s to reach out to and meet the needs of non-Lutherans. One member noted that this new service came about because the congregation's leaders were worried that Zion might "become a club rather than a church." Another member reported that they adopted a praise music service because "we realized that, unless we changed worship, we were going to die." The guiding assumptions here (as at Faith Lutheran) are (1) that the so-called traditional Lutheran worship service (i.e., one conducted in accordance with the *LBW* and replete with organ-led classic sacred music) required inside knowledge and skills that created an exclusive culture and thus would keep visitors away; and (2) that seekers, the unchurched, or people in general are not interested or capable of participating in explicitly liturgical services.[23] In 2002 the congregation restructured its worship schedule by replacing a 10 a.m. service that followed the Lutheran rite of Holy Communion with a "blended service" that followed the Lutheran liturgical order but used praise music. The senior pastor explained in a newsletter article that the switch was "being done intentionally to maximize the reach of our contemporary service . . . for the purpose of attracting new people." At the congregational meeting to discuss the proposed change, the worship committee chair defended the schedule and style shift by argued that "if Zion's mission was to invite people into a personal relationship with Jesus and if worship is the primary way that happens, then we need to offer a service that appeals to guests, new Christians, and those who currently don't attend Zion." She then cited several unnamed studies that demonstrate that "people in our community prefer a blended service, which means a service with a traditional structure but a contemporary style."

Members of Zion were asked to comment about the proposed changes and how they fit in with the new mission of the congregation (a new mission document was produced and discussed in a sermon series and small-group meetings during the fall of 2001). Uniformly, members reported that they supported the goal of reaching out to the unchurched or non-Lutherans and were willing to rearrange worship and abandon some parts of the worship tradition to meet this goal. One older member echoed the rationale for change offered by the pastor and the chair of the worship committee when he responded to my question about why the church was changing the 10 a.m. service: "We need to change the middle service to make it more alive and vibrant so other people will want to attend." Another member spoke about how the old middle service is "too contemplative, too quiet, and too Lutheran to attract non-Lutherans. It's never full and when visitors come they don't see our exciting contemporary service." Her comment implicitly reflected the pastor's argument that "10 a.m. is prime time

when most visitors arrive at church, and we need to offer them a worship experience that is comfortable, meaningful, and life changing." Another member also
identified the problem of inaccessible and meaningless worship, and especially
classic church music, as barriers the congregation needs to overcome to successfully reach out to the unchurched:

> Change is really hard, but without change you get stagnant. And we were
> getting stagnant. I think traditional liturgy and traditional worship are
> wonderful for traditional Lutherans, but there aren't a whole bunch of
> them still coming off the boats here in California. And quite honestly peo-
> ple just weren't getting it. New people coming in off the streets just weren't
> getting the liturgy. So, I think we've recognized that we're in a different era
> now. People who grew up with Sesame Street like a different style of music.
> What we're trying to do is adapt to that new reality without losing the core
> of the gospel.

In short, Zion's leaders articulated both pragmatic and evangelistic reasons for
adopting praise music and abandoning a distinctly Lutheran worship service in
favor of one that offered music in a familiar musical style that would make non-
Lutherans feel "comfortable," more able to participate, and thus more likely to
find the service meaningful. Ultimately, worship was understood as a means to
witness to the unchurched and persuade them to consider becoming Christian.

At Faith Lutheran in the Oakland suburbs, the senior pastor, John Lincoln,
explained the shift from classic to praise music in two of their three worship
services by similar appeals to making church relevant and accessible to people
who are unfamiliar with Lutheranism. In the congregation's mission document,
he identifies evangelism as their top priority ("sharing our faith by building relationships with unchurched people, living our lives of faith before them, and
inviting them to join us in worship") and worship as the means to do this. In
one sermon the pastor claimed that the spiritually dead churches are those that
fail to "adopt new methods that allow them to adapt to the culture of their day
in order to reach people for Jesus Christ." The sermon was given in the context
of ongoing unrest over shifts in the worship schedule that relegated the "traditional" worship to the earliest and least desirable time slot.

During one of my interviews with Pastor Lincoln, he spoke about their shift
toward a more evangelical emphasis in worship by arguing that "Communion
is our altar call; it is the time for people to invite Jesus into their lives again."
He even claimed that if he presided at Communion more regularly (he usually
preached, and as is the custom in Lutheran churches with multiple clergy, the
preacher does not preside at Communion), he would use the phrase "altar call"
in the service.[24] This change in language suggests that a strategy of reframing
was used. When I pressed him to explain why he would adopt the language of
evangelicalism and more generally the forms of worship from that tradition, he

turned to the strategy of reconnecting to show how the tradition allowed for this kind of borrowing:

We Lutherans have overemphasized baptism as a one-time event that saves us, and so we think we can't do anything more, out of a fear of relying on good works. Baptism is only the initiation. Everyday we need to be reborn; each day we should say the sinner's prayer like Luther did—"I believe that I cannot by my own reason or effort believe in Jesus Christ my Lord, or come to him." [25] Each day I need to respond to God's yes with my own yes. I need Christ to empower me to live as a Christian, and in Communion we invite Jesus to do this. Even though we are saved through baptism, there have been points in life where we have to make decisions to choose God or not choose God if we are to remain Christian. And I need God's help to make those choices. Now we use a contemporary music because we need to find ways to speak to the unchurched in the language or forms of our culture. Luther used contemporary language and music in worship. If we are a church that is always reforming, then we should use contemporary forms.

Thus, while Faith redefined worship as a tool for conversion, a cornerstone of the evangelical tradition, it understood this shift as congruent with Lutheran theology and the practices of Luther. So rather than seeing the addition of praise music as a radical change in the tradition, this congregation saw it as a means of fulfilling the tradition and also helping the church make its worship service appealing to non-Lutherans, especially those from more evangelical backgrounds. [26]

The addition of praise music led to some subtle and some not-so-subtle changes in the theological content or meaning of worship. First, the addition of a large band (usually six to seven instruments and three singers) created a new focal point spatially for the worshipers. In both congregations a large space to the right of the chancel (i.e., where the pulpit, altar, and large cross are located) was set up for the band, and thus the eyes of members were drawn away from the central architectural features of the sanctuaries that symbolized three important ideas in Lutheran theology—Word (the pulpit), sacraments (the altar, where Holy Communion was celebrated), and grace (symbolized by the empty cross of the crucified and resurrected Jesus)—toward the band and, at Faith, the large video screens on which the words to the songs were projected. [27]

Second, the addition of a band and amplified music modified the structure of the service, which in turn redefined its purpose. The services at Faith and Zion more closely resembled the three-part order of the evangelical tradition insofar as the section in the Lutheran service that emphasized the Word—when the stories of God's saving words and deeds are told through scripture readings, hymns, prayers, and the chanted liturgy—was given less attention, and more attention or emphasis was placed on the singing of praise songs. [28] These songs, much like the song service of the revivals in the frontier tradition and today in many megachurches, were designed to create a particular emotional mood (e.g.,

Table 3. Content of Praise Songs at Zion Lutheran Church

Theme	Count (%)
Personal benefits of faith/personal relationship with Jesus (peace, joy, comfort, guidance, hope, freedom; Jesus as friend, savior, guide)	34 (35%)
Evangelism (old vs. new life, brokenness, save me, change me)	9 (10%)
Praise and thanksgiving	20 (21%)
Attributes of God (power, mercy, glory, righteousness, faithfulness)	21 (21%)
Lutheran themes (sin, grace, the cross, death and resurrection, blood, water/baptism, bread and wine)	13 (13%)

Note: I assigned key words and phrases to one of five themes: personal benefits of faith/personal relationship with Jesus; evangelism; praise and thanksgiving; attributes of God; and Lutheran themes. Given the repetitive nature of these songs, I counted a theme only once even if it appeared multiple times.

joy and excitement) and to set expectations about participation. Because the music is amplified and led by professional-sounding singers, there is a disincentive for the audience to join in, and passive observation is much easier.[29] Moreover, by replacing much of the chanted liturgy of the Word section with praise music (either collectively sung or performed by the band), these contemporary services minimize the level of participation and the call-and-response structure of the Lutheran liturgy.[30]

The addition of praise music also emphasized some of the other key features of the evangelical tradition: experience, emotion, and the individual. These changes were evident in both the lyrics of the music and members' comments about how praise music had altered their experience of worship. Sargeant and Senn both note that praise music closely resonates with the therapeutic religious culture of Protestantism that has become the dominant mode of religiosity in recent decades.[31] This type of music places the individual and his or her personal relationship to Jesus or God at the theological center and presents a vision of the Christian life as one freed from worldly troubles through this relationship. The up-tempo, light rock music and lyrics that emphasize the positive dimensions of the Christian faith also serve the pragmatic purposes of creating celebratory experiences for worshipers and providing examples of or rationales for conversion (meeting the evangelistic purposes of worship). A comparison of the praise songs used at Zion with songs from the *LBW* illustrates the emphasis on the individual and the personal benefits of faith that characterize the evangelical tradition.

A content analysis of fifty-three songs used in nine different worship services at Zion illustrates how borrowing the musical forms of evangelical worship reshaped the theological emphasis of worship. Table 3 provides a numerical count of the themes that appeared in the songs and suggests a strong emphasis on key themes from the evangelical tradition. About one-third of the themes in the songs stressed the personal benefits of being a Christian or having a relationship with Jesus, and although explicit evangelistic themes accounted for only 10 percent of the total themes, the message about the personal benefits of Christianity can be read as evangelistic insofar as it describes a new life of joy, peace, and comfort for those who accept Jesus as their savior. "Spirit Song" exemplifies the therapeutic and evangelistic nature of many of the praise songs sung at Zion:

O let the Son of God enfold you with His Spirit and His love,
Let Him fill your life and satisfy our soul.
O let Him have the things that hold you and His Spirit like a dove,
Will descend upon your life and make you whole.

O come and sing the song with gladness, as your hearts are filled with joy,
Lift your hands in sweet surrender to His name.
O give Him all your tears and sadness, give Him all your years of Pain,
And you'll enter into life in Jesus' Name.

Similarly, the song "The River Is Here" presents the Christian life as one of utter joy in which there is no pain, suffering, or doubt:

The river of God sets our feet a-dancing
The river of God fills our hearts with cheer.
The river of God fills our mouths with laughter,
And we rejoice for the river is here.

Such songs present an inoffensive, simplistic faith in which the reality of evil, suffering, and the costs of discipleship are not articulated. In this way, praise songs maximize the possibility that seekers or the unchurched will want to join the church because the Christian life seems to promise so many benefits.[32] Moreover, praise music in general, and the songs used at Zion, tend to emphasize the private dimensions of faith and minimize the public dimensions. Few of the songs used at Zion spoke about Christianity's (and Lutheranism's) call to serve the neighbor or stressed that being Christian should radically de-center the individual. The songs tend to identify the duty of Christians as giving God thanks and praise and allowing God to comfort, heal, or guide the individual. While many classic hymns in the *LBW* have similar themes, they also focus attention on the public role of the Christian and emphasize how the Christian life is centered on God and loving service to others. For example, in "O God of Mercy, God of Light," the believer asks God to "Teach us the Lesson Jesus Taught: To feel for those his blood has bought, that ev'ry deed and word and thought may work a work for you."

Praise songs also tend to present the Christian story and notions of God in relatively simple, reductionistic terms so that the difficult, ambiguous, and negative aspects (e.g., sin, sacrifice, death) of Christianity and Christian theology are avoided. Even the songs that speak about classic Lutheran themes of sin and grace, the cross and resurrection, tell an abbreviated story that minimizes the sacrifices required by Christian disciples, the inescapable condition of human sin, the righteous anger of the hidden God, or the agony of Jesus' death. For example, in one of the commonly used songs, "Lord I Lift Your Name on High," a verse summarizes the life and death of Jesus without providing any details about the reasons for Jesus' death nor the divine and human costs of sin:

> You came from heaven to earth to show the way,
> From the earth to the cross,
> My debt to pay,
> From the cross to the grave,
> From the grave to the sky;
> Lord I lift your name on high!

Compare this with Luther's hymn "To Jordan Came the Christ, Our Lord," in which Luther tells the story of Jesus' baptism in the first four verses and then outlines the call to discipleship and the necessity "to abandon sin and come to true contrition." The final two verses present the Lutheran understanding of sin and grace, the inability of humans to earn salvation through good works (part of the Lutheran doctrine of justification), baptism, and the cross:

> But woe to those who cast aside
> This grace so freely given;
> They shall in sin and shame abide
> And to despair be driven.
> For born, in sin, their works must fail,
> Their striving saves them never;
> Their pious acts do not avail,
> And they are lost forever,
> Eternal death their portion.

> All that the mortal eye beholds
> Is water as we pour it.
> Before the eye of faith unfolds
> The pow'r of Jesus' merit.
> For here it sees the crimson flood
> To all our ills bring healing;
> The wonders of his precious blood
> The Love of God revealing,
> Assuring his own pardon.

In general, Lutheran hymnody is grounded in classic sacred music from the sixteenth through the twentieth centuries and presents complex narratives about God, Jesus, the Holy Spirit, and the nature of the Christian life. Moreover, the hymns are tied to the specific seasons of the church year (e.g., Christmas,

Epiphany, Lent, Easter, and Pentecost) and to the weekly assigned readings in *The Common Worship Lectionary*. As such, the hymns relate stories about the events, biblical stories, or themes of the season (e.g., hymns during Lent focus on the sacrifice of Jesus and on human sin and alienation from God and may point to the promise of Easter) and, therefore, are an important means of teaching and reinforcing particularly Lutheran understandings of the Christian faith. Conversely, praise music is theologically thin, and because of its simplicity (one member at Zion called it "7–11 music"—seven words repeated eleven times) it cannot explain matters of faith in any depth. It does not serve a didactic purpose but is intended only to touch the emotions or cultivate an attitude of prayer. Moreover, the music used at Faith and Zion rarely reflected the mood or theological themes associated with the various liturgical seasons and thus again lacked the ability to help people live through the joy of Christmas or the penitential preparation of Lent.[33]

Sacred music, whether classic or contemporary, is a primary means of communicating and teaching the beliefs, values, and formal doctrines of a religious body. As suggested by the example above, Lutheran sacred music both teaches and reinforces a particularly Lutheran way of understanding Christianity and a particular confessional identity.[34] The widespread use of praise music at these congregations modified the tradition in three ways. First, such music did not teach or articulate some of the core theological doctrines and commitments of Lutheranism. Second, it replaced Lutheran theology with a different theology that emphasizes a therapeutic and personalistic understanding of Christianity in which the individual chooses to be saved and then goes on to live a life free of sin (this is markedly different from Lutheran theology, which claims that salvation is a unmerited gift from God and that humans must contend with the reality of sin every day). Third, it helped to redefine the purpose and structure of worship (away from the proclamation and response format and emphasis on Word and sacrament in the Lutheran tradition) toward individualistic, evangelistic, and pragmatic goals and thus created a fundamentally different type of worship in which experience and emotion became the criteria by which to measure the authenticity of worship and, more importantly, the authenticity of Christianity.

While both congregations claimed they were merely borrowing the forms of evangelical worship, the preceding analysis suggests that they also unwittingly imported the theological content carried by those forms. Some clergy and lay leaders at Faith and Zion argued that praise music was theologically neutral—a tool to facilitate church growth that transcended denominational traditions—and thus they did not see any relationship between the musical form and the explicit theological content.

Yet the literature on the relationship between cultural forms and explicit meaning carried by those forms suggests that the two cannot be easily separated. Cultural forms, such as musical genres, carry meaning in several ways. First, cultural forms operate according to an internal logic (a set of rules or organizing principles) that identifies the purpose and meaning of a particular form.[35] For example, the genre of romance is organized around an adventure story in which the hero is seriously challenged by inner faults, the world, or assorted "bad guys" but ultimately overcomes them. The genre affirms the belief that good will triumph over evil and thus promises social security and integration to its audience.[36] Praise music is organized around a simple, repetitive, upbeat musical form that mirrors the optimistic and uncomplicated theological message of the lyrics. Its internal logic makes it difficult to address issues like doubt and despair or suffering and evil.

Second, formal conventions constrain choices about content, just as the overt content limits which forms can be used. For example, Blain's work on Nazi discourses illustrates how form sets boundaries around content and how content animates the conventional features of a particular form. He shows how Nazi leaders relied on the form of melodrama to mobilize mass support for the war and their anti-Jewish program. The form demands clearly defined villains and victims, but the particular villains (the Jews) offered in their discourse were so widely accepted because they were grounded in the particulars of German literary and popular culture (e.g., the *Volk* tradition, Teutonic myths of blood and race, and Wagnerian opera). Nazi discourse worked because the content, which is based on local knowledge, is located within the conventional meanings of melodrama.[37] Similarly, the genre of praise music operates according to a logic that sets audience expectations and limits the overt theological meaning that can be communicated by the form. This musical genre is designed to help people express positive emotions such as joy or thanksgiving and does so in part by relying on up-tempo and very singable music (e.g., by using major keys and the midrange of notes). This effectively limits the kinds of theological claims or themes the music contains because it would be difficult and inappropriate to sing about evil, death, or suffering, for example, in this musical genre. Moreover, the simple lyrics and the repetitious nature of praise music suggest that the genre is supposed to operate as a way to enter into a state of prayer rather than convey or teach complex doctrine. It is impossible to explain the Lutheran doctrine of justification or the sacraments in a handful of words.

Third, ritual and symbolic forms used in worship communicate and reinforce the specific theological claims articulated in a hymn or litany of confession. Aune argues that how congregations worship (e.g., "the manner in which we proclaim, pray, or share the Lord's Supper") makes the theological claims of the rites or practices concrete and thus fosters particular ways of faith or being Christian.[38] Praise music signals certain claims about what kinds of religious experiences or activities are authentic and normative for Christians.[39] Praise music tends to present an image of the Christian life as one filled with joy (singing and dancing are favorite images in this genre) in which the Christian has no problems or is somehow immune from the perpetuation or effects of poverty, racism, injustice, ill health, unemployment, or divorce. The conversion motif also plays a prominent role in this style of music insofar as the lyrics often encourage individuals "to surrender to Jesus," "join the kingdom," or "fall in love with Jesus" or compare the broken life of the sinner before conversion to the healthy, joyful life of the new Christian. The genre does not allow for instruction in how Christians sustain or grow in faith, nor in how they weather the inevitable problems that life presents.

In short, the music borrowed from the evangelical tradition reconfigures the message and meaning of Christianity by emphasizing the individual's decision to convert (as opposed to the Lutheran understanding that God comes to humans and that the work of salvation is not accomplished by any human act), by offering a truncated and potentially unrealistic view of the Christian life, and by defining emotion and experience as the criteria of authentic worship. In contrast, the historic liturgical and hymnody tradition of Lutheranism is couched in an understanding of the Christian life as a journey. Rituals such as the confession and Holy Communion mark different stages on the journey (e.g., the daily recognition of one's sinful nature and the gift of God's grace or forgiveness that can help the Christian live in a new way), and hymns tell the story of God's involvement with humans on this journey.[40] Together they make the theological claims of Lutheranism regarding sin and grace, justification and salvation, concrete or real to participants.[41]

By borrowing the musical form of the evangelical tradition, these two congregations necessarily, even if unwittingly, also borrowed and institutionalized some of the theological claims of that tradition. In doing so, the churches lost some of the historic Lutheran ways of thinking and enacting the faith and, de facto, baptized other, once-foreign (and possibly contradictory) experiences and activities as normative.

Lutheranizing Evangelicalism

The changes to the tradition were not wholly unobserved by the leaders (at the least, the clergy) of Faith and Zion. While these innovations in worship were seen as critical in the attempt to recruit non-Lutheran members, church leaders also acknowledged the problem of ensuring that the worship remained sufficiently tied to the Lutheran tradition to maintain legitimacy among those seeking a Lutheran worship experience. In other words, both congregations were forced to attend to the problem of how to preserve some Lutheran content amid the powerful influence of evangelical form. Thus, the reworking of the tradition at Faith and Zion also included an attempt to make the evangelical practices more Lutheran, or at least to make them fit within the tradition. This is how the isomorphic process was tempered as leaders intentionally avoided adopting particular theological ideas or practices from the evangelical tradition or tried to "Lutheranize" them.

The leaders and most members of the two congregations saw the changes in worship either as an attempt to blend the two traditions or as a simple borrowing of evangelical worship forms without also incorporating the theological content of those forms. Some of the key lay leaders and the clergy of both congregations strongly denied that their church had become evangelical, Baptist, or fundamentalist, suggesting that, like Roof's "Mainstream Believers," they drew clear boundaries between overzealous evangelicals and more moderate and tolerant mainline Protestants.[42] The youth and family pastor at Faith,[43] for example, reported how he specifically stressed to the high school students that he and the church are not Baptist even as the young adults participate in a program in which they write their own testimonies of coming to faith and compile a "hit list" of friends whom they will invite to church and for whom they will pray for conversion.

An older member of the congregation claimed that because so many young people "don't want to have anything to do with Lutheranism," the church, led by Pastor Lincoln, "is trying to string together Lutheran and evangelical traditions, but we're downplaying our Lutheran identity." When I pressed her to explain what those traditions are, she identified the key theological claims of both traditions—the Lutheran claim that God offers grace to humans who then respond to this gift out of love in acts of thanks and service versus the evangelical tradition that emphasizes the individual's choice to believe and then strive for moral/religious perfection or sanctification—but was unable to say exactly how they were blended:

> The Lutheran tradition is based in the idea that God comes to us first; we accept him and then we go forth in service. The evangelical tradition is that we accept Jesus Christ as our personal savior and then we are on a pathway to improve ourselves. I guess I hear the first in the sermons, but there is a group of fundamentalists in the church who seem to want to make having a personal relationship with Jesus the measuring rod of faith.

Several leaders at the congregations denied that they were trying to become another Willow Creek, Saddleback, or Community Church of Joy—all megachurches on the evangelical side of the religious spectrum—arguing that their blended worship service was rooted in Word and sacrament. A lay staff member at Zion argued that the church

> will not become Zion Community Church. I think foundationally we are people who believe in the grace piece of Luther and want an opportunity for liturgy. It's important to stay Lutheran but we have to lose some of our Lutheranness in order to reach the unsaved because they are turned off by things that are too Lutheran. But our contemporary service is liturgical; people just don't know it.

Similarly a council member at Faith argued that his church was "theologically rooted in the Lutheran understanding of Grace, Word and Sacrament, *sola scriptura,* and all that, but we've gotten rid of the whole cultural element, you know, all that Scandinavian stuff." In one of his first newsletter articles, Pastor Lincoln told the members of Faith that it would be a mistake to copy "what's working at boomer churches like Willow Creek and Saddleback because this will put us out of touch with the next generation coming behind the boomers." And in one interview, he claimed that their goal was not to become the next Willow Creek, in part because such churches have trouble "channeling people into opportunities for growth." Instead, he argued that Faith had merely taken some of the best ideas from the megachurches and church growth literature about making church accessible and doing outreach.

A number of leaders involved in planning or leading worship defended their contemporary or blended service as Lutheran because it was liturgical or followed the tradition's order of worship based in the Common Rite. For example, a member of the band at Zion passionately defended the blended service there as liturgical and hence Lutheran:

It [the blended service] has gotten more liturgical than the traditional service. It's easier to identify as liturgical. I mean, it walks you doggone through the whole thing, and we print it all in the bulletin for you to see. You can say you don't like the style, but you can't say it's nonliturgical. Man, I tell you, it's as liturgical as it can possibly be.

One of the developers of the blended service at Zion shared the story of how the service came about, what elements from the Lutheran tradition were kept and why praise music was added:

We sat down with the *LBW* and said, "What's important here?" We listed them out and decided what parts were essential. Everything in the blended service is intentional; it's where it is for a reason. We were concerned that we do a Lutheran worship service with integrity. We wanted to make sure that whatever we did we would continue to look Lutheran. Basically, we followed the format from the *LBW*. We kept the confession because we thought it was important to have the words of forgiveness as part of each and every Sunday service. We kept the creed, not because we don't know what we believe, but because we need to continue to stand fast and say this is who we are; this is what we believe. We kept the "Kyrie" and "Hymn of Praise" but we changed the words. We added an opening medley of praise songs and other praise songs instead of hymns. I think the biggest difference between traditional and contemporary worship is the music. Praise music is heart language, and if you cut off that style, you are cutting off something that resonates in the hearts of individuals and really cutting them off from church.

Her account suggests that the congregation believed they were keeping the structure and core ritual elements of the Lutheran tradition (although the "Confession" and "Kyrie" are optional elements, and the sacrament of Holy Communion, a more important part, was left out) while adding music from the evangelical tradition because it offered something their own tradition could not provide—a way to make religion emotionally resonant and powerful. Her account also echoes the concern with evangelism and the need to make worship accessible and meaningful to non-Lutherans, which are both elements of the congregation's causal story.

The institutional account of changes in worship at Faith echoes Zion's concern to alter the tradition in order to grow while still preserving the essential parts of the tradition. Pastor Lincoln's predecessor had started a true seeker service in 1994 that was led by a Pentecostal music director. The service was modeled after Willow Creek's seeker service and replaced the Lutheran liturgy and the rite of Holy Communion with praise songs led by a rock band and with a sermon. The service was not well received by many members, in part because too much of Lutheranism had been sacrificed. One member who often worshiped at other area churches during this seeker service era commented that this service was so disturbing because it undermined the Lutheran identity of the congregation and herself: "I didn't know if I was in an Assembly of God church or a Lutheran church." Within a year of assuming his position, Pastor Lincoln ended the seeker service and replaced it with a blended service that included Holy Communion. His rationale for doing so relied on the strategy of reconnecting that would become a key part of his and other leaders' defense of the new blended service in the coming years: namely, that Lutherans are a church of Word and sacrament.

Pastor Lincoln, like some of his lay leaders, defended the inclusion of praise music because it helped individuals tap into the emotional side of faith. In one interview, he explained that they use praise music in their blended services because it offered an element missing from Lutheranism that would make Lutheranism more complete and thus more relevant to younger generations, for whom integrating emotion into their worship experience is considered essential if they are to become part of a congregation.[44]

> Let's talk about how praise music works here. It really has more of a mantra-like effect, in terms of how it's sung. Some of our older, longtime Lutheran members say, "Why do you sing that damn thing two or three times?" Well, because in every singing of that chorus again, it kind of filters to a deeper level inside—experientially, emotionally—and so this type of music is affecting us in different ways. Intellectually, does it do for our minds what "O Sacred Head Now Wounded" did? No. Does it feed us and touch us at an emotional level in a much different way? Yes! When you put "Holy, Holy, Holy" alongside of "We Cry Holy," and you sing those two things together, you've started off, in a sense, in your head, you've got to a place of emotional kind of depth, and you come back out of that in an integrated kind of way, it seems to me. So I would argue that we need both styles of music. This is one of the reasons we no longer just do praise music at the 11 a.m. service. We need hymns. Remember, the intellectualism and the

theological depth of our hymnody were in an age of enlightenment in which it was about our heads. And we have got to see that this generation is as much about the heart as they are about the head.

The evangelical impulse was tempered at these churches by a commitment to preserving a liturgical worship service that included Holy Communion and some of the core theological ideas of the tradition (i.e., grace, sin, the cross and resurrection, and Christocentrism). An examination of the structure of worship and the content of the sermons reveals how these congregations remained Lutheran while incorporating the forms and ideas of evangelicalism.

Table 4 summarizes the order and elements of the generic Lutheran and evangelical worship traditions and those used at the blended services at Faith and Zion. I have italicized the key departures from the Lutheran tradition at the two congregations. At first glance, the services at Faith and Zion look remarkably similar to the generic Lutheran tradition: both maintain the four-part structure, both offer Holy Communion (Zion offers it only twice a month), both keep some of the optional elements of the Lutheran ordo such as the rite of public confession and absolution, the "Kyrie," and the recitation of the creed. Some members of the churches argued that they were Lutheran because they always have the confession of sins in the service. The recognition of the reality and inescapability of sin and God's action through Jesus to defeat the power of sin over humanity are hallmarks of Lutheranism. This theological commitment was evident in a sermon deliver by Zion's pastor John Andersen, who argued that Lutheranism's awareness of sin makes it different from the megachurches and evangelical tradition more generally. He began the sermon by unpacking a prayer in the Lutheran rite of baptism in which the pastor asks God to give the baptized person the spirit of wisdom, understanding, counsel, and might and fear and joy in the presence of God. He made the comparison between Lutheranism and evangelicalism in his comments about the joy of being in God's presence:

Why do you think we have more celebratory music in worship at Zion? To make being in God's house more joyful. But we also have confession and absolution at the beginning of the service. Now church growth experts say, "Don't start with confession and absolution; no one wants to be told right from the start that they are not good or remind them of how bad they are." But we recognize that when we enter into the presence of God, we recognize that we are unclean. Have you ever had the experience of not belonging—like when you're wearing casual clothes at a formal event? That's the kind of uncomfortableness you might feel coming into God's presence. You know it's not right and that's why we start with the confession and absolution; so that we can worship with joy.[45]

In this comment, Pastor Andersen used the strategy of reconnecting to remind his congregation how they are different from evangelicals insofar as they do not sugarcoat the reality of sin and daily need for forgiveness. At the same time, he suggested that they are unlike other Lutherans, whose traditional worship seemingly does not allow for a very full expression or experience of joy. Sargeant contends that, although the nondenominational megachurches acknowledge the reality of sin, they tend to define it in individualistic and psychological terms in line with the therapeutic notions of religion common in contemporary Protestantism. He writes that, "while seeker church pastors do discuss the basics of Christian orthodoxy, including the seriousness of sin and the reality of judgment, they often frame this discussion in terms of how sin harms the individual rather than how it is offensive to a holy God. Sin, in short, prevents us from realizing *our* full potential.[46]

At Zion it was rare to hear sin talked about in these terms. Instead, in the litanies of confession and forgiveness used at the blended service, and in sermons, sin is framed as an inherent condition of being human that is often manifested in acts of injustice, exclusion, hatred, greed, or indifference to the oppressed (e.g., "We live as broken people in a broken world. Too often we are content to look away instead of confronting the injustice we see."). Sin is also conceived of as an affront to God (e.g., "Lord, we confess that we have not lived our lives in ways that honor and serve you"). However, the pronouncements of forgiveness used in the blended service tended to reflect the more individualistic notion of sin and salvation Sargeant sees in use at the megachurches, and often forgiveness was explicitly connected to the congregation's evangelizing mission. This is illustrated in the following "Words of Forgiveness": "We can rejoice! God has forgiven our sins through Jesus' death on the cross. We are alive in Christ through this resurrection power. We are free to live lives fully transformed by God's love and grace. We are free to live out our calling to grow in faith and to share our faith in the world."[47] Thus, Zion combines a more explicitly Lutheran understanding of sin insofar as sin is conceptualized as the inescapable condition with which humans must struggle every day, and a more evangelical notion of sin and forgiveness insofar as it stressed highly individualized and therapeutic understanding tied to both the call to share one's faith with unbelievers and the theological emphasis on the ability of humans to live morally perfected lives.

Similarly, at Faith, there is a strong commitment to a Lutheran understanding of sin and grace. At nearly every blended service I attended, the congregation recited the "Confession" found in the *LBW*. Pastor Lincoln was personally committed to the Lutheran doctrine of *simul justus et peccator* (the belief that humans are simultaneously saint, justified by God, and sinner) and claimed that this belief was generally shared by the members of the congregation (in response to my question about what aspects of Lutheranism they appreciated or believed were important to preserve, several members mentioned this belief). Occasionally, the clergy spoke about the Lutheran understanding of sin in their sermons. For example, in a sermon entitled "Plugged into Salvation," Pastor Lincoln began by showing a clip from the film *Saving Private Ryan* where Captain Miller is dying and tells Private Ryan that he must earn his rescue. The sermon largely

Table 4. The Structure of Lutheran Worship and Evangelical Worship

Generic Lutheran (Four Parts)	Generic Evangelical (Three Parts)	Faith Lutheran	Zion Lutheran
Gathering • Brief Order for Confession and Forgiveness* • Entrance hymn • Greeting to the congregation • "Kyrie" and "Hymn of Praise"* • Prayer of the Day	**Preliminaries and Call to Worship** (led by band) • Welcome • Opening song(s) • Drama or performed music	**"We Prepare Our Hearts to Meet God"** • *One or two upbeat praise music songs* • *Confession and absolution* • *Drama/video presentation and/or praise song* • *Prayer of praise*	**Gathering** • *One or two praise songs* • Welcome and announcements • *Confession and absolution and "Kyrie" (often different from the versions in the LBW)* • Praise song
Word • Reading of the scriptures (the four appointed texts in the lectionary) • Sermon • Hymn of the day • Recitation of the creed* • The Prayers[a] and the Peace[b]	**Message** • One scripture reading • Sermon	**"We Listen to God's Word"** • *One scripture reading (may or may not come from Common Lectionary)* • Message	**Word** • *Children's message* • New Testament and Gospel readings • The message • Praise song • *Apostles' Creed* • Offertory • Prayers of the community

Meal		"We Respond to God's Word"	Holy Communion
• Preparation of bread and wine	• Communion is usually omitted	• *Praise song/hymn set to rock music*	• Rite of Communion (every two weeks)
• Offering and offertory		• Prayers of the people	
• Prayer over the offering		• The peace offering	
• Rite of Holy Communion		• Rite of Holy Communion (weekly)	
Sending	**Altar Call, or Harvest**	**Sending**	**Sending**
• Prayer	• Call for decision to accept Jesus	• Benediction	• Benediction
• Benediction	• Praise songs	• *Praise song*	• *Praise song*
• Closing hymn*	• Sending prayer		

Note: * signifies optional elements in the Lutheran tradition. Departures from the Lutheran tradition at the two congregations are italicized.

a The official name used for these prayers in the hymnal.

b "The Peace" is a ritual greeting.

Sources: Michael B. Aune, "*Lutheran Book of Worship*: Relic or Resource?" *Dialog* 33, no. 3 (1994): 174–82; *Lutheran Book of Worship*, Minister's Desk Edition (Minneapolis: Augsburg Publishing House; Philadelphia: Board of Publication, Lutheran Church in America, 1978); Gordon Lathrop, "New Pentecost or Joseph's Britches? Reflections on the History and Meaning of the Worship Ordo in the Megachurches," *Worship* 76, no. 6 (2001): 521–38; Kimon Howland Sargeant, *Seeker Churches: Promoting Traditional Religion in a Non-traditional Way* (New Brunswick, NJ: Rutgers University Press, 2000); James F. White, *Christian Worship in North America* (Collegeville, MN: Liturgical Press, 1997); Frank C. Senn, "'Worship Alive': An Analysis and Critique of 'Alternative Worship Services,'" *Worship* 69, no. 3 (1995): 194–224.

focused on how a Lutheran understanding of sin and salvation sin is at odds with American culture:

> Ask the average American if they believe they are going to heaven and they will say, "I hope so." Ask them on what basis they believe they'll get into heaven, and they answer, "Because I've lived a good life." Most Christians in the U.S. of all sorts think there are things you can do to earn salvation; that if you live a good life you will go to heaven. This is our American theology. It is the theology of the young man who came up to Jesus that day on the road. "What must I do to inherit eternal life?" the young man asks. "Earn it," says Captain Miller. And you can see the anguish in the voice of Private Ryan as he pleadingly says to his wife at the cemetery scene, "Tell me I've lived a good life. Tell me I've been a good man." This should be shocking to Lutheran Christians, who are taught that we are saved by grace through faith. I was really angry when I saw this movie. This is the American theology, and it's all a lie. It rests on the assumption that eternal life can be earned. There is nothing we can do to be saved; the disciples ask who can be saved and Jesus says nobody; but God will save us. This is at the heart of what it means to be a Lutheran Christian.

Yet the evangelical therapeutic understanding of sin (i.e., sin as a barrier to personal fulfillment), and more generally an overemphasis on the personal benefits of faith, are also present in the sermons at Faith Lutheran. For example, in a sermon entitled "The 12 Steps to Faith," Pastor Lincoln used the self-help language of Alcoholics Anonymous to speak about the need to confess, repent, and receive God's forgiveness. He began by reviewing the first four steps in the process: "Step 1: Admit you are powerless to stop sin. Step 2: Admit Jesus Christ has the power to heal you. Step 3: Put your life in Jesus' hands every day. Step 4: Do a spiritual inventory. Step 5: Admit to God, yourself, and others the true nature of your sins." The sermon focused on step 5 and how to help people "overcome the human propensity to keep God out of our lives because we are afraid we won't be lovable to God." He concluded the sermon with a call to convert: "If you're looking to turn your life around, then confess your problems to God and your loved ones and he will forgive you." Pastor Lincoln borrowed not only a therapeutic notion of sin that is common in evangelical religiosity but also the evangelical tradition's framing of sin in terms of conversion.

As suggested by the preceding discussion of sin, some of the ways in which the evangelical tradition has reshaped worship or has been blended into the Lutheran tradition at Faith and Zion are not apparent from simply looking at the structure of the worship service. They became apparent only by looking at what actually happened at the services. For example, it is clear from table 4 that both congregations rely on evangelical praise music and, as discussed in the preceding section, this type of music both sets a mood and emphasizes heart (or emotions) over head (or intellect). The members I interviewed who supported the blended services uniformly reported that these services were more exciting, joyous, or meaningful for them and were a noticeable change from the Lutheran worship they associated with the tradition. A woman in her late twenties responding to my question about what she most likes about worship at Faith said, "I love that people are just fired up about God. There's so much energy there. And it's not just stand up sing a hymn, sit down and have a reading, stand up, sing hymn, sit down, you know. There's just this tremendous feeling of joy when you get into the song and you're singing and I feel the band is really singing to the glory of God."

The worship leader at Faith also mentioned how "the congregation had finally come to realize that it's [i.e., worship] not just coming and standing by yourself every week year after year, but it's about realizing when you hear a song or something Pastor Lincoln says in a sermon that you're in the presence of God and he's right here with you." She continued by connecting the worship experience to the therapeutic work of improving or creating the self:

> People came to embrace the contemporary music because they found themselves really getting into it and becoming engaged and finding themselves worshiping and getting really touched by the music. They would say, "Whoah! I never felt this way about singing 'Built on a Rock.'" I think they just really realized that through music they could open up their selves and get down to business.

Another member commented, "Now I see joy on people's faces and I feel it too. There's this energy in worship that doesn't happen at the traditional service. Whenever my dad comes to the 9:30 service, he says, 'Wow! No wonder you're happy. This church is alive.' I think it's the music that really gives worship that energy."

Several members of Zion also noted the higher level of energy at their blended service and attributed it not only to the praise music but also to the new words used in the "Confession" and "Kyrie" each week; as one person said, "the wording of the liturgy is a little bit new every week, and that makes me think about what I'm saying and it makes me really feel like I'm worshiping God." These comments suggest that the praise music creates a worship context in which individuals feel joy and the presence of God and that this does not happen with the music and liturgy that use organ music and pre-twentieth-century hymns and that follow the Common Rite in the *LBW*. These comments also reflect the individualistic and personalistic idiom of evangelicalism and more generally post–World War II Protestantism, in which God is decentered and individuals attend worship to get psychosocial or emotional benefits.

Organizational Moves toward Evangelicalism

In addition to embracing a more evangelical style of worship, these congregations also borrowed a number of organizational techniques and resources from evangelical sources. Clergy and elected leaders at Faith and Zion freely adopted the decision-making structures, hospitality plans, marketing practices, and educational resources from megachurches and church growth companies and seemed to have little concern that doing so could change the religious commitments of the congregation. Both congregations followed the "purpose-driven church model"[48] to maximize their ability to effectively reach out to or attract the unchurched in their communities. Yet no one I interviewed expressed any concern that the model rests, first, on Baptist theology, in which the central purpose of Christianity and the congregation is to convert unbelievers, and, second, on a hermeneutic that accepts biblical inerrancy (literalism), which is not part of the Lutheran tradition per se.

Faith and Zion, in particular, adopted the mission of conversion advocated in the model and its stepwise process in which visitors or the unchurched are invited into church, taught the basics of the faith, encouraged to join a small group to become mature in their faith, and finally to become evangelists themselves. Each congregation offered similar versions of a four-course sequence which they understood as the best way to recruit and keep new members. Faith Lutheran began to strongly encourage its new members to attend the theologically conservative Episcopal program Alpha (in which the basic teachings of Christianity are laid out in a nonthreatening manner) as the first step in the process of moving from new Christian to mature Christian. Both congregations taught the Willow Creek course on personal evangelism entitled "Becoming a Contagious Christian," in which members are taught how to share their faith and the joyful experience of being a Christian with friends and coworkers without relying on the high-pressure sales pitch often associated with door-to-door or curbside evangelists. Faith Lutheran commissioned an "Assimilation Task Force" (this use of the term "assimilation" comes from Willow Creek) to figure out the most efficient ways to make the church hospitable, friendly, and memorable to visitors so that they would return and join. The task force created a process that funneled visitors into worship (after being welcomed in the parking lot and escorted into the building, a practice developed at the megachurches), then into a separate visitors' coffee hour where they could meet current members and see a video about the church, and then into membership classes. Most new members were channeled into small groups to make them feel more at home in the large congregation. They attended a spiritual-gifts class, which used the booklets and testing materials from Willow Creek, to help them identify their gifts for ministry and to place them into organized ministries of the church.

Both congregations adopted the marketing advice of the model in which the congregation identifies its "target" audience(s) and then shapes worship and programs to meet the religious needs and interests of that audience. Both groups targeted families with young children who were either lapsed Lutherans or Catholics, former evangelicals, or members of the unchurched population. This was particularly evident at Zion during the reworking of the worship schedule, as they "sold" the changes on the basis of market research about the worship preferences of young adults (ages twenty-five to thirty-five) in their community.

Finally, both groups almost exclusively used educational materials from Willow Creek or other evangelically oriented megachurches. Such materials emphasized specific theological ideas, such as the importance of developing a personal relationship with Jesus, the imperative to share one's faith with unbelievers, and an overarching determinism in which God is understood to be absolutely in control of all events at both the individual and global levels (e.g., some interviewees who participated in small groups at the congregation spoke about trying to discern God's plan or purpose for their lives). While this did not mean that members of the congregation would become evangelical simply by reading the booklets or watching the videos from non-Lutheran sources, it did mean that they were far less likely to hear or learn about a specifically Lutheran approach to such topics as evangelism, studying scripture, or ethics. In my interviews with small-group or Bible study leaders and staff at both congregations and observations of classes at Zion and a men's group at Faith, I saw three ways in which education and small groups mirrored contemporary evangelicalism and the theological messages advanced in the megachurch materials.[49]

First, some members of the small groups adopted the language of evangelicalism to describe their own experience of being Christian.[50] For example, at Zion, the leader of a group studying the world of the Old Testament repeatedly used such phrases as "being in the Word" or "giving your life to the Lord" and spoke about how his own faith had been formed less by the Lutheran church (he was a lifelong Lutheran) and more by his time in Campus Crusade for Christ (an evangelical organization that serves college-aged adults) and his reading of literature by such figures as James Dobson and Robert Schuler (he mentioned in our interview that he also regularly watches Schuler's *Hour of Power* television show). One member of Faith Lutheran reported that her participation in a small group after her divorce helped her "reinvite Christ into my heart and develop that personal relationship." Another member said that her small group "helps me grow; it helps me get more into the Word; it helps me keep a mind-set on eternity rather than on this life only."

Similarly, most of the nine participants in the men's group at Faith used the language of evangelicalism to talk about their faith, the Bible, and their understanding of service. Two men used the language of "muscular Christianity" favored by the Promise Keepers organization: they talked about being "Jesus warriors" or "prayer warriors" and used the language of male headship when they talked about their roles as fathers and spouses.[51] One week we spent most of the session answering the question "When did you first meet Jesus?" Three of the men claimed they were Lutheran or Episcopal before having some type of born-again experience, at which time they actually became Christian, reflecting the evangelical distinction between being authentically Christian and being an unconverted member of a church. Not one member of the group spoke about his baptism, confirmation (the educational process in the Lutheran church whereby teenagers are taught the doctrines of the church and then publicly reaffirm their baptismal vows), or the experience of meeting Jesus every day by acknowledging one's own sin and God's forgiveness through the cross and resurrection—all of which are responses rooted in Lutheranism.

Second, some of the small groups had an explicit goal of evangelism. This was particularly true at Faith. The men's group I attended was studying biblical teachings about service and doing some service activity one a month. For a few weeks the group brainstormed about the possibility of delivering breakfast to the homeless population in Oakland or San Francisco, less because they were needy and more because it would be a way to "preach the gospel" to them. At a training meeting with the small-group leaders at Faith, the staff member who oversaw the small-group program reminded her charges that one of the commitments they had as leaders was "to cultivate personal relationships with unbelievers and meet them where they're at in their own journey. We have lots of unchurched members at Faith and you can't assume they know the Bible or know how to pray. You need to be very intentional about serving them at their point of struggle." At the same meeting, the leader of the men's group testified that participating in the group was a "great conversation starter at work. When I say I'm in a men's Bible study, no one seems interested, but when I mention doing construction at the battered-women's shelter, people listen. It's a way I can invite people to the gospel and church." The leader of a group that met in her firm in downtown San Francisco claimed that the simple presence of the group "gave me an opportunity to make my faith public," and it "invited conversations with coworkers whenever they asked what we were doing." Thus, the small-group program at Faith, and the classes at Zion to a lesser extent, became the organizational means to teach and implement each congregation's goal or mission of evangelizing the unchurched.

Third, some members of both congregations, and especially those who participated in small groups at Faith, used the anticultural/antisecular-society language of evangelicalism that Smith argues is foundational for the construction of an embattled subcultural identity.[52] For example, at the small-group leaders meeting discussed in the preceding paragraph, the senior pastor spoke about "servant leadership" and offered the following comment about how Faith's positioning itself against secular culture will help it fulfill its mission of evangelism:

I truly believe all people are on a spiritual journey. The road is broad in our culture but it ends at a precipice. Our job is to provide a net at the edge of the precipice. Our culture tells us we can do it on our own; we don't have to go to church. If we think we can talk to God on the golf course, then we will never hear the true message of Christianity, and the values of our culture will dominate our lives. . . . Our job as spiritual leaders is not to convert people; our job is to share how God has changed our lives.

The men's group at Faith also identified themselves as occupying a minority position at work and in American culture. For example, during a discussion of the lesson on breaking out of the "Me-First Mindset" (chapter 1 in *Serving Lessons*, a Willow Creek study guide authored by its founding pastor, Bill Hybels), the men talked about the pressure they feel at work to seek positions of power and to make money and how difficult it is to preserve their Christian values at work. Another indicator of the religious exclusivity and elitism engendered by evangelicalism was seen in interviewees' responses to my question about how many friends they had in and out of the congregation. Eighty percent of those who answered the question at Faith, and over 90 percent of those who answered it at Zion, reported that a large majority (from 75 to 100 percent) of their friends were members of the congregation.[53] Furthermore, many of those respondents noted how they wished or needed to cultivate more friends outside the church, largely for the purpose of witnessing to them.

In sum, the commitment to follow evangelical models of church growth and organization and to use non-Lutheran educational resources also pushed Faith and Zion toward a more evangelical identity. As in the case of borrowing evangelical worship models and resources, both congregations were unable simply to adopt the form without also adopting some of the theological claims carried by the forms. The organizational and educational forms of evangelicalism reinforce the changes made in the worship tradition and thus helped both congregations create a unified identity and mission centered on fulfilling the Great Commission.

PRESERVING THE LUTHERAN TRADITION

Two other congregations in the Silicon Valley, St. Peter's and Resurrection, also borrowed organizational models from megachurches or evangelical church growth experts, yet these congregations took the path of preserving rather than blending or altering the Lutheran tradition. They were able to do this because the congregations had a different relationship to the tradition than Faith and Zion did and because they approached the borrowing process in terms of pragmatism (i.e., in terms of finding ways to make the congregation work more effectively) rather than ideology (i.e., in terms of changing the tradition to make it more meaningful and more attuned to the task of evangelism). In other words, rather than relying on an integrated change strategy, these two congregations turned to what I call the strategy of *retooling*, in which the goal is to borrow or adapt organizational practices from external religious traditions to help the congregation solve specific problems associated with the nuts and bolts of operating a voluntary organization. As such, changing the tradition is not a high priority for the congregation, and thus it is effectively buffered from change.

St. Peter's had the strongest self-identity as a Lutheran congregation of the nine congregations in the study. Its clergy and members consistently described the church as firmly committed to the Lutheran principles of "Word Alone," "Grace Alone," and "Faith Alone." One council member commented on this commitment in his response to my question about the importance of Lutheranism for himself: "Being Lutheran is important to me. The basic message about salvation through grace; faith alone; grace alone; word alone—these three things really ring true to me. I think Luther's work is true to the Bible and that's important to me." Another member described the new associate pastor as thoroughly Lutheran (which was why she thought he was such a good addition to the congregation): "I think that he believes that there is such a thing as sin, death, and the power of the devil. And that he does believe that Jesus came to overcome that for us. And that therefore by that grace, and it is only by grace, that we're drawn back to God. Now that's about as Lutheran as you can get." The congregation's four-hour-long new-member class was largely an introduction to Lutheran doctrine, and the pastor told the attendees: "This is what we believe." The pastor then told the attendees, "If this isn't what you believe, you should look for a different church, but do look for a church because God wants you to be a member of a church." The pastors also periodically offered adult classes on the Augsburg Confession and Luther's *Small Catechism.*

Moreover, the congregation was a member of the Word Alone Network—a parachurch organization seeking to renew the denomination by more closely following the Lutheran confessional documents, adhering to a more conservative way of interpreting the Bible, and making evangelism a more central task of local congregations. This network supported the organization's activities by hosting conferences and giving money.[54] St. Peter's was actively involved in speaking out against the alleged pro-gay agenda of the ELCA (i.e., what is perceived by the congregation and many Word Alone congregations as an attempt to legitimize the ordination of gay and lesbian persons and same-sex marriage by the national church) and the perceived ecclesiastical betrayal of Lutheranism's tradition of congregational polity by the 1996 formal agreement with the Episcopal Church USA.[55]

The congregation also adopted the "purpose-driven church model," but, unlike Faith and Zion, clergy and lay leaders reported that they felt responsible to "Lutheranize" the model by de-emphasizing the Baptist preoccupation with the Law (or God's judgment on sinners) and emphasizing the Lutheran doctrine of justification and grace. Lay leaders involved in the study and adaptation of the model reported that it had been adopted on pragmatic grounds. One person noted that the senior pastor suggested the council explore using the model because it was a "tool that would help with our spiritual health and growth." Another claimed the purpose-driven church model as "just something we borrowed to give the congregation a focus; really, it's just a means to an end." For most leaders, the model was theologically neutral and as easily adapted as any other business technique, as suggested in the comment from one leader:

> In my business I often ask, "Why are we doing this? What's the reason for it?" ... So yes, it's similar concepts. You don't have to do the same program [as Saddleback's] and be successful, but you do have to ask those questions, "Why are we doing this?" "Well, because we've always had this kind of potluck every year." If it isn't successful, then do something different.

Others, including the senior pastor and council president, claimed that the congregation adopted the model only to help the congregation more effectively accomplish its mission, which is fulfilling the five basic purposes of ministry given to the Church by Jesus as enshrined in the Great Commission and Great Commandment:

Membership: *"baptizing* them in the name of the Father, and of the Son, and of the Holy Spirit"
Maturity: "and *teaching* them to observe all that I have commanded you."
Ministry: "and you shall *love your neighbor* as yourself."
Mission: "Go, therefore, and *make disciples* of all nations."
Magnification: "You shall *love the Lord* with all your heart, and with all your soul, and with all your mind."

These five tasks correspond to the general tasks all congregations must fulfill: recruitment and sustaining membership through fellowship, education, service, or outreach to the community, evangelism, and worship.[56] The Saddleback model gave the leadership of the church a new organizational structure. This structure allowed them to divide the core tasks among different "teams," thus freeing the pastors from having to do it all and, more importantly, making the Lutheran principle of strong lay participation and leadership in the church (i.e., the notion of the "priesthood of all believers") more concrete, as they organized programs, classes, and activities around fulfilling each of these tasks.

The leaders at Silicon Valley's Resurrection Lutheran Church also took a pragmatic approach to borrowing ideas or models from evangelical or nondenominational church growth experts, but they also were more critical about the non-Lutheran ideas. Recall that leaders of the congregation had been reading several church growth books and had begun implementing several programs that emerged from their reading, including becoming a "permission-giving" church[57] and adopting the Willow Creek materials on spiritual gifts. They did so not so much because they believed it would help the congregation convert the unchurched but in order to address several practical organizational problems: a perceived need to increase lay involvement in all areas of church life because the congregation had only one full-time minister after a retirement in 2000; a perceived organizational need to integrate newer members, as the church had grown and faced the perennial problem of high membership turnover; and a perceived need to make the church more accessible to the growing Hispanic population in the community.

At the same time, Lutheran theology and its worship tradition served as a check on this pragmatic approach; not every idea could be adopted or made to work at the congregation if it required them to compromise on their collective commitment to Lutheranism. Pastor Barbara Williams spent a three-month sabbatical reading widely in the church growth literature, attending church growth seminars, and visiting growing congregations, and upon her return we spoke about what she had learned and hoped to adapt for use at Resurrection. She identified a few ideas such as the permission-giving congregation but on the whole remained skeptical of this material. This skepticism or critical appropriation of non-Lutheran models of doing church was evident in her comments in that interview:

> I know we've gone from being a family church to a program church, but I'm not sure McIntosh's [a church growth expert] advice will fit Resurrection. A lot of the church growth literature holds out a particular practice, like praise music, as the key to creating a vital congregation, but so much of this stuff is from the 1980s and I'm not sure it will work in the twenty-first century. I don't want to simply impose someone else's ideas on Resurrection; we need to look closely at Resurrection's core values and the theological perspective of Lutheranism and see if some growth program will fit us.

She continued by noting how members strongly value the Lutheran doctrine of justification by grace. If she did not preach this in the pulpit and, for example, substituted the more decisional theology from the Baptist tradition that underlies the purpose-driven church model, "I would hear about it from the lay theologians in the church. One of them would quietly invite me to coffee and ask me what I was doing." The knowledge of and commitment to the tradition, shared by laity and clergy, led the congregation to buffer the tradition from certain kinds of changes, even as they struggled with growth and adapting to a new demographic and cultural environment in their community.

Members spoke passionately about their love and appreciation of the Lutheran liturgical worship and the theological focus on grace, justification, and the sacraments in worship. Although there was talk among some members of adding a "contemporary" service, there was no consensus on the desirability of such a service. Nearly every member raised questions about or voiced opposition to adding an evangelical-style worship service like those in place at Faith or Zion, saying they did not want to "dumb down" the liturgy or lose it even if doing so would allow them to grow numerically. This commitment to not compromising the tradition was captured in one member's critique of evangelical seeker worship services:

> The whole premise [of seeker services] is wrong. You know, Sunday morning church should be the gathering of believers, not a place where outsiders are catered to. Outsiders should feel welcomed and not turned away. But we shouldn't be changing anything just to make outsiders feel comfortable. Look, if it's Christmas Eve and we're doing all our family traditions, we're not going to stop doing those traditions just because a neighbor comes in who doesn't believe in Christmas.

Thus, Resurrection and St. Peter's largely protected the tradition from change even as they adopted particular decision-making models and programs from non-Lutheran traditions. Their strong commitment to preserving the tradition and pragmatic (as opposed to ideological) approach to the borrowing strategy limited how much change could be made to the tradition.

St. Luke's in Oakland is the other congregation that largely protected the tradition from change, but in contrast to Resurrection and St. Peter's, they did not look for help from non-Lutheran traditions. Stan Nielsen, the congregation's pastor, claimed that the purpose of the congregation is to "deepen individuals' faith" and that the church growth literature does little to further this goal. He also noted that the theology that he taught and that was followed by most members was unabashedly Lutheran and, as such, not very congruent with the pietistic theology underlying this literature. Worship at St. Luke's followed the classic Lutheran ordo as written in the *LBW*. The church also was one of several Lutheran churches in the San Francisco Bay Area with an openly gay pastor and thus had faced discipline from the national church when they refused to fire their pastor.[58] The experience of the trial solidified membership and increased commitment among the vast majority of members who stayed. It also placed the congregation on the local map as a church open to gay and lesbian persons and involved with HIV/AIDS issues and with gay, lesbian, bisexual, and transgendered persons' rights. Perhaps because of the local prominence the church gained and the members' desire not to simply become a "gay church," the congregation remained steadfastly tied to the tradition.

THE RISKS AND BENEFITS OF SELECTIVE ISOMORPHISM

Faith and Zion borrowed and copied some of the central features of contemporary evangelicalism: its up-beat, rock-and-roll-based music, an emphasis on conversion, and the strong emphasis on the individual, emotion, and experience. Roof's description of this style of evangelicalism as "a more 'conversion-oriented' and/or 'spirituality-oriented' faith, one denoting personal transformation, and . . . an expressive, joyful, soulful mode of religion [in which] personal assurance, inward joy, and spiritual presence are key traits," is strikingly similar to the style of worship and the theological orientation at Faith and Zion.[59] Elements from the evangelical tradition were not borrowed uncritically, nor did they simply replace their Lutheran counterparts. Instead, leaders at these two congregations tried to preserve what they considered the essential or core elements of the Lutheran tradition. They tried to make sure that this core provided both the theological criteria to guide their borrowing and a theological corrective to any objectionable beliefs and practices from the evangelical tradition. Yet the core was not completely shielded from change. Particular theological claims, emphases, or assumptions within the contemporary evangelical tradition, such as the centrality of converting the individual, decisional theology, and the elevation of informality, emotion, and experience in worship over formal rituals and intellect, were imported, and they crowded out such core pieces of the Lutheran tradition as justification by grace alone.

Sargeant notes, "A change in ritual signifies both a change in the *context* (patterns of social organization) and in the *content* (doctrine) of religious groups."[60]

and it is clear that the adoption of praise music and evangelical organizational models changed the structure of worship and the theological commitments of the two congregations. In the end, Faith and Zion appear to have created a hybridized tradition—neither fully Lutheran nor fully evangelical.

Blending, or selective isomorphism, became the preferred and dominant strategy of change (rather than the strategies favored by the congregations discussed in chapter 4) because these congregations operated under a different set of organizational and cultural conditions. Zion and Faith were embedded quite strongly in the evangelical religious world. Institutional embeddedness is important for two reasons. First, the religious networks within which congregations are embedded limit exposure to and familiarity with alternative traditions, especially when the congregations are tightly embedded in exclusionary organizations. Faith and Zion increasingly looked to evangelical and nondenominational organizations for resources and ideas for education, worship, and governance and minimized their connections to the ELCA, the local synod, and other area congregations.[61] Faith's embeddedness, for example, ranged from formal affiliation with the Willow Creek Association and staff participation in a network of evangelical musicians, worship leaders, and educators, to congregational support for evangelical missionaries and local Young Life programs (a nondenominational, evangelical, parachurch organization dedicated to helping teens come to faith), to members' regular participation in community Bible studies led by evangelical ministers. Moreover, the kinds of organization with which they were connected tended to advocate against tight connections to the national denominational body and argued that the future of Christianity lies in the direction of nondenominationalism. This antidenominational position was evident in the clergy's attacks against the ELCA and the congregation's willingness to shift monies away from the denomination.[62]

This institutional embeddedness increased the congregation's exposure to, and familiarity with, evangelical ways of thinking and talking about congregational life. Leaders, both lay and ordained, commonly spoke in the language of the evangelical tradition and reported in interviews that they felt at home in the evangelical worship tradition. Many of the elected and appointed leaders who served on the church councils or ad hoc task forces at the congregations tended to more strongly identify themselves as evangelical, or at least as generically Christian, and not Lutheran. Relocating the congregation to the evangelical world meant that leaders did not need to engage in reframing, because their task was not to redefine the tradition or update the language of the tradition but to make the tradition itself more evangelical.

Second, historically, the congregations had a loose relationship to the tradition, and a majority of their members were not strongly committed to preserving Lutheranism or, in the case of non-Lutheran members, even learning about it.[63] And unlike several other congregations, such as Good Shepherd or Christ, discussed in the previous chapter, neither Faith nor Zion had a powerful minority of members who were strongly committed to the tradition and who were willing to fight to keep it intact. This meant that neither of the congregations needed to expend much energy on a reconnecting strategy to legitimize changes.

At the same time, clergy, lay leaders, and rank-and-file members of these congregations were still committed to preserving some features of the Lutheran tradition. Many members did not want to become a nondenominational megachurch or become aligned too closely with Pentacostalism. Perhaps the long association many members had with Lutheranism and its emphasis on ceremonial or formal worship practices served as a check on the movement toward the more informal, enthusiastic form of worship favored by the evangelical tradition. While Faith and Zion were clearly pulled into the orbit of evangelicalism, a baseline commitment to preserving certain Lutheran theological ideas such as *sola gratia,* the rite of Holy Communion, or the liturgical order helped each congregation maintain a tenuous hold on the tradition and a Lutheran identity. Yet it was a relatively weak identity and one easily overshadowed by the addition of evangelical language, ideas, and worship practices. Small minorities at both churches protested or lamented the loss of Lutheran hymns and worship practices and voiced suspicion about the evangelical direction of their churches, yet conflict over what to keep and what to change in the tradition was easily contained and defused largely because most members were not at all concerned about losing the tradition; being distinctly Lutheran was not a very high priority among many. Yet the dissenting members recognized, albeit incompletely, how evangelicalism had subtly but profoundly changed the identity and faith commitments of their churches.

In the next chapter I explore the question of why some strategies of change succeeded and why others failed. As intimated by the analyses presented in chapters 4 and 5, part of the answer lies in the degree of fit between the proposed or actual changes in the tradition and the existing understandings of religious authority and styles of religiosity held by members.

Chapter 6

CONFLICT, COMPROMISE, AND CONSENSUS

AT GOOD SHEPHERD Lutheran Church a small group of members responded to changes in the tradition first by initiating what amounted to a smear campaign against the clergy and eventually by charging the senior pastor with heresy. After the local bishop examined and cleared the pastor, over one hundred members left the church, claiming that Good Shepherd was no longer Lutheran, but Unitarian. At Grace Lutheran Church, a long-simmering dispute over replacing a pipe organ threatened to escalate into a conflict over what constituted legitimate worship, until several members reminded others at a congregational meeting how the fight was undermining the foundational values of the congregation. Eventually, the pro-organ and anti-organ factions were able to agree on a less expensive plan to purchase a new organ and place it in the sanctuary while retaining the sanctuary's non-Christian appearance. However, at Faith and Zion, the two congregations making the most far-reaching changes, the process of altering the tradition proceeded with little opposition and, in general, with loud support by the congregation. Why did the process of change lead to conflict in some cases, compromise in others, and consensus in several congregations? Why does change seem to work in some congregations and fail in others? Are there specific organizational, cultural, and environmental conditions that facilitate success or guarantee failure?

In this chapter I rely on a series of case studies and direct comparisons between congregations to answer these questions and, more generally, to explore when, why, and how change succeeds and fails. Existing work on religious change suggests that the degree to which attempts to change a congregation's tradition will be successful depends on how the changes fit or articulate with the external environment (e.g., market conditions or demographic shifts) and/or internal context (e.g., existing congregational culture). For example, Finke argues that innovative congregations succeed because they protect the core teachings of the tradition while adopting organizational structures, liturgies and hymns, and communication technologies from outside sources that allow these congregations to adapt to changes in the religious market.[1] Similarly, in her study of congregations in Oak Park, Illinois, Becker shows how innovative congregations succeeded when organizational changes fit within the dominant religious model or culture of the congregation.[2]

While such explanations are intuitively persuasive, their post hoc character raises suspicions about their accuracy.[3] One way around this problem is to begin to specify the more general conditions or mechanisms of articulation.[4] Articulation or resonance refers to the process whereby a cultural object—in this case, a religious tradition—connects with or fits with the interests and expectations of its targeted audience and the wider social setting in which the object is located. For example, leaders of congregations who attempt to change the Lutheran tradition are more likely to be successful to the degree that the change fits members' expectations of what is or is not in the tradition and its importance for their individual and collective religious lives, as well as the degree to which it fits the particular social setting facing congregations in northern California (e.g., a general lack of interest in organized religion and heightened interest in spirituality, the rise of nondenominationalism and evangelicalism, and a strong culture of choice that permeates both religious and social life in the Bay Area).

Another way in which explanations based on the concept of articulation may be made more robust is to attend to the ongoing processes by which cultural change is produced and received—in this case, the way in which congregational leaders attempted to alter the Lutheran tradition, how those changes were received by members, and what degree of opposition or support shaped subsequent efforts to institutionalize or amend the changes.[5] Thus, my goal for this chapter is to look closely at how the process of change shaped the different outcomes. In particular, I develop an explanation that yokes interactionist ideas about the negotiated order with the concept of articulation and with specific organizational and cultural conditions under which particular outcomes or trajectories of change will be more or less likely.

CONFLICT AND SCHISM AT GOOD
SHEPHERD LUTHERAN CHURCH

Good Shepherd Lutheran Church had been fighting since the pastors and council decided, based on a congregational survey of worship preferences, to change the worship schedule in September 2000. A small group of older members mounted a campaign to overturn that decision, but from the very beginning the opposition had broader concerns, and they voiced these concerns privately to mobilize other like-minded members and publicly to undermine pastoral changes in worship, theology, and governance. In particular, the "traditionalists" objected to the senior pastor's theology because it did not conform to several orthodox doctrines concerning sin, atonement, and the literal physical resurrection of Jesus.

Breakdown of the Negotiated Order

The initial shift in worship schedule was quickly followed by more substantial changes in the content of worship as the new minister of worship and music changed the language, liturgical order, and music of both the traditional (in accordance with *The Lutheran Book of Worship*) and the contemporary service. After several weeks, members began making their unhappiness with the changes known by withholding their offerings, complaining to the clergy and members of the church council both publicly and privately, and forming an ad hoc group to pray and seek ways to reverse the changes. When I began attending the monthly council meetings in the autumn of 2000, the issue of worship was always on the agenda. In early November I conducted a focus group interview with twenty upset members. Their responses to my questions about why they were unhappy with changes to worship and with the clergy introduced many of the themes that would animate the conflict as it escalated. The council meetings and this focus group interview also revealed how the "negotiated order" of the congregation had been challenged by the changes and the pastors' defense of them. The negotiated order is "the sum total of the organization's rules and policies," along with any other unofficial or tacit agreements, working arrangements, role expectations, and decision-making structures or processes.[6] In the case of congregations, the negotiated order may include the official polity and the customary ways in which power and decision making are handled (e.g., if a congregation must vote on all financial decisions but leave programming decisions to the clergy or a specific committee), role expectations for pastors (e.g., generalist vs. specialist), the identity and mission of the church, and the set of conventions, customs, or rules by which the congregation organizes its life.

Members spoke angrily as they described the effect changes in worship were having on them and the rest of the congregation. Several men complained that the pastors were running a "dictatorship" and had violated the democratic principles by which the church should be run (e.g., "one man [*sic*], one vote"). Part of the problem, according to the interviewees, was that the congregation had been surveyed about their worship preferences, and then the pastors had disregarded the wishes of two-thirds of the members, who wanted to retain the old schedule, in which the traditional and contemporary services alternated between the early and late services every other week. Repeatedly, I heard members complain that the survey was a "vote" and that the pastors, in overturning the vote, were acting as "dictators" and not as pastors. For these members, an important part of the congregation's negotiated order was that the decision-making process should follow democratic principles. Several members claimed that the pastors and council were acting like Roman Catholics rather than American citizens in their disregard for the importance of democratic values. One interviewee reported that he told the pastors after they changed the worship schedule, "You know, this church isn't run by a pope. We don't have a pope here!" In a similar vein, after failing to persuade the council to reverse the changes in worship, a council member reminded the pastors and other council members, "You can't ignore the will of the majority and let the minority dictate worship decisions. We're not Roman

Catholics; we're a democracy." Curiously, no one explicitly linked democratic decision making with the Lutheran polity or the Lutheran tradition, perhaps because this group possessed relatively thin or limited knowledge of Lutheranism and perhaps because many members of this group conflated American citizenship with church membership (the latter became evident after 9/11, when they attempted to place the American flag in the sanctuary against the expressed theological convictions and principles of the pastors).

Pressed to explain why the pastors' allegedly unilateral actions to change the worship schedule and the content of worship were illegitimate, one member groused that "the pastors are our employees. They're paid, and in my mind, overpaid, to do what we tell them to do."[7] Throughout the two years of fighting, the clergy consistently were referred to as hired employees rather than as "called" by God to serve the congregation—the latter is the official Lutheran way of thinking about the pastor's job. Another member suggested that the pastors' job is to make sure that "the sheep are spiritually fed," and that, by switching the worship schedule and then "radically" changing worship, "they were putting their own agenda ahead of caring for the flock."

For these members, the pastors had violated the implicit role expectations and authority structure of the congregation. Authority was ultimately held by the congregation and not by the pastors, who were understood to be mere employees. Their decisions to alter worship were interpreted as an illegitimate unilateral act by pastors who had overstepped their authority. It appeared that the clergy, and to a lesser extent the church council, were trying to change the "negotiated order" of the congregation, and members were resisting. That is, Good Shepherd's leaders were trying to change the overt and covert rules, agreements, and policies that guided behavior and defined roles and that, more generally, organized congregational life. The group of disaffected members who were so vocal in interviews had little interest in changing the order. Part of the problem, they argued, was that the church's leaders had not been forthright about their desire or the organizational need to change the negotiated order. It appeared to them to have occurred without warning or a clear explanation, even though the senior pastor had written several newsletter articles outlining some of the changes in the decision-making structure and pastors' roles.

If an organization is to successfully change its structure (including its culture), it must revise the negotiated order, but from the very beginning neither the upset members nor the clergy at Good Shepherd seemed willing to engage in a collective process of revision.[8] The former argued for a return to the past while the clergy argued that preserving the tradition wholesale would ultimately lead to decline and, more importantly, a betrayal of the biblical call to form disciples in a community of faith. During the focus group interview, I asked several questions to determine if this group would be willing to compromise and on what issues. Few people expressed any desire to accept the pastors' reworked negotiated order or learn how to incorporate the worship changes into the existing culture and structure of the congregation. Several members recalled the past when the pastors "ministered to the congregation" and "the congregation ran the church." When I asked if this group would be willing to allow the clergy to rewrite the liturgy but retain all of its various elements, one woman vehemently rejected this by asking, "Why does he have to rewrite anything? What's the matter with what we've got?"

For their part, the clergy and several elected lay leaders defended the changes to worship as biblical and necessary to make the congregation relevant to a post-denominational, post-Christian, postdoctrinal world (in this endeavor they relied on the authenticity causal story discussed in chapter 3). For example, at one council meeting, Pastor Thompson defended some of the changes by claiming that what they were doing was biblical and necessary to make church relevant to the growing number of unchurched Californians:

> Mission is having worship be a way of life. In our present world, the way we used to worship doesn't work anymore. Postmodern people are very interested in spirituality; but they don't care about church. They are looking for a life transformed. Some congregations, like ours, are abandoning certain things. What we are doing is biblical. Read Acts and the Old Testament. You know, people often said Jesus wasn't doing religion right.

Clergy repeatedly said they were willing to lose 20 or 30 percent of the members in order to make the changes they envisioned. At a post-council-meeting debriefing session with the pastors, I asked the clergy to explain how they were managing the change process. "Well," said one, "according to the Alban Institute [an ecumenical, nonprofit consulting firm], we should expect to lose 30 percent of the members and experience a lot of conflict. What we've been telling people is that if they don't like what we're doing, then we suggest other congregations that might meet their needs better. We'll give you our blessing to go." Later that evening Pastor Thompson defended their unwillingness to reverse the changes on principle: "People either need to get on the bandwagon or get off. The church is a radical institution, not a country club."

One of the commonly voiced complaints of members is that the pastors were violating the unspoken but very real expectation that pastors should act to keep members rather than alienate them. It was unacceptable to many of the focus group interviewees that a pastor could encourage someone to leave the church for another; as one angry member said at the meeting: "Pastor Richard's basically telling us, 'It's my way or the highway; take it or leave it.' It's not right for a pastor to talk this way. He should be respectful and polite and certainly not do anything that would lead someone to leave the church." A former president of the congregation also identified this cavalier attitude about losing members as a driving force of the conflict: "It's a very offensive thing to say, 'If you don't like it here, why not go somewhere else?' This is our church. We've worked hard for it. We've invested in it. The pastors don't seem to respect how people feel when they change things or tell people to leave. They can't keep saying it's okay to lose 70 percent of your members when you change. No wonder people are mad."

Thus, the notion that the pastor should be a shepherd and seek to keep the flock together was another part of the negotiated order that some members perceived to be under attack.

The negotiated order also included the largely implicit expectations or understandings about what it meant to be Lutheran and what parts of the tradition, especially worship, were essential for these members. Interviewees challenged the pastors' goal of making worship more accessible to the unchurched and dismissed their reliance on church growth experts, whom they often quoted to justify the changes. One woman, in tears, spoke at length about how the pastors' changes to worship violated these understandings. But her views, shared by those in attendance, also revealed what kinds of religious authority this group considered legitimate and what they understood to be the principal identity of the church:

> What I understand is that there's three parts of the Lutheran church. It's supposed to have the gospel, it's supposed to have the Lord's Prayer, and it's supposed to have the creed. The first Sunday with the new service there was no Lord's Prayer or creed. I began to wonder where I was. You know, people got up and walked out of that thing. The creed is a Christian's acknowledgment and belief that Jesus is the Son of God, the Messiah, and our Savior. We also confess our belief in God the Father and the Holy Spirit. Without the creed, who are we? If I want to be entertained, I go to the theater or the symphony or whatever. I come to church to hear God's Word, to pray, and have Communion as well as fellowship with other Christians. Let us remember those words of Romans 12:2, "Do not conform any longer to the pattern of this world, but be transformed by the renewing of your mind." James 1:27 says, "In part, keep yourself from being polluted by the world." I don't come to hear hippie music [i.e., amplified guitars and drums]. It didn't give you a feeling of being in the sanctuary of God, being able to worship God and get something out of the service. I got absolutely nothing out of that service. Nothing.

First, she appealed to the authority of tradition narrowly defined as the time-honored, unaltered ritual forms and practices of worship. In her view, legitimate Lutheran worship must include the recitation of a creed (an optional element in the *LBW*) and the Lord's Prayer and the reading of a passage from one of the Gospels (for Luther the gospel is the good news that God has acted decisively in the person of Jesus Christ to save humanity, and it can be found, theoretically, in any book of the Bible). Yet she did not mention any of the core theological emphases or claims articulated in Lutheran worship (such as the centrality of justification or the sacraments of baptism and Holy Communion) to defend her appeal to preserve the tradition. Tradition is something that should not be changed; doing so undermines its authority and legitimacy and caused her to question the degree to which the congregation remained Christian.

Second, she grounded her complaint in a particular type of biblical authority (her literalistic interpretation and application of two texts to discredit the "hippie music" by aligning it with the secular world) and experience ("I got absolutely nothing out of that service") and did not even consider the new service to be worship: she called it "that thing" because it did not seem biblical nor did it provide her with an experience of the sacred. These two understandings of religious authority would become increasingly important as the conflict deepened because there was no simple way to determine whose religious experience should be defined as normative for the congregation and, more broadly, because scripture's content and the nature of its authority were contested. The traditionalists' literal hermeneutic provided little room for compromise.

Finally, she defined the church as a group of people who believe or follow doctrine or a set of beliefs (which was the very identity the clergy and lay leaders were trying to eliminate). She claimed that the work of the clergy and the purpose of worship were to reaffirm doctrine and help her dwell in God's presence. These views sharply diverged from those held by the clergy, who saw their role as helping people discover an authentic faith community and an authentic faith and who argued passionately that doctrine had no place in public worship.[9] Moreover, her complaint that she "got nothing out of" the new service reflects the kind of individualistic, consumerist orientation to religion that the pastors of Good Shepherd were hoping their parishioners would disavow. From the beginning then, the conflict revolved around competing religious cultures and the attempt to replace the old with the new: one emphasized a "spirituality of dwelling" and affirmed the necessity of doctrine and preserving the tradition and thus offered the religious security of unchanging tradition; the other emphasized a "spirituality of seeking" and minimized the importance of doctrine and tradition and thus offered the religious insecurity that comes with remaking tradition.[10]

The Misarticulation of Religious Cultures

A year later, in the fall of 2001, two groups of disgruntled members at Good Shepherd joined forces after a pastor removed the flag from the sanctuary that a member had dug out from a closet after 9/11. One group was primarily concerned about changes to worship, and the other, smaller group was concerned about the theology of the pastors. Led by a women's prayer group and several retired men, the group that I called the "traditionalists" circulated a petition among members whom they believed would sign.[11] The petition demanded that the pastors teach and preach orthodox Lutheran theology. In particular, they charged the senior pastor with heresy, claiming that he had broken his ordination promises because he did not believe in or teach the literal resurrection of Jesus, the virgin birth, or original sin, and that he did not accept the Bible as the "inspired word of God" or as the authority of the historic creeds.[12] The petition ended with an ultimatum for Pastor Richards to either conform to their demands to preserve the tradition and teach only a literal interpretation of the confessional documents and the Bible or resign:

> It is inconceivable that an ordained Lutheran pastor would openly proclaim doctrine that is not consistent with our confession of faith. . . . In stating this, know that we hope and pray that God will lead you to confess that Jesus Christ is risen Lord who atoned and provided for the forgiveness of the sins of mankind [*sic*] by his suffering and death on the cross. Without the saving power of Jesus Christ we are lost. If the words you affirmed at your installation do not reflect your true faith and belief, then it is with a deep sense of sadness that we request that you relinquish the honor of being pastor of Good Shepherd Lutheran Church.

One hundred and forty members signed the petition (just over 10 percent of the congregation). During the next six months letters circulated via e-mail among the traditionalists and the members they tried to recruit to their cause and in print from the council and pastoral staff in response as rumors and unsubstantiated accounts of the pastor's theological misdeeds circulated. The church council hired a conflict resolution consultant to mediate the conflict but failed to broker a compromise. In the winter of 2002 the traditionalists asked the synod's bishop to determine whether or not the senior pastor was Lutheran and, more importantly, Christian and therefore fit for office. As the conflict unfolded, it began to revolve around fundamentally different religious cultures that had very different understandings of the Lutheran tradition and its value, different ways of interpreting the Bible, and different views about the mission and identity of the congregation.

In a series of congregational meetings and documents circulated within the congregation (some were letters from the clergy to all members, others were essays in the biweekly newsletter, others existed in cyberspace) from January through March, both sides explained their positions, sought to garner support, and revealed two competing understandings of what it means to be a church, what tradition should govern the life of the congregation, where authority is to be vested, and how it is to be exercised. More generally, the conflict also revealed two reasons why it ultimately resulted in schism and the failure to institutionalize a reconstituted tradition: first, the inability of church leaders to make their changes to the tradition articulate with the religious culture of the traditionalists; and, second, the inability to reach consensus on what constituted the core of the tradition.

The traditionalists called for conserving Lutheran traditions regarding doctrine, ritual, and biblical interpretation. They claimed to represent the true Lutherans in the congregation and often referred to themselves as the defenders of the Lutheran confessional documents or official denominational beliefs. In the letter that accompanied the petition, they reprinted the ELCA's ordination

service and documented how the executive pastor had broken most of his ordination vows.[13] Throughout the conflict they also urged the pastors and the congregation to provide "Christ-centered and biblically based sermons" and to return to
the order and content of worship as written in the *LBW* and thus only use "language in the service that [is] clear and direct, without allegories and euphemisms
that blur, soften, obscure, and distort the meaning of creeds, hymns, and liturgy."
At the final meeting where the bishop delivered his ruling that Pastor Richards
was theologically sound and within the pale of Lutheranism, several traditionalists demanded to know how the ECLA could support this pastor when he did not
adhere to the "essential beliefs of Christianity that the ELCA confirms regarding
the virgin birth, the physical resurrection, . . . and the New Testament as the
firsthand account of those who lived through the life, death, and resurrection."
At the heart of this view of the tradition is the idea that theological and biblical
documents define the core religious beliefs; those beliefs are not to be altered or
abandoned, because they were given to humanity by God, and they are to be
read or interpreted literally. Several traditionalists claimed the pastors were "re-
writing the creeds to fit the times" and that by denying the reality of Jesus' literal
physical resurrection they were destroying the foundation of their faith.

In short, the inherited doctrines, creeds, and liturgies as well as the Bible were
considered the fundamental religious authorities for the traditionalists. They relied on a literalistic interpretive strategy and claimed it was the only legitimate
way to read scripture. They often argued that, if something was written plainly
in the Bible, then it must be true and, if the creeds were true for ancient Christians, then they ought to still be true. This type of religious authority supported
a type of piety (or way of being religious) that is centered on adherence to a set of
truth claims about the nature of God, Jesus, salvation, and the church (e.g., the
physical resurrection happened as reported in the Bible, and this event was necessary for God to forgive my sins). I call this "propositional piety" because the
Christian faith is reduced to a set of intellectual propositions or right beliefs. The
tradition is understood, first, as the corpus of doctrines and creeds, passed down
from generation to generation, that provide identity and security and, second, as
the forms of worship that teach, reaffirm, and hence preserve the belief system.
At Good Shepherd, altering the tradition was perceived by the traditionalists as
undermining these foundational beliefs, the religious authority they carried, and
the identity of the congregation as Christian.

At the same time, an alternative understanding of religious authority and piety existed. The pastors and elected lay leaders claimed to represent the silent
majority in the congregation, for whom the more liberal theology of the pastors
resonated with their own experience and beliefs. They championed an alterative
tradition that was grounded in liberal Protestantism, "lay liberalism," "golden
rule Christianity," and seeker spirituality more than in Lutheranism per se.[14]
This alternative tradition rests on a more tenuous understanding of religious
authority—one in which individuals' religious experience is given much more
weight, and in which scripture plays an important but secondary role because

it provides the stories out of which people construct their faith rather than clear truth claims that demand intellectual assent. For example, one member urged the congregation to adopt an American Roman Catholic approach to faith in which each "faith is like a cafeteria; we all choose what we believe." At nearly every public meeting, one or two people invoked the value of tolerance and the idea that the congregation should operate like a "big tent" in which various styles of worship, ways of reading the Bible, and putting together one's faith were allowed.

"Seeker piety" emphasizes the ethics of Christianity, or lived religion; rejects an uncritical acceptance of orthodoxy and tradition; understands faith as a journey in which doubt and exploration are allowed; elevates tolerance (for a plurality of journeys and different ways to live one's faith) over obedience to orthodoxy. This alternative religious culture was evident in the senior pastor's letter to the congregation defending himself from the traditionalists' charges of heresy. In response to the charges that he did not hold Christian beliefs, Pastor Richards claimed:

> First, I am a disciple of Christ. That means I follow the one who says I am the way the truth and the life. I don't just believe things about Jesus in my head, but I am adjusting and shaping my life so that I might live in a new way. This is what faith is to me. It is not an academic proposition; it's a way of living my life shaped by the gracious gift of Jesus. How we live is what we believe. . . . At its heart this way of being a Christian allows for us to not simply take the Bible as an inerrant document penned by the divine, but as a compilation of writings born out of layers and layers of traditions, historical contexts, local challenges and huge cultural influences. It is our task to explore these stories to see clearly the power of God active in their lives and to allow that activity to speak meaningfully to us today. . . . We are seeking to understand [biblical stories] in their context and find meaning in them for our Christian lives today. That means this congregation will approach the study of and reflection of the scriptures differently than a fundamentalist church, or many evangelical churches, and even the Missouri Synod Lutheran churches.

Several exchanges at the public meetings illustrate the tension between the two religious cultures within the congregation and the difficulty of finding a way to reconcile the two. At one meeting, an elderly man stood up to complain about how the senior pastor explained his belief in the resurrection. His statement illustrates the way in which tradition functions authoritatively:

> Now the pastor in his letter says "live the resurrection." That's not very clear. This isn't meaningful to me. Do you believe in the resurrection? "I live the resurrection" is a roundabout way—it's not an answer to the question. But [*in a loud voice*] I believe in Christmas and Easter. Without

the resurrection of the body, I would suffer in my belief and how my belief would be acceptable to God. I was raised with the Apostles' Creed—and that tells us that Jesus was raised from the dead and we will be raised bodily too. What we need from the pastors is a clear statement that we need to follow the Nicene and the Apostles' Creed. Now the men who wrote the creeds had wisdom—we don't need to make up theology today; we need one we can follow. Lay people aren't capable of getting to this profound wisdom, so we need to look to the bishop. We don't need another nebulous statement about the resurrection but a concrete theology that we can give to our children and grandchildren. To me, Martin Luther is a great Lutheran when he wrote "A mighty fortress is our God / A sword and shield victorious"—now that means something to me. [*Long pause.*] I don't think "I live the resurrection" is an answer—it was an actual happening. I know it. I respect it.

A woman responded with a defense of seeker spirituality and echoed several themes from Pastor Richards's letter: the necessity of interpreting biblical stories to find the truth for her life, the legitimacy of doubt, and the importance of tolerance as individuals struggle on their faith journeys:

I know that coming into a nebulous situation with one's faith isn't comfortable . . . many times in my past something happened to shake my faith. I remember when I learned that there were two creation stories, and it shook my faith. But just because there are two versions of the creation stories doesn't mean they aren't true. They deepen or broaden my faith. Maybe a whale didn't swallow Jonah; maybe it was a way of God for telling us what happens when we don't go. How you make it through those nebulous times is important. I understand your discomfort, but for me the umbrella is broad—50 percent of the references in the Bible to resurrection refer to resurrection today and 50 percent to resurrection in the future. We tend to focus only on the future and not on today—but my umbrella is broad.

Two alternative and incompatible views of scripture (i.e., how to interpret it and its authority) played a major role in the debate as supporters of the two sides clashed. The bishop himself suggested that the problem really came down to the question of how we should interpret what is in the Bible. He rejected literalism and suggested that the hermeneutic to the Lutheran tradition is more contextual and focuses on discerning how particular stories or texts convey God's love and grace for members of a given community:

The ELCA's stance that scripture is inspired doesn't mean we are bound to a literal interpretation. No one can interpret scripture literally. We all bring knowledge and prejudices, and this figures into our reading. And this is why we must read scripture in community. The community provides the norms for interpreting it. Yes, I know Pastor Richards prefers not to speak of a physical resurrection, but I see references to the living Christ in his sermons, and you can't believe in a living Christ without believing in the resurrection. . . . He works at interpreting scripture in ways that may be unfamiliar but that doesn't mean what he teaches is in conflict with the Lutheran church. As Lutherans, we say that we are saved by grace through faith; that the Bible tells us that God is reconciling the world through Christ; that God is present in the sacraments. Pastor Richards teaches these things.

Various members pressed the bishop to say if he believed in the physical resurrection or the virgin birth, to which he said yes but he refused to make literalism the authoritative approach for the tradition. Members also argued among themselves, revealing the two different hermeneutic traditions at odds in the congregation. For example, one woman asked the bishop if she was a "heretic" like her pastor because "I don't believe in the virgin birth or the physical resurrection, and if it was proved not to be a fact, that wouldn't alter the fact that I want to live my life according to Jesus' teachings. I don't need them to be a Christian. . . . If I'm not allowed to question, then I'm a heretic and then there's no room for me [here]." Immediately, another woman jumped up to refute this view by arguing that it was impossible to defend what she perceived as their relativistic interpretive strategy:

Where do we draw the line? When don't I have to honor my father and mother? When is it okay to kill? When I decide I don't believe the Ten Commandments? Where does the ELCA stand on the physical resurrection? I was raised Lutheran and my faith stands on the physical resurrection. It is the great miracle that gives me hope. . . . If everyone is allowed to interpret scripture on their own level, then what will we have?

Thus, two competing theological and hermeneutical traditions were in use at the congregation and their misalignment was at the center of the conflict. Moreover, the two sides disagreed about who properly represented Lutheranism. Periodically, the clergy reminded the members that they were part of the "reforming" church tradition—citing Martin Luther's practice of transforming drinking songs into hymns—to justify or explain their use of colloquial language or contemporary musical forms in worship. In his four-page letter defending himself and the changes to the tradition he initiated, Pastor Richards employed the strategy of reconnecting to make the case for a more liberal hermeneutic that would foster seeker piety rather than propositional piety. In the letter he reminded the congregation:

Within our Lutheran faith tradition, the use of the Bible provides enough room for critical thinking and engagement. I am proud and invigorated by a tradition that does not demand any of us to be bound by a single literal interpretation of scriptures, but that asks each of us to engage deeply in our texts to find meaning for today. This brings diversity and depth to our life together. I am committed to a community that does just that.

His argument was picked up and used by some members during the final congregational meetings of the conflict. For example, when one traditionalist quoted the ELCA's official position on scripture (i.e., "it is the inspired word of God and the authoritative source and norm for [the Lutheran church's] proclamation, faith, and life"), another member finished the quotation, stating that, "while Lutherans recognize there are different ways to read or interpret the Bible, it is still the norm of faith" and then continued, "So I guess there is room for all of us here." Ironically, the nontraditionalists seemed to have a firmer grasp of the tradition than traditionalists, who exhibited a limited understanding of the Lutheran tradition. While the bishop and pastors spoke about core Lutheran theological ideas such as justification by grace through faith, the traditionalists made appeals to the Augsburg Confession by title without being able to speak about its content. Perhaps the latter's largely toothless appeal to the authority of tradition was doomed to fail in a congregation where most members cared little for preserving the tradition. Conversely, the antitraditionalists' ability to identify specifically how and which parts of the tradition were authoritative articulated neatly with the authenticity causal story and seeker piety they championed.

Finally, the conflict centered on two competing understandings of the congregation's identity and purpose. Throughout much of the two-year conflict, the pastors laid out their vision for a new collective identity and congregational mission, drawing implicitly and explicitly on the advice of experts. Early in the conflict, the pastors and council encouraged members to watch a video of a church growth consultant speaking about how to reverse the decline of mainline congregations by creating worship and programs to meet the particular religious needs of different generations. Repeatedly, the pastors wrote and spoke about congregational change strategies they were learning from the Alban Institute, invoking the authority of experts that the traditionalists refused to deem legitimate. In oral and written form, the pastors argued that the church exists to serve the world. They spoke about the church as the living community that exists primarily to help people live as Christians in the world and not as an organization that exists primarily to pass along doctrine or tend to the needs of members.

For the traditionalists, the congregation is a place where the correct doctrines are preached and taught; where the historic creeds and confessions are recited in worship and not altered in any way; where the Bible is interpreted in a literal manner and understood as providing clear moral rules; and where pastors provide assurance of each individual's salvation. More pragmatically, the church is a "home" or "family." The majority of traditionalists had been members for twenty or thirty years, and many had long-standing and deep friendships with other members. They had also built the present building and spoke in ways that suggested a strong sense of being invested in the congregation. They had a deep sense of ownership of the "family business." Yet it was this very deep sense of connectedness and ownership that nontraditionalists rejected. In interviews, several members complained that the congregation had functioned for too long as a country club, and they welcomed the new initiatives to serve the community, explore the meaning of authentic faith more deeply, and struggle with living as Christians in a pluralistic society.

In the end, the majority of Good Shepherd's members supported their pastors and agreed with the bishop's ruling, although most of the traditionalists and perhaps another thirty or forty persons left Good Shepherd and joined other Lutheran churches in the area. The conflict over changing the tradition at this church may be seen as a result of a severe articulation problem that was exacerbated by the inability of both sides to revise the negotiated order of the congregation in a cooperative manner. The clergy, with at least the tacit support of most of the members, began to redefine the mission and identity of the congregation in ways that disconnected it from much of the Lutheran tradition (especially its worship practices and theological language). They thought of the tradition in minimalist terms—as providing orienting guidelines and a few theological commitments (e.g., the centrality of grace). Such an approach did not fit with the traditionalists' understanding of tradition as a set of unalterable doctrines and ritual practices that the congregation must follow as a piece and without question.

Traditionalists and antitraditionalists held vastly different understandings of religious authority and supported incompatible pieties. Seeker piety is grounded in the authority of experience and celebrates the values of diversity and tolerance. This operative authority and these religious values shaped how members thought the congregation should be organized as a place to help individuals on their specific religious journeys. In theory, this should have meant that theological, hermeneutic, and aesthetic differences would be equally welcomed, but in practice it did not work that way. The clergy were reluctant to preserve those parts of the tradition that the traditionalists believed were central to their own identities or to invest resources in their preservation. The traditionalists, for their part, defended their position on the basis of the authority of tradition and biblical literalism; the latter, almost by definition, makes compromise all but impossible.[15] At the same time, they argued that their individual religious experience of one manifestation of Lutheran worship and theology should be normative for the whole congregation. The congregation had no way to adjudicate whose experience should be considered normative except by vote of the majority or an appeal to an outside expert (in this case, the local bishop and a few church growth experts). When members of the congregation were forced to articulate their views about the tradition, they ended up drawing lines in the sand and left little ground for compromise.

How the changes were undertaken also intensified the conflict. The clergy and lay leaders revised the congregation's negotiated order with minimal input from the general membership, and the traditionalists refused legitimacy to any of the changes in pastoral roles, congregational mission, worship styles, or ways of believing implemented by the clergy and council. This eroded trust and encouraged the division of the congregation into warring camps (decades-long members literally stopped speaking to one another). Finally, two organizational conditions facilitated the emergence of conflict and the schismatic outcome. First, the bulk of Good Shepherd's members were loosely committed to the Lutheran tradition, and many seemed to be uninformed about the specific theological claims or ritual practices in the tradition. In other words, they did not think of themselves or the congregation as distinctly Lutheran or believe it was very important to be Lutheran. This made the majority of the congregation largely unreceptive to the appeals and protests of the traditionalists. Second, changing the tradition would not have led to conflict without the presence of a minority who were deeply committed to preserving the tradition and who possessed the resources and ability to organize protest. Overall, the misarticulation of two incompatible religious cultures that supported opposing understandings of the centrality and vitality of the Lutheran tradition, together with a combative style of interaction, turned the process of religious change into conflict and schism.

REARTICULATION AND COMPROMISE AT GRACE LUTHERAN CHURCH

Like Good Shepherd, Grace Lutheran also experienced conflict over worship, but members and pastors overcame a misarticulation problem created by competing understandings of the tradition and how it had been changed. Recall from chapter 4 that Grace had been engaged in reframing the tradition by translating Lutheran theological language into the contemporary language of spirituality and psychology and by creating new worship traditions, often incorporating new rituals or practices from non-Western religions into the liturgical format of Lutheran worship. Yet they not only retained the Lutheran liturgical order but also its Christocentrism and its theological emphasis on grace and Christian freedom.

Grace was still adjusting to its one-year-old building and significant influx of new members when I began studying it. The new sanctuary was an open-beamed, light-filled, pastel-colored space, intentionally designed for use by non-Christians and Christians alike (e.g., a cross was not permanently placed on the back wall of the sanctuary as in many churches, nor were there any permanent explicitly Christian symbols in the worship space). Many members had worked with the religious artist who designed the stained-glass windows, artwork on the back wall, and layout of the sanctuary. Years of planning and building together had created a strong sense of ownership among many old members, and the nonchurchlike appearance appealed to many new members. The new sanctuary also was designed to allow for experimentation in worship. It looked and functioned more like a theater than a church, with painted concrete floors; a large, wooden, two-tiered platform at the center of the sanctuary that looked like a stage and held the altar; modular, padded seating (not pews) arranged in a half circle around the platform; and the absence of a pulpit and a choir loft. This minimalist design allowed worship leaders to bring in different props (such as the twelve-foot Mardi Gras Jesus puppet) and facilitated audience participation in new rituals, in part because such activities did not seem out of place in a more informal space and because it was easy to move around in the sanctuary or have different sections of the audience engage in interactive tasks (such as responding to a question in a sermon).

The changes to the tradition and the new building were not approved of by all the members, however. A small group—perhaps fifteen to twenty members—intensely disliked the new building and did not find the experimentation and retraditioning in worship meaningful. Most in this group preferred routinized liturgical worship anchored by an organ and classic sacred music over an eclectic and ever-changing structure. The wife of a former pastor summarized the group's opinion of the new building at one congregational meeting and hinted at this group's understanding of what constituted legitimate Lutheran worship: "This isn't my idea of a church. It's like a noisy barn; it's noisy. I can't worship here. It won't be a church until you get some proper music in here." This group, sometimes called the "old guard" by newer members, began a fund-raising campaign to build a pipe organ for the new sanctuary as soon as the congregation moved into the new church. The new sanctuary had an old, failing electric organ from the old building, and apparently either a new organ was not even considered during the design phase or the decision was made to delay installing one.[16]

The organ and, more indirectly, the changes to the tradition became the focus of a short but turbulent conflict in the winter and spring of 2001. The conflict's roots extended back to 1999 when the congregation authorized the organ committee to enter into a contract with an organ manufacturer and to engage in a fund-raising campaign. However, the sanctuary was not designed aesthetically or acoustically for a large pipe organ, and the senior pastor and some lay members had serious concerns about how a pipe organ could be incorporated without radically altering the worship space. In the fall of 2000, the church council asked the organ committee to stop raising funds because they saw this campaign as draining money from the general fund. They also asked the committee to work closely with the artist who designed the sanctuary to address aesthetic concerns (e.g., how the ranks of pipes could be placed without obscuring the artwork on the walls or the stained-glass windows) and build the organ with whatever money they had raised. When the organ committee refused to work with the artist ("he didn't know anything about organs," said one member) and was unable to raise the necessary funds to pay for the contracted organ (they were about $50,000 short), the church council canceled the contract before the no-penalty exit clause expired.

The cancellation of the contract set off the public struggle that had largely been contained in discussions between committee and church council. The cancellation was announced at the annual congregation meeting in February 2001.

Members of the organ committee circulated a resignation letter and a call for a congregation vote to overturn the council's decision. In the first meeting about the organ, council members and the organ committee and its supporters largely debated the history of the decision-making process and argued about whether or not the congregation's negotiated order had been violated or changed without congregational approval. Organ supporters questioned the council's authority to cancel the contract without congregational approval and hence the legitimacy of both the decision and the council. Council members defended their action by citing the church constitution and bylaws, which gave them power to act, and charged the committee with failing to take into account the aesthetic and financial concerns the council had raised months earlier. It was a heated debate with finger-pointing, raised voices, and tears.

At the end of the meeting, the congregation voted overwhelmingly to hold a special meeting to review the issue and take a final vote on whether to overturn the cancellation or support it. People began leaving, but the council president refused to end the meeting with the vote and instead called on the church to pray together and tried to defuse the acrimony and focus attention away from the decision-making process and on the foundational values and identity of the congregation. Only about thirty people stayed to pray, and after they gathered in a circle, holding hands, the council president turned to the religious language and images that many members shared and that would come to dominate the final public meeting over the organ: "We are like children: we play, we fight, but we sit down to a meal together [i.e., Holy Communion] and look to be fed; and we are a family. Let the Spirit of God blow through us and transform us. Amen."

In the month between meetings, several prominent members announced they would stop attending church at least until the conflict had been resolved; and the choir disbanded (many supported the music directors, who also were leaders on the organ committee). The council hired a conflict mediator to assess the organizational damage and outline how best to resolve the situation. Her recommendations were revealed at the final meeting in March as part of a surprise presentation by Pastor Tom Irons that began a process whereby the congregation talked themselves out of the conflict and into a compromise.

Pastor Irons passed out a one-page letter and then read it with some additional comments. He reviewed the history of the conflict and the way in which "the facts" had become distorted to such a degree that the very life of the congregation was at risk. He used the metaphors of illness to describe the conflict and its effects on members. He claimed that the relationship between the committee and the congregation's leaders had "become toxic" and that the "spreading poison of mistrust" meant that neither side could hear or work with the other. He then urged the congregation to accept the conflict mediator's recommendation to stop pursuing plans to acquire an organ for at least six months and seek forgiveness and reconciliation before beginning again. The most powerful moment of his presentation was when he spoke about the strong negative effects the conflict was having on members:

People of great integrity have been trashed by this disturbing experience. Our council president has resigned and refuses to be here—it is too toxic, too poisonous for him; it complicates his health. Six choir members no longer sing. At least a dozen called me and said they would not attend the meeting. They can't stand it and want nothing to do with the process. One council member has received three threatening phone calls warning that if she doesn't stop interfering with the organ building there will be consequences for her family. I don't know who is making the calls but it is sick and it testifies to how out of control the process is. If you want to wreak havoc and infect more friends at Grace with this insatiable and cancerous virus then press on, but if you desire to restore trust among us, then admit we are contaminated with a bad spirit, refuse to pursue the organ, and acknowledge the necessity of Christ's reconciling love, forgive, and act from a fresh start.

For the next forty-five minutes members responded to their pastor's strong words and spoke to one another about how they had betrayed the fundamental religious values that had guided the congregation and the necessity to reaffirm and live by those values. Several members spoke about how the congregation had "lost its way," "lost its ministry," or "lost what Grace is all about." One council member urged the congregation to reclaim its vision and identity that were grounded in the gospel values of justice, compassion, and service: "The organ is like a car—IT'S A THING! I wish I saw the passion around the organ also focused on the homeless, AIDS, and children. I don't hear these kinds of passionate conversations around these things. It's wrong to spend $280,000 on an organ. Let's just drop the whole thing and return to who we are called to be." Other members echoed the notion that a thing, the organ, had become more important than relationships, than the community, than their individual and collective identities as Christians. Some asked for forgiveness, other expressed remorse at having perpetuated the conflict, and nearly everyone agreed to drop the issue. Near the end of the meeting, someone asked a technical question about how to build the organ with the monies on hand, and before an organ committee member could fully respond, another person jumped up and said, "Stop. I don't care about the organ. Can't you see this is about people—people and relationships that have been hurt?" That comment seemed to signal that an agreement had been reached to end the discussion and the conflict, and the meeting quietly ended with prayer. Over the next few months, the congregation's leaders agreed to a six-month moratorium on the organ and then agreed to begin the process anew. In 2004 a new, much-less-expensive electric organ was purchased, and the original artist returned to repaint a section of the sanctuary to celebrate and highlight the role of music for the congregation.

There was wistfulness in some of the comments as several members spoke about the congregation they had once loved and realized that their collective experience of a community committed to one another and a radical understanding of Christianity had been violated. My field notes conclude with the following observation about the meeting:

> Pastor Tom's letter seemed to have awoken the congregation. After he spoke, several members argued that the issue at stake wasn't the organ but what kind of church they were or would be. They talked about how the conflict revealed the ways in which they had put an object ahead of people; how they had not treated each other with forgiveness, tolerance, compassion—the core values of the congregation; and how the congregation they had once known had disappeared in the conflict.

In short, the meeting became an opportunity for the congregation to reconnect or rearticulate their core values and identity with their actions, and to reaffirm the way in which they had been expanding and translating the tradition. Repeatedly in the interviews with members and clergy following the conflict, I heard them describe the congregation as a place of inclusiveness, openness, nonjudgmental acceptance, and reconciliation. The organ conflict revealed that the congregation had collectively lost sight of these values. Moreover, most members understood the purpose of worship to be transformation, and for many newer members, worship that followed the *LBW* and organ music week after week was not transformative. The new rituals, new music, and new language of faith they experienced in worship services challenged them to put their faith in action.

Although few members spoke about the conflict in relation to Grace's retraditioning and reframing of Lutheranism, when they did, they tended to speak about reclaiming the core values of the congregation or using resources for the justice and outreach ministries of the congregation. However, Associate Pastor Karen Douglass did make the connection between the conflict and the Lutheran tradition and argued that ultimately the fight was about preserving a mythical, unchanging version of Lutheranism or continuing to transform the tradition so it could be meaningful to people who are relatively indifferent or unconcerned with Lutheranism per se:

> The organ is a symbol; no, an icon. I want to give it more power than just to say it's a symbol. It's the icon in the minds of a core group of people who, for lack of a better word, are stuck, completely stuck. These are the people who keep saying the building doesn't work. What we're doing in worship doesn't work. They're tired of being shook up. They want to go back. They don't want to transform the tradition. They want to go back to be secure in it. . . . It's an icon for all the changes Tom has made. I've been reading a new biography about Luther, and I was struck by how we Lutherans have been trying for centuries to get back to the church of the Reformation. But that is a mythical place; there never was some perfect version of Lutheranism. So what the fight was about was getting back to that mythical, nonexistent place, and the pipe organ is the thing which defines that place. It's

funny, at the February meeting Tom's report was as Lutheran as could be—
"I preached the gospel every Sunday and administered the sacraments"—
and that's not enough for this group.

The process of talking and listening to one another helped the congregation
recall the values and identity of the congregation and reconnect values, identity,
and behavior. This meant they had to acknowledge that the fighting over whether
or not to build a pipe organ had led the congregation to betray their commitment
to their values, and then they needed to reaffirm that worship not only should
be guided by these values but should embody them. In the process of talking
and listening, members of the congregation appealed implicitly to the authority
of the gospel (e.g., Jesus' model of forgiveness, inclusion, justice-oriented service) and explicitly to the authority of their collective experiences of having been
transformed by the new liturgies and rituals of worship at Grace.

THE CONDITIONS FOR CONSENSUS

Faith, Zion, St. Peter's, and Resurrection had a high degree of consensus regarding the nature and direction of change. They were able to reach consensus about
altering the tradition because several interrelated organizational conditions that
facilitated change were met: a close fit between each congregation's culture and
the specific changes to the Lutheran tradition it implemented; the perception
that the core of the tradition was buffered from change; leaders' ability to work
with, rather than in opposition to, each congregation's negotiated order; the absence of an organized opposition and/or the absence of multiple and conflicting
church cultures; and the timing or history of changes to the tradition.

The Timing and History of Change

The timing and history of change appeared to have facilitated change at several
congregations. Zion and Faith were early adopters of contemporary worship using praise music and other techniques from evangelicalism. Zion began experimenting with praise music and rock and roll in 1989 and Faith in 1995. Both
had experienced worship wars (i.e., conflict over the legitimacy and desirability of contemporary worship versus the preservation of traditional forms of Lutheran worship) when the congregations added a contemporary service and lost
some members.[17] Yet both congregations weathered the storms with relative ease
in part because the changes to worship evolved slowly; Faith had experimented
with two acoustic-guitar-based liturgical services in the years prior to the
change, and Zion did not add amplified music for several years after starting
their contemporary service. Another important factor was the congregations'
historic missions to reach the unchurched. And these histories were still alive. A
council member at Zion, for example, noted that "the roots of the church go back
to being a mission church. Many people speak with great respect for the first

pastors and how they weren't shy about going door to door and really putting the emphasis on members that they too needed to do evangelism. There are people still here that have a memory of that and we tell that story." Longtime members of both congregations reported that initially there was a high level of discomfort, but that many recognized the changes were necessary in order to grow.

The fact that these churches were early adopters made their subsequent changes to worship or the tradition easier for three reasons. First, these changes were framed as a means to revitalize the animating vision and identity for each congregation. Second, they were shown to be biblical, which carried great weight in congregations that tended toward literalism. Third, they were defined as being congruent with or improving upon the tradition. An octogenarian at Faith remarked that at first she hated the contemporary worship service, but then, "Pastor Lincoln really had a way of making people realize that we aren't here for ourselves. He's out to spread the message of Jesus Christ." She also acknowledged that Lincoln ended the Willow Creek–styled seeker service, reinstated weekly Communion, and added more traditional hymns to the contemporary service (albeit set in the genre of rock and roll), all of which signaled to some of the traditionalists that the church was returning to its Lutheran roots. Few members of Zion objected to adding a second praise music service in the fall of 2002. Most viewed the change as necessary to ease the overcrowding at the existing contemporary service and to reach out to the unchurched population of the community, for whom rock and roll and a more informal style of worship were attractive. In a sense, the congregations' histories of early adaptation and strong identity as outreach-minded congregations made them more receptive to incorporating the practices and ideas of evangelicalism.

In contrast, the history and timing of changes at Good Shepherd did not facilitate consensus or an easy transition to a reworked tradition. Like Faith and Zion, Good Shepherd was an early adopter of contemporary worship, but the church's leaders apparently forgot all of the lessons learned about how to implement change. In the late 1980s, the congregation created a service that substituted guitar for organ music and set the Lutheran liturgy to folk music. They slowly introduced each new part of the liturgy every few weeks and explained how each was similar in content and form to the more formal liturgical elements in the *LBW*. However, when the new clergy moved to change the worship services in 2000, they did so without warning the congregation and without providing an explanation for how or why they were changing them. And unlike Faith and Zion, Good Shepherd radically changed both the formal, liturgical *LBW* service and the existing "contemporary service," which followed the historic Lutheran liturgy and was instituted by a beloved and dying former pastor (Faith and Zion each dedicated one service to the older style of worship). Here the rapid pace of change and the way in which it violated the congregation's expectations about the process of change based on their history delegitimized the attempt to reframe the tradition and helped fuel conflict.[18]

The history of a congregation thus can shape attempts to change the tradition by providing a frame of reference that members use to evaluate the congregation's leaders. A more positive example comes from St. Peter's Lutheran Church. There the current pastor was hired after a period of decline in which the congregation had two interim ministers (by one account the congregation lost five hundred members in a few years), and he quickly made growth a top priority and person-ally recruited many of the young families that became mainstays of the church. Older members also report that he brought back sound Lutheran theology and biblically based teaching (apparently missing during the interim period), which convinced some members who had left to return. In this case, the congregation saw the success of the new pastor set against the backdrop of a recent and pre-cipitous decline and gave him permission to try new things, like adopting the purpose-driven church model and adding praise music to one service.

The Perception of Change

As suggested in the previous section, how members perceive change is an im-portant part of determining its success or failure. In particular, members' per-ceptions about the tradition—its importance and the degree to which its core is buffered—and about the process of change are critical for building consensus. At Emmanuel in Oakland, for example, the congregation readily accepted the ad-dition of the gospel music and spirituals from African American Protestantism because it would help the congregation appear more similar to other churches in the community. However, members saw such additions as a supplement to the largely beloved Lutheran tradition, and leaders told me they were not try-ing to turn these proud Lutherans into some other type of Christian. They were not being asked to become "a shoutin' church"—a strategy that would have ul-timately failed according to most of the interviewees—just one that was more closely aligned with African American culture. Similarly, at Christ Lutheran on the other side of town, by retaining the liturgical structure and sacramental the-ology of Lutheranism, most members did not perceive the addition of African American music, theology, or preaching styles as a threat to the tradition.

One reason Faith and Zion had a relatively easy time changing certain forms of the tradition was because the tradition was not meaningful to the majority of members nor did traditional forms ground their religious identity. Losing ele-ments of the Lutheran liturgy or Lutheran hymnody, for example, simply did not matter very much to members at these congregations. A few members re-ported that they were happy to lose the "ethnic" or "cultural" features of Luther-anism because a Scandinavian or German identity was apparently unmarked for so many, especially the unchurched. Yet, to those for whom it did matter, the changes in worship and theology appeared to affect only the nonessentials. There was a sense that the core of the tradition remained untouched and pro-tected. Few people at Faith and Zion felt like they were being asked to abandon the Lutheran emphasis on grace and the sacraments or jettison the liturgy alto-gether. Members wore their Lutheranism lightly at these congregations, often placing their Christian identity above a denominational one. One member of Zion summarized the feelings of several older members when she said, "We're willing to try new things. We still respect our heritage but we're open to going into the next century. Our understanding is that although we may be uncomfortable with it, times change and worship changes." Another commented that most people at the church believe that "Christ is the center of our faith. It isn't about Martin Luther. It's all about Jesus as God's son. I've seen too many other people get into their own denominations to the extent of revering their theology and their practices more than they revere God. Not at Zion."

In other words, there appeared to be a willingness at these two congregations to subordinate the tradition to the larger goal of making the faith and the church accessible and relevant to non-Christians, and to cultivate a more general Christian identity rather than a distinctly denominational one. This respectful but loose hold on the tradition made it easier to change and easier to identify those few elements of the tradition that the congregations took pains to preserve.

This study largely supports Finke's argument that buffering the core of a tradition is necessary for successful innovation, as evinced in the effort to Lutheranize evangelicalism at Faith, Zion, and St. Peter's (recall that members of St. Peter's, for example, perceived the adoption of the purpose-driven church model as an administrative move to increase the efficiency of the congregation rather than as an attempt to change the tradition).[19] Finke's argument, if extended, might suggest that attempts at innovation and change will be more likely to gain widespread support if a congregation's negotiated order is buffered from drastic change or redefined collectively and cooperatively, as demonstrated by the Good Shepherd case study. Resurrection Lutheran, in the Silicon Valley, also provides support for this extension of Finke's argument. This congregation had a history of strong lay involvement in the decision-making process, and the pastor reported that a top-down leadership style would never work at Resurrection: "I would never even try to make some change without having conversations with members." Process and reaching consensus were central features of the congregation's negotiated order. I saw this at work during the congregation's months-long discussion about a new vision and mission document. Part of that discussion was about how to grow the church and whether or not to adopt some suggestions from the evangelical church growth literature. The result of many public and private conversations among pastors, elected lay leaders, and rank-and-file members was not to follow that advice (e.g., adding a praise music worship service) but first to study how to make sure that the advocated changes in worship would fit with the congregation's commitment to Lutheran worship and theology; to develop the skills to share one's faith with nonchurchgoing friends in ways that would be congruent with an individual's Lutheran identity; and to discern how best to serve the larger community, which might mean that the church would not necessarily grow in members—basically placing the Lutheran call to be a "Christ to one's neighbor" ahead of numerical growth.

However, Faith, Zion, and St. Peter's successfully changed the decision-making processes and ways in which power was organized. They did so, especially at Faith and Zion, to more effectively reshape the tradition. They succeeded because the leaders of these congregations were able to frame the shift in the negotiated order as a matter of administrative efficiency rather than as a substantial reworking of congregational identity or the core of the tradition, and because they were able to make changes in the negotiated order articulate with the business culture familiar to many church members.

All three congregations had histories of strong lay involvement in the decision-making process—really a commitment to strong congregational polity—and a consensus model of decision making. All three adopted a more diffuse system in which many decisions were made by small groups, largely outside the oversight of the congregation as a whole. Each church created an executive council that handled all administrative and financial matters, an elected church council that focused on setting the church's vision, and various ministry teams (some permanent, some ad hoc) that developed specific programs (from adult Bible studies to service projects) with little or no opposition from the congregation. St. Peter's adopted the purpose-driven church model about a year prior to the start of my fieldwork, and by all accounts it was well received by members. Lay leaders involved described the decision to adopt the model as a "no-brainer." It made sense to them because it mirrored the same kind of leadership structure used in their corporate settings, and because it made it easier to accomplish tasks and involve more members in the day-to-day programs of the church (one council member noted that they had tripled the number of members involved in ministries since adopting the model). One of the key leaders involved in implementing the model recalled:

> Pastor Erik [the senior pastor at St. Peter's] came back from Saddleback Community Church and said, "Ron this is just incredible. You've gotta see it." So we sat down and went through the tapes from the session he went to, and I said, "This is great. I have to tell you this is exactly like a model we use to fix broken companies." Then I explained it to him: the model provides the infrastructure that helps new leaders evolve and helps existing people in the company better understand the values, goals, and mission of the company.

Another member, using corporate language, noted that the model "created more leverage for spending time on figuring out how to meet the ministry goals of the church." In our interview, he described the model and emphasized how it made the church run more efficiently by delegating tasks and decisions to small teams and by freeing up the congregation's leaders to concentrate on thinking about how best to reach their goals of recruiting the unchurched and of developing disciples:

> It created leverage because before, the old way, we had a list of thirty things we had to do—and who wants to do number twenty-two, who wants to do number twenty-three, we were constantly trying to find people to do those thirty things. The purpose-driven model broke it into six groups of five

each. . . . When we were trying to wrestle with thirty things it was hard, but now you have these five things [as a council person]. Just make these five things work and it's only five things. Okay, now I have five individuals—one for each—who are the subleaders of those five things, and the council person is the leader of five subleaders who are doing their thing. It makes it a lot easier. Another thing, a number of years ago we would literally spend 80 percent of the council meeting on things unrelated to the key purposes of the church. We'd spend an hour on should we build a fence along the side yard. But we were spending very little time on how do we reach more people, how do we enhance the service, what classes should we hold. These days we don't spend much time at all on the administrative items. It's probably reverse. It's 20 percent administrative and 80 percent what should we do in terms of our ministry. The other side of that was, if you try to get sixteen people to decide on what kind of fence to put up, you're not going to get there.

Not only did the borrowed organizational model from a California mega-church mirror some members' corporate experience of leadership and decision making, but it helped the church capitalize on a unique feature of work in the high-tech capital of the world. Engineers, as many Silicon Valley interviewees told me, tend to be very task oriented, entrepreneurial, and independent, but they often lack the ability or interest to think about the overarching vision of a company. The purpose-driven model delegated the visioning task to a small group and then turned the task-oriented people loose to do much of the on-the-ground work of running the church. A council member who worked in the high-tech industry noted:

The area is full of people who can implement. Engineers, by and large, are very good at accomplishing a task. What this area lacks are people who have a vision, a plan, and who can express it well. We are blessed with a few people who are good at that and who can communicate our message effectively, and we have an overabundance of engineering types. The model lets us exploit that.

The restructuring plan also was received without opposition because it was framed in terms of heightening the efficiency of the congregation and, in turn, of helping it fulfill its mission. As at St. Peter's, Zion's leaders proposed both to centralize the financial, administrative, and visioning tasks in a small executive council and to give ministry teams and ad hoc groups more power to design new ministry programs. At the meeting where the council asked formally for the congregation's permission to do this, the council president urged the members to vote yes because "the council continues to spend more time on business issues than on ministry development and leadership." As part of the restructuring plan, the ministry heads who had been council members would no longer be on the council, and this would free them up to develop their particular programs by recruiting and training more members to take on leadership responsibilities and to use their spiritual gifts.

In a video presentation, the restructuring plan was sold on an appeal to the congregation's "entrepreneurial spirit" and its mission of developing disciples. The head of the social-justice team made one such appeal on the video, arguing, "This is an exciting proposal because it will get more people involved in ministry. It's how we can be a missional church and carry out God's will on earth. We need to develop leaders and programs to equip all the members to carry out God's will. The restructuring will allow this to happen." Another member spoke up in favor of the plan and reminded the congregation: "We've got a lot of high Q people here—that's what we call people with a lot of talent in the electronics industry.[20] They just need an initial start and boom; they'll take it from there. That's what this restructuring proposal will do." When it came time to vote on the proposal, not one dissenting vote was cast. Here the proposed change to the administrative side of the negotiated order was tied to fulfilling the congregation's mission and not explicitly connected to the ways in which the tradition had been or was being changed. However, when the council presented the proposal to replace a traditional service with a second praise music service, they encountered resistance. Most members were not opposed to the addition of a more evangelical service. They opposed not being consulted about this shift in the tradition, suggesting that changes in the negotiated order affect the tradition in certain ways. Changing the substance of worship, which is often seen as the foundation of a tradition or central in the life of congregation, is a much more important decision than changing the organizational structure of a church council, and congregations may balk at making the changes when they are not consulted or asked for their opinions. In this case, members' opposition forced the congregation's leaders to delay the vote and spend several more months listening to members' concerns. Eventually the congregation implemented the proposed changes to the worship schedule.

Leaders of these congregations, in general, were able to persuade members to give up an older consensus and democratic model of decision making for one in which power was exercised by small groups outside the congregation's oversight. They succeeded by showing how the restructuring would allow the congregation to fulfill its mission (largely understood as making disciples and reaching the unchurched), by making the changes to the negotiated order fit or articulate with the entrepreneurial business culture of members, and by framing the issue in terms of efficiency and not connecting it explicitly to changing the tradition.[21] At Zion, church leaders played to the business culture of members by using market research (they conducted a survey of members' worship interests) and developing marketing materials (e.g., the video) based on the results to "sell" the restructuring plan as well as the shift in worship schedules and the addition of video screens in the sanctuary. At Good Shepherd and Grace, by contrast, clergy and lay leaders made no effort to sell their changes to the tradition or the congregation's negotiated order. Because some of the changes at these two congregations involved engendering an anticonsumerist approach to religion, marketing or selling change may have been unacceptable or even unimaginable. Moreover, at Good Shepherd, the traditionalists were able to show how the changes in the congregation's rules and procedures allowed church leaders to subsequently change the tradition, whereas at St. Peter's, Faith, and Zion, changes in the negotiated order largely were disconnected from the Lutheran tradition.

Fitting Change to Congregational Cultures

An important factor that contributed to consensus at several congregations (Faith, Zion, St. Peter's, and Resurrection) was a relatively unified congregational culture. Unlike Good Shepherd and Grace, where competing congregational identities and pieties created the conditions for conflict, these other congregations operated according to a shared identity, a shared piety, a shared set of religious or organizational values, and a shared understanding of religious authority. While there was some dissent regarding the changes to the tradition at Faith and Zion, the dissenters were never able to organize protest or prevent change in part because the tradition itself was not seen as central to the faith lives of individuals or the congregation as a whole, and in part because many members seemed to value pragmatism and efficiency more highly than preserving the tradition. For example, a sixty-nine-year-old member of Faith commented that Pastor Lincoln had upset some members when he first arrived and began changing the worship practices and religious language of the church, but that in the end the resulting growth in numbers offset any sense of having lost parts of the tradition:

> I'm sixty-nine years old and the traditions are unimportant to me. Pastor Lincoln has come in and changed everything. We're going to have a new format to this; we're going to call everything different. That bothered some people. Not me. You can say what you want, but he's attracting all kinds of younger people. So whatever gets people into the church building and into the sanctuary, that's what's important. The church is pushing the envelope constantly, to reach more people with the Word. And in order to do that you have to make some pretty radical changes. And the congregation as a whole is not opposed to doing that.

Members of the consensus churches also shared the value of religious choice more than members of Grace and Good Shepherd did. At the latter two churches, the ethic of choice and consumption that drives much of American religious life today was being challenged intentionally by the congregations' leaders. One result of that challenge was that, when the congregations changed the tradition, they tended to eliminate worship options. At Good Shepherd, initially, the old styles and services of worship disappeared, and at Grace, the constantly changing worship service meant that members looking for a "traditional" worship service could not predict when such a service would be offered. Leaders of these congregations removed options or refused to institutionalize an ethos of religious choice on principle. They were trying to force members to choose to worship and, more broadly, to live their lives according to values that were incongruent with the values of consumerism. However, an oppositional stance against religious choice and consumerism was not shared by all members of the congregations and became one of the concerns of the dissident groups. Conversely, at Faith and Zion members were given the option of traditional or contemporary worship, and members spoke appreciatively about having the choice to worship in a style that they personally found meaningful, but they also appreciated that others could find a style that suited their own needs or tastes.[22] A staff member expressed the importance of choice in her description of what makes worship so vital at Zion:

There's a group who think it's very, very exciting to worship on Sunday at the contemporary worship because it's fun. And it's bursting with energy and enthusiasm. So naturally, someone of a somewhat contemplative nature is not comfortable in that kind of a worship setting. Where conversely, the person who likes that zippy-zippy is not comfortable in a quiet, more meditative worship service. And we do provide both styles. I know some large, large churches, like Church of Joy, essentially they threw the baby out with the bathwater. They said to people if you don't want to worship this way, and you want to use the green hymnal [i.e., the *LBW*], then go someplace else. We decided not to throw out the traditional service. We wanted to give people the choice.

The consensus congregations differed from the churches with conflict in the degree to which members shared a common piety and held common views about the saliency and import of the Lutheran tradition. Recall that at Grace and Good Shepherd, there were competing understandings of how to be religious and how the church should use the tradition to promote the religious life. These conflicting pieties encouraged and fueled conflict. At St. Peter's, members largely shared a propositional piety in which religiosity was organized around assent to a set of truth claims about God, Jesus, and the Christian life. The Bible provided clear answers about these claims, and worship taught and reinforced these beliefs. In particular, members at St. Peter's spoke about the Lutheran doctrine of "justification by grace through faith" as the cornerstone of their faith and consistently described the worship as the event in which "Christianity 101" was taught. Compared to the other congregations in the study, worship at St. Peter's was unremarkable—the music was mediocre in quality compared to the very professional bands at Faith, Zion, and Resurrection; the ritual activities lacked the originality and passion at Grace; and the service in general lacked the kind of experimentation I witnessed at Grace, Christ, or Zion. Yet, members always raved about how meaningful worship was and how they always heard a sermon that conveyed the saving message about Jesus Christ's death on a cross. I suspect that members cared little about high-quality music or being ritually innovative because they went to church to be reminded of the fundamental tenets of the Christian faith.

This form of piety tends to be conservative (members commonly used the term "conservative" in their descriptions of the congregation) and thus made the congregation more receptive both to preserving the theological tradition of Lutheranism and to embracing the Biblicist and evangelical theology of the purpose-driven church. As one member claimed: "This congregation is very conservative. Maybe that sounds like a stretch using a Rick Warren's Baptist metaphor [i.e., the purpose-driven church model], but we actually adapted him to our conservative place. This ELCA congregation really is a lot like the LCMS [the more conservative Lutheran Church—Missouri Synod]."

Members at Faith and Zion tended to practice what I call "therapeutic piety," in which belief and religious activity emphasized wholeness, healing, and growth. The Christian faith is centered on the individual's personal relationship with Jesus and how that relationship brings healing and wholeness. Worship in this form of piety is expected to provide a warm, uplifting experience of the sacred (as one member noted, "it opens up my heart") in which the Bible's religious teachings are made applicable to people's daily lives. The centrality of relevant, applicable, and personal religiosity was evident in members' answers to my question about what they like best about worship at their churches:

> He gives you sort of a real-life, current-day thing, then gives you Bible information, and then ties it back together so that you got some sort of take-home message. I like how he pulls in movies or he pulls in current events that help you figure out how how what he's saying applies to your life. There are some mornings where I sit there and I think I am the only one in church that he's talking to.

> Pastor John's sermons are great. You know I can't tell ya how many times I'm wiping my eyes, you know, and walk out of there saying, "Boy, he talks." Not all the time, not every time, but he was talking to me.

This type of piety de-emphasized the tradition insofar as members were willing to discard it if the religious language or worship practices did not make Christianity relevant, accessible, and personally meaningful to members or outsiders. Moreover, the tradition was not very important to most members of either congregation. While there were small groups within each church that valued Lutheran worship traditions more highly or had clear identities as Lutherans, most members had little interest in cultivating a distinctly Lutheran identity, most disliked the formal liturgy of the historic Lutheran worship, and most were committed to preserving a handful of theological ideals that they named as uniquely Lutheran (e.g., *sola gratia*). This relative unanimity about the tradition, especially the low level of commitment to it, made it easy to change much of the tradition or repackage it in new forms and languages, in comparison to congregations where members were divided about the core and peripheral elements of the tradition and at odds regarding its overall importance for the life of the congregation.

Finally, some of the congregations in the study were able to reach consensus about changing the tradition because those changes were justified or explained in ways that fit neatly with the congregations' operative understandings of religious authority. Authority is important because it provides the grounds to legitimize change and help members make sense of why the tradition must be altered.

For example, Faith, Zion, and St. Peter's framed their explanations or defenses of changes to worship or church structures by appealing to the authority of experts or biblical authority. The evangelism causal story described in chapter 3 illustrates how Faith and Zion defended the use of evangelical praise music and downplayed denominational distinctiveness because growing churches, as described by megachurch pastors and organizational consultants, did so. Pastors commonly relied on church growth and decline statistics to make a point about why their church had to change the tradition or die. Expert authority combined with pragmatism is a key characteristic of late modernity and postmodernity according to some sociologists and certainly part of the larger cultural milieu of these congregations. Appeals to expert authority are congruous with the American culture of pragmatism or utilitarianism.[23] It appears that there was a tight fit between the kind of authority congregational leaders used to defend changes to the tradition and the kind of authority under which members lived. Adopting evangelical praise music or the purpose-driven church model seemed like the right thing to do for many members because, according to the experts (those who actually led growing churches or observed them), it worked.

At the same time, the vision documents, mission statements, and causal stories were peppered with Bible verses and commentaries upon them to show that change to the tradition would make the congregations more closely aligned with the ancient church. Miller notes that this turn to embrace the model and practices of the early church is one of the key reasons for the growth of new-paradigm congregations, and ultimately it rests on a form of biblical literalism.[24] Similarly, several congregations in this study described themselves as "biblical" or "Bible-oriented" and, on matters related to church growth, evangelism, and the purpose of the church, tended to engage in proof-texting to push their claims. For example, when the clergy at Faith spoke about transforming the church into a discipling, or evangelizing, church, they often quoted the Great Commission from the Gospel of Matthew, followed by such phrases as "the Bible is clear" or "the Bible tells us."

Unlike appeals to experience (used at Good Shepherd, for example), appeals based on biblical or expert authority provide more definitive grounds for changing the tradition. It is difficult to argue against a change that is based on the Bible when most of the congregation consider the Bible to be the ultimate authority to guide the life of the congregation and believe it provides unambiguous rules, models, or teachings about how to organize the church. Similarly, arguments based on expert authority carry great weight among professionals whose own corporate experience validates the legitimacy of expertise and who are willing to apply the lessons learned from one arena of social life to church life.

PATHWAYS TO CONSENSUS AND CONFLICT

In this chapter I have shown that there are multiple pathways to consensus, compromise, and conflict when congregations attempt to change the religious tradition that governs their collective lives. I have offered a conjunctural argument in which different configurations of organizational variables lead to different outcomes. In particular, I have argued that these outcomes vary based on the degree of articulation among a congregation's culture, the cultural and religious codes that orient public and private life in the United States, and the specific changes to the tradition. Congregations that shared a common single culture tended to avoid conflict and successfully implement change, whereas congregations in which multiple cultures existed that were seen as incommensurate by members did not. The key is not so much the nature of the culture as the degree to which it is shared. For example, although Resurrection and Faith had very different cultures—one embracing the Lutheran tradition and one in which the tradition was largely seen as optional—each congregation was able to successfully navigate the process of change because the changes did not violate or undermine the common values of their respective cultures. Conversely, a religious culture rooted in propositional piety and a static understanding of the tradition at Good Shepherd and Grace was incongruent with the shift to a culture in which doubt and ambiguity and personal experience and a commitment to fully live the radical demands of Christianity were emphasized. However, at Grace the conflict was resolved when the senior pastor and other members reminded one another, in the midst of brewing conflict, that the radical and seeking religious culture (specifically, the radical gospel of reconciliation) was why many members had committed themselves to the congregation.

As suggested above, articulation or misarticulation was facilitated by a congregation's relationship to the tradition and the type of religious authority considered normative for the church. Congregations that had a relatively weak relationship to the tradition had an easier time abandoning it or augmenting it with elements from other traditions in part because the organization and its members were not vested in preserving it; in part because they did not know what they might be losing by changing it; and in part because they were able to define a very few elements as essential and most others as peripheral. This was true especially for Faith and Zion. Moreover, these congregations replaced many of the Lutheran practices and ideas with those from the evangelical tradition dominant in American religious culture, with its strong emphasis on an individualized and private faith. The type of religious authority that undergirded efforts to change the tradition also shaped the outcome of the process. The churches that relied on biblical and expert authority were more adept at providing clear and compelling defenses for the changes than those that relied on the authority of experience.

Some congregations were also able to generate consensus because the changes and/or the explanation for the changes articulated with belief systems and organizational structures from the larger cultural context that were familiar to members. Appeals on the basis of pragmatism and choice appeared to have facilitated change at several congregations, whereas the effort to remake the tradition in the image of seeker spirituality and liberal theology drove a wedge between members at two churches where some members saw such spirituality and theology as incompatible with Lutheranism.

An important reason for the success of several congregations was the tight fit between the embrace of the evangelical tradition and the broader cultural codes of pragmatism and consumerism. These codes have deep roots in American religion—from the rejection of tradition for whatever technique would bring about conversion in nineteenth-century revivalism to the rise of televangelism and Christian bookstores within contemporary evangelicalism. Perhaps these congregations were so unified on the nature and process of change because the changes fit so easily into the logic of the market that permeates nearly all aspects of social life in the United States. The codes of pragmatism and consumption (especially the notion of choice) are reinforced by institutions and practices outside religion, which makes them very powerful. This was evident in the way in which members of St. Peter's and Zion, for example, compared the evangelicalization of the tradition and their congregations' negotiated order to the standard way in which business operates. They saw no problem with extending the logic of the market to the work of the kingdom. The revival tradition and evangelicalism, rather than mainline Protestantism, intentionally capitalize on these values and yoke them to the opportunity to convert the nation and the world, as suggested in the following comment about revivalism by historian R. Laurence Moore: "Religious leaders delightedly seized upon market logic, . . . because it brought their mightiest dreams of doing God's work into the realm of possibility. . . . Revivals became businesses because markets showed the way to evangelize the far corners of the globe. Market logic promised universal salvation."[25]

The codes of pragmatism and consumer choice also are structured to lead to consensus. By offering members a range of worship choices, for example, Faith and Zion did not require members to sacrifice or compromise on the religious values and practices that were personally important to them. Individuals at these congregations to whom Lutheranism—its liturgical worship or theological ideas—provided meaning and comfort still had a traditional service to attend; meanwhile, contemporary music and nondenominational praise services were available for those for whom the tradition was considered expendable. Similarly, pragmatism breeds consensus when it is operationalized in a context where the goal of the organization is, not to preserve or defend specific principles, values, or traditions, but to do whatever it takes to succeed. This was the case at Faith, Zion, and St. Peter's.

In contrast, traditionalists at Good Shepherd and Grace were given few options and in a sense were asked to sacrifice their personal interests regarding the tradition in order to cultivate a new religious culture that transcended Lutheranism and refocused it by returning to the radical roots of Christianity (i.e., a religion that demanded that its members fully live according to its moral precepts—to love and forgive unconditionally, to change the world through self-sacrificing love, to promote the needs of the community over the needs of the individual). The form of liberal sectarianism advocated at these two congregations did not fit neatly into a culture dominated by individual choice and markers of success equated with growth (e.g., growth in members or in the weekly offering). At Good Shepherd, the clergy were willing to lose a substantial number of members (anywhere from 10 to 70 percent) and defended this position by appealing to certain religious principles or values they believed were rooted in the life and teachings of Jesus and in the ancient forms of Christianity. "Principalism" does not sit well in a culture dominated by pragmatism, and it was clear that the clergy's stance and "principled" actions did not sit well with the dissidents. In some ways, the conflicts at Good Shepherd and Grace were not so much about the tradition as they were about the larger meaning systems that were harnessed to preserve or alter the tradition.

Finally, process proved to be important insofar as the way in which the process of change unfolded or was managed fueled conflict, compromise, or consensus. Change that was done slowly, clearly explained, and connected to a shared congregational identity and mission, as in the case of Zion and Faith, for example, facilitated consensus and the move toward evangelical Lutheranism. Whereas change that was done too quickly or without sufficient explanation or that defied the perceived identity and mission of the congregation generated conflict, as in the case of Good Shepherd. Moreover, by staking the changes to a set of theological and ecclesiological principles, leaders at Grace and Good Shepherd encouraged conflict. The consensus congregations made change more palatable by preserving choice and showing how the changes to the tradition would help the congregation realize their goals of "reaching the unchurched" and thus fulfilling the Great Commission.

Part of the change process included managing the perception of change and, in particular, the perception that the core of the tradition was protected. At Good Shepherd and Grace, leaders and members struggled to determine what actually constituted the tradition and then which parts of it to protect. Leaders of these two churches encouraged conflict when they abandoned or reframed parts of the tradition that the organized minority believed was part of the core. At Faith, Zion, and St. Peter's, reconnecting, although used less frequently than at Good Shepherd and Grace, reassured members that the congregations were still fundamentally Lutheran despite the move to more explicitly embrace evangelicalism; reconnecting failed miserably at Good Shepherd because neither side could agree on what the tradition was, nor was their any consensus on whether the leaders had saved the essential elements of it.

The last three chapters have analyzed the connections among the process of transforming one particular religious tradition in local congregations and several broader cultural themes that animate American religious and public life: individualism and privatization, pragmatism and consumerism, and the search for community. In the final chapter, I explore these themes and connections and summarize my approach to understanding religious and cultural change.

Chapter 7

TRADITION AND CHANGE IN THE AMERICAN RELIGIOUS LANDSCAPE

SCHOLARLY AND POPULAR accounts of the restructuring of American religion suggest that the culture of religious choice, seeker spirituality, and the move away from denominationalism have weakened the relevancy and authority of specific religious traditions. At the same time, these larger changes within American religion have set off a concerted search by individuals and congregations to rediscover and re-create traditions as they find themselves disembedded from the rituals, theologies, and stories that serve as the foundation for community.[1] This study has provided a window onto the ongoing process of religious change at the onset of the twenty-first century and suggests that the familiar story of restructuring needs to be amended in three ways.

First, the extant story describes and explains the decline of old mainline Protestantism and concomitant rise of evangelicalism and nondenominational church bodies, while at the same time it shows how churches within these different traditions reside in separate religious worlds. However, it has not helped us understand how and why evangelicalism and nondenominationalism have impacted congregations within the old mainline. The account in this book suggests that the old boundaries that kept evangelicalism and mainline Protestantism in separate religious worlds are breaking down as churches within the old mainline adopt the worship practices, theological language, and identities of evangelicalism and nondenominationalism. It appears that evangelicalism and nondenominationalism are colonizing mainline Protestantism. Second, the process of colonization has become the means by which the larger religious culture of consumption, choice, and pragmatism that has fueled the growth of nondenominational and evangelical traditions has decentered the Lutheran tradition. This in turn weakens the ability of these Lutheran, and other, congregations to serve as communities of memory. Third, the process of religious change is not driven by unfettered bricolage as suggested by Roof's most recent study of baby boomers, nor is it simply a response to competitive pressures in the local religious market as suggested by ecological and market approaches.[2] Rather, changes to the tradition are catalyzed by constructed crises of membership and meaning as congregation leaders attempt to manage the felt isomorphic pressures from a national religious market by selectively incorporating elements from alternative traditions.

In this final chapter I discuss how this study of Lutheran congregations contributes to the larger account of religious change in America. I begin by examining how the colonization of Lutheranism by evangelical and nondenominational religious forces has altered the historic tradition. I then show how these changes have affected the nature of community at several of the congregations. I conclude with a discussion of how this study contributes to our understanding of the more general processes of religious and cultural change.

THE COLONIZATION OF LUTHERANISM

Lutheranism in the United States has been an insular religion—separated from much of the rest of Protestantism by its ethnic (i.e., Scandinavian and German) exclusivity, by its complicated liturgical service and use of classical sacred music, and by its emphasis on education and intellect (i.e., its emphasis on biblical, theological, and liturgical literacy). As such, until recently Lutheranism had lacked the central features of the indigenous pietist tradition that have become the dominant way in which Protestantism is organized and expressed in America: nonliturgical worship that relies on the idioms of rock and roll and self-help to make it accessible and egalitarian, an unambiguous theology that emphasizes conversion, personal morality, and the benefits of belief, and the privileging of individual self-expression, emotion, and experience over institutional concerns.[3] One of the surprising findings of this study is the degree to which the pietist tradition, as expressed in contemporary evangelicalism, the church growth movement, and nondenominational seeker spirituality, is replacing, augmenting, or bolstering the Lutheran tradition. Moreover, the underlying codes and logics of pietism—namely, individualism and experience, consumption and choice, pragmatism and efficiency—increasingly are shaping life inside these congregations and, in so doing, pushing many of the congregations to minimize the historic Lutheran tradition.[4]

The process whereby the ideas, codes, and practices from the pietist tradition become the primary means of organizing Lutheranism or at least influence the ways in which Lutheranism is expressed is what I consider colonization. It entails both the intentional marketing of nondenominational, evangelical, or seeker ideas and practices among religious entrepreneurs and the willing acceptance of these goods and services by church leaders who see them as the cure-all for the mainline decline. Colonization is powerful because it is not simply that Lutheran congregations have replaced all or some of their own worship traditions with the music and theology of evangelicalism to make their congregations appealing to church shoppers, but they also have incorporated the underlying logic and values that animate the pietist tradition. Pietism emphasizes the conversion of individuals and is organized to help individuals grow in their personal relationship with God. The church often is viewed instrumentally as a context that may facilitate conversion and personal faith but is ultimately not necessary since God works through the individual's heart rather than human institutions.[5] In contrast, Lutheranism (part of the confessional tradition) emphasizes, not the momentary decision to convert, but instead the process of becoming a Christian and thus the ongoing life of faith. The tradition, especially the rituals of worship, serves as the vehicle through which individuals are introduced to and sustained in a corporate life of Christian faith.[6]

The imperative to bring about conversion has encouraged a pragmatic orientation toward tradition within pietism: revivalists and congregations have been quick to innovate and experiment in order to save souls. The genius of pietism is that it borrowed and sacralized the more general cultural codes, values, and logic of the market and American individualism in order to sell God and Christianity to nonbelievers. In other words, evangelicalism and the church growth movement speak in the language of business and the shopping mall, of individual choice and experience, and of expedient efficiency and, in so doing, make their version of Protestantism familiar, relevant, and appealing to Americans whose daily lives are organized by the codes of individualism and the marketplace.

Signs of the colonization of Lutheranism are evident most clearly in the central role that nondenominational, evangelical megachurches and church growth experts played in the lives of the study congregations. Part of the new restructuring story from this study is about the ways in which megachurch pastors, church growth experts, and management consultants provide information about the causes of congregational decline, the interests of seekers and the unchurched, and the solutions to the problems facing congregations. These information brokers consistently blame the mainline malaise on an outdated tradition and urge churches to minimize or abandon it in order to survive into the twenty-first century. Much of their literature and many of their seminars are built around cases studies of successful (i.e., growing) churches from across the United States, suggesting that a given recipe for revitalization will work in any geographic or cultural setting. Thus, the experts encourage congregations, whether intentionally or not, to ignore the local context or market and instead rely on profiles of the unchurched, worship models, or outreach strategies that may or may not apply in a local setting.[7] Not only do experts introduce congregations' leaders to a national market of religious ideas and products, but they act as an important bridge between the nondenominational and evangelical worlds and the Lutheran world. They make the unfamiliar world of the megachurch or evangelical congregation familiar to Lutheran churches and legitimate the turn away from the tradition.

At the same time, the process of colonization implies a willingness on the part of some of the natives to welcome the foreigners and their new ideas and to champion these new ideas. Leaders at Zion and Faith were the most active advocates for replacing the Lutheran tradition with the practices, ideas, and language of evangelicalism. Faith regularly hosted training seminars by leading megachurch and church growth experts, both Faith and Zion were members of the Willow Creek Association, and both congregations were at the center of a small network of California Lutheran congregations committed to remaking Lutheranism in the image of evangelical Protestantism. Leaders from five of the other congregations also attended the seminars, used the resources, and followed (some more than others) the organizational models and worship practices advocated by megachurches and church growth experts.

The impact of pietism's instrumental and consumerist approach on the Lutheran tradition also was seen in the creation of marketing teams at two congregations and in the variety of ad hoc study teams or committees convened to examine how adding amplified praise music and video screens for use in worship or the creation of specialized worship services and programs for members of the baby boomer, baby busters, and millennial generations might make the congregation appealing to audiences unfamiliar with the Lutheran tradition.[8] Pietism's influence was also evident in the language that leaders and members commonly used to describe their church's identity and goals. Members at Faith, Zion, St. Peter's, and Good Shepherd routinely spoke about becoming an "outreach-oriented church" and about "reaching people with the Word." They talked about the need to be "relevant" and thus to stop using the language and worship practices of Lutheranism because they prevented non-Lutherans from feeling welcome. In this manner, the adoption of pietism's consumerist approach to member recruitment and worship contributed to the decentering of the Lutheran tradition.

The decentering of the Lutheran tradition was evident, as well, in the diminished authority it exercised or was accorded in the study congregations. During conflicts over change, experience and expertise were the most common types of authority members invoked to defend given positions and resolve differences. Even when the authority of the tradition was marshaled, as in the heresy fight at Good Shepherd, it failed to settle the conflict, however. This was because so few members possessed a working knowledge of the tradition's teachings on scripture and doctrine that they were unable to evaluate the claims made by the traditionalists and because there was little consensus on what was in the tradition. Several congregations (Faith, St. Peter's, and Zion), however, were able to achieve widespread consensus about changing the tradition because many of their members (who worked in high-tech or managerial occupations) shared a belief in the primacy of expert authority and in the power of instrumental reason. They were willing to alter the tradition because credible experts and consultants with records of successfully revitalizing congregations claimed that preserving Lutheranism would not foster growth or help the congregation operate efficiently.

Pietism affected more than organizational and cultural forms. It also was evident in the rationales for change that congregation leaders devised to defend and win support for their attempts to alter the Lutheran tradition and in the attitudes members of these congregations held toward the tradition. Many leaders, citing church growth experts or pointing to the model of growing evangelical churches, claimed that their churches were not growing or would soon go into decline (as aging members died) because they now lived in a religious world where inherited, denominational traditions were alien, inscrutable, and off-putting Relying on the language of consumerism, they argued that the tradition had to be changed in order to make it user-friendly and appealing to non-Lutherans. Many elements of the tradition—its hymnody, its sixteenth-century theological language, its liturgical order, and its ethnic heritage—were seen as expendable or at least as candidates for modification in order to make Lutheranism and their congregations' programs relevant to prospective members, who were believed to be uninterested in following the tradition. Many of the members and some of the clergy in the study congregations were indifferent and even ignorant of the tradition and identified as generically Christian rather than distinctly Lutheran. These antidenominational identities, coupled with an orientation toward growth as the primary goal of the congregations, illustrate the degree to which pietism's pragmatic or utilitarian attitude toward religious traditions came to hold sway in the congregations.

While colonization may have decentered the Lutheran tradition, it also brought benefits to several congregations in the study. It encouraged some of the congregations to seek greater balance between intellect and emotion in worship (and, perhaps unintentionally, helped some of the congregations reconnect to some ethnic Lutheran subtraditions that had a greater emphasis on emotion and experience). It encouraged several congregations to translate the language and ideas of Lutheranism into more familiar idioms of spirituality, self-help, or evangelicalism in order to make participation easier for nonmembers and demonstrate that these churches were not closed to outsiders.

At the same time, colonization is rarely uncontested, and the congregations in the study did not simply become evangelical megachurches or havens for New Age spirituality. Instead, the tradition served as a threshold or a guide for clergy and lay leaders. It set limits on just how far they would go to redefine the congregation's identity and rework its ritual practices, theology, and language of faith. Still, there was no consensus about what actually constituted the core or essential elements of the Lutheran tradition. Each congregation selected certain ritual or theological elements that they wished to preserve and embodied them in different ways. For example, Good Shepherd, Grace, and Resurrection emphasized the Lutheran understanding of God's grace and love of neighbor. Good Shepherd chose to express these commitments through the language of contemporary spirituality and a collective attempt to create an authentic Christian community. They did so to meet the perceived religious needs of their members and of prospective members in the East Bay suburbs who they believed were spiritual but not religious (in the way Roof describes) and who were in search of a place to belong.[9] Grace and Resurrection remained committed to expressing these ideas through the historic Lutheran liturgical order but did so in remarkably different ways. Worship at Grace was highly experimental and reflected members' interests in the arts, non-Western religions, and social justice. Worship at Resurrection reflected members' love of classical sacred music.

St. Peter's and Faith, both more heavily influenced by evangelicalism than some of the other congregations, adhered to the Lutheran theology of sin and justification by grace through faith but stressed different sides of the doctrine. The self-identified conservatives at St. Peter's welcomed sermons that stressed the inherent sinfulness of human beings, God's gift of forgiveness, and God's demand for changed lives in response to this gift amid the narcissistic and affluent culture of Silicon Valley (reflecting evangelical notions of conversion). The baby-boomer majority at Faith resonated with the therapeutic framing of sin that they heard in sermons and at Bible studies, and they welcomed the upbeat message of joy and the assurance of God's love that they heard each week in praise music songs. Emmanuel and Christ, in Oakland, remained committed to the Lutheran understanding of God's radical acceptance of all humans and the central role of the sacraments as the vehicles by which God's acceptance is experienced, but they tried to express Lutheran theology through the musical forms and language of the black church in order to communicate more effectively with African American members and prospective members.

A local essentialism seemed to operate in the study congregations. Leaders of the congregations selected different elements of the tradition to preserve and reinterpret in light of the perceived religious needs and interests of their members and prospective members, the particular culture of the congregation, and the networks of advice and association (e.g., megachurches and church growth experts) in which they were embedded. In addition, the two primary strategies of change—reframing and hybridization—influenced which elements the congregations chose to preserve and how they went about maintaining or altering the tradition. For example, Emmanuel's strong identity as a black Lutheran middleclass church (often articulated in the phrase "we're not a shoutin' church") limited how far its leaders could incorporate worship practices of the historic black church as they tried to contextualize the tradition. Thus, spirituals rather than more upbeat gospel music were favored for inclusion in worship, and they were placed within the standard liturgical order rather than in the three-part evangelical order of worship used by most black churches. Similarly, the ministers included ideas from black liberation theology in their sermons but did not ordinarily use the call-and-response style of preaching more common in other black churches.

The analysis of how the Lutheran tradition has been influenced by the congregations' encounters with evangelicalism, seeker spirituality, and the nondenominational church growth movement suggests that the boundaries between old mainline Protestantism and evangelical Protestantism are weakening. In short, the operative reference groups have shifted away from other Lutheran congregations and the denomination to a variety of evangelical and nondenominational organizations. By adopting the forms of worship and music, organizational models, and consumerist orientation of the broader pietist tradition, these Lutheran congregations also were adopting its underlying theology. It is a theology in which the individual replaces God and church as the primary religious actor and in which growth is elevated to the highest organizational and religious value. Thus, choice, innovation, and experimentation come to be prized as the means to achieve growth while preserving or rediscovering the tradition comes to be devalued because it cannot accomplish the necessary work of conversion. The study also contributes to the account of American religious restructuring by showing how the process of bricolage and choice are negotiated in the congregational setting and constrained by local congregational cultures, religious networks, and the lack of alternatives to the overabundance of resources from the pietist tradition.[10]

Finally, the study confirms other scholars' contention that we have entered a period of de facto nondenominationalism for all but those congregations that intentionally cultivate a denominationally specific identity.[11] Unlike congregations studied in previous analyses, these Lutheran congregations did not exhibit much interest in rediscovering, preserving, or mining the tradition in order to cope with the religious instability and anomie that arise from the dominant culture of religious choice and seeker spirituality.[12] This is somewhat surprising, especially in light of the several national studies that show that the majority of ELCA Lutherans report that being Lutheran or being part of the ELCA is important and that their congregation clearly expresses its Lutheran heritage.[13] Instead, the congregations in this study seemed more interested in downplaying the distinctive markers of Lutheranism to make their congregations appear relevant to members and prospective members thought to be either irreligious and/or uninterested in Lutheranism per se.[14] It may be that the congregations' location at the geographic and cultural periphery of American Lutheranism, and the broader context of irreligiosity and unchurchedness in the San Francisco Bay Area, pushed many of the congregations away from making Lutheranism their primary organizational identity.

At the same time, the changes described in these northern Californian congregations reflect larger shifts in worship and identity among some Lutheran and other mainline Protestant congregations. Recent work drawing on two national surveys, the Faith Communities Today Survey (FACT) and the U.S. Congregational Life Survey, suggest that congregations with significant growth rates (over 25 percent in the past five years) are more likely to adopt the worship practices and identities that mark evangelicalism. "Fast–growing" ELCA and PCUSA (Presbyterian Church, U.S.A.) congregations are more likely to prefer contemporary worship and music than other congregations in their denominations, are more likely to have started a "seeker service," and are more likely to use electronic music and visual projection equipment and have participants raise their hands in praise—all characteristics of worship in the evangelical tradition.[15] Both surveys also suggest that although the majority of Lutherans and Lutheran congregations embrace their historic identities, are strongly tied to the denomination, and do not rely primarily on the worship practices from evangelical or nondenominational seeker churches, a significant minority (roughly 20 percent) have weak denominational identities and weak ties to the traditions and institutional infrastructure of Lutheranism. The largest and fastest-growing congregations tend to be part of this minority.[16] This trend is not limited to Lutherans. Wellman's overview of sectarian evangelical churches and their impact on Protestantism in the Pacific Northwest suggests that, while most mainline congregations remain firmly entrenched in their denomination, some of the large and growing mainline churches, especially in the PCUSA, have clear evangelical identities and are associated more strongly with evangelical church or parachurch bodies than denominational ones.[17] Roozen notes that vital old Protestant congregations appear to have discovered the importance of experiential, subjective, and emotive worship, and he suggests that the example of such worship in successful seeker churches may be one of the causes for this discovery.[18]

In short, while the churches in this study different significantly from the majority of ELCA congregations in matters of denominational identity, worship practices, and theological orientation, they appear to be part of a larger movement within mainline Protestantism to adopt evangelicalism to revitalize their congregations in a context that leaders perceive as indifferent to denominational distinctiveness.

REMAKING RELIGIOUS COMMUNITY

The loss of community or at least a concern about the nature and viability of community has been a perennial theme in sociology. The recent outpouring of research on civic or political community in the United States suggests that Americans' ties and commitment to communities have become attenuated.[19] The communities to which we belong often have a short-term, ad hoc, instrumental, and personalistic character. Local congregations have been seen as one of the few institutions where community with a gemeinschaft character—strong bonds of solidarity, commitment, and mutual obligation—still remains. Religious traditions are seen as the basic building blocks for community. Tradition supplies the stories—founding or heritage narratives, accounts of shared suffering, or stories of exemplary persons of faith—that connect church members to the past, provide members with their religious identities, and serve as the shared ground for interaction. Tradition provides the repertoire of practices (e.g., hymn singing, rituals of baptism and Communion) that build commitment and solidarity among church members and embed them in a shared history and way of life. In this way, congregations may act as "communities of memory" in a social world where "communities of interest" or "communities of limited liability" dominate.[20]

Yet congregations are not automatically constituted as communities of memory. Bellah and his colleagues note how congregations are profoundly influenced by the cultures of individualism and therapy and become "communities of empathic sharing"—communities that provide personal support—rather than communities of memory.[21] Coleman suggests that the commodification of religious goods and services undermines tradition and the ability of congregations to operate as communities of memory:

> Markets are not very good at tradition. Markets thrive on innovation, on the "new"—at their worst, on ephemeral fads and fashions. They itch for new products. There is irony in the fact that, in America, religion—which is inherently traditional and deals with the passing on of values and beliefs across generations—leans so heavily on a mechanism that undermines and disvalues tradition. A community of memory, such as a religious tradition, has to sometimes run counter to market individualism to survive. Its logic as a community of memory and commitment must undermine rather than reinforce market logic.[22]

The move to treat the tradition as an outdated commodity at several of the study congregations eroded one of the foundations for community and pushed the congregations toward the more individualistic and voluntaristic embodiments of community. Even though elements from the pietist tradition were added to or blended with the Lutheran tradition, pietism's emphasis on innovation and newness, and its belief that all traditions should be changed if they do not produce results (i.e., bring in new converts or church members), meant that this alternative tradition could not effectively serve as the new basis for communities of memory at the congregations. Community at the study congregations was grounded primarily in strong personal ties of friendship and support, shared commitments to particular values or congregational goals (e.g., growth and evangelism at Faith, Zion, and St. Peter's; tolerance, inclusivity, and social justice at Grace), and, to a lesser extent, a shared congregational history.

Although members spoke about the particular traditions (tradition with a small *t*) that their congregations held on to—the annual seder meal at Grace; the Labor Day family camp-out for members of Zion; the annual crab feed and quarterly mission trips to Mexico of Good Shepherd—the Lutheran tradition itself was rarely mentioned; and when it was mentioned, members relied on a minimalist and simplistic understanding of the tradition (e.g., this congregation follows Luther's doctrine about grace, or we believe in the centrality of the sacraments). The stories that held the congregations together tended to be personal in nature and, at best, thinly tied to the tradition: stories about how the churched cared for ill members, weathered financial crises, or provided members' children with a moral foundation for adult life. What was largely absent from members' descriptions of their communities was a sense of how the Lutheran liturgy teaches people about the nature of God and God's relationship to humanity, how participation in the rituals of the church connect members with the imagined community known as the "body of Christ," the universal Christian church.

The different strategies of change weakened the ability of the tradition to provide the stories and rituals of commitment for members. For example, reframing at Good Shepherd and Grace made the tradition unrecognizable for some members, while the contextualization strategy used at Christ Lutheran led some members to leave when they no longer could sing the old familiar hymns. The creation of services based on contemporary or praise music at Faith, Zion, and Good Shepherd created separate congregations within each. Members who worshiped at different worship services rarely, if ever, interacted with one another. In this way, the congregations became more like communities of interest than communities of memory, with a strong emphasis on options and choice. In addition, the incorporation of the evangelical music, language, and theology (with its emphasis on the personal benefits of faith) or a variety of spiritual practices for religious seekers (with its emphasis on helping individuals gain access to or experience the sacred) allowed some members of the congregations to understand the church as a center for personal religious exploration rather than as a community of shared history, obligation, and accountability.

Yet the erosion of tradition as the basis for community was not the only story in this study. There were small pockets of traditionalists in several of the congregations who were bound together by Lutheran hymns and liturgy, its theology of grace, and even its ethnic heritage. Similarly, there were moments when the tradition was remembered and embodied and thus united members and connected them to the larger history of Lutheranism: baptisms at Grace; the confession and forgiveness of sins at Resurrection; new-member classes at St. Peter's; the abrupt shift from worship in the black church tradition to the rite of Communion at Emmanuel. Thus, the tradition was marshaled, in largely unconscious or unintended ways, to resist the pressures of consumerism and individualism that always threatened to push the congregations toward becoming communities of individuals bound only by personal history or instrumental goals.

RETHINKING RELIGIOUS AND CULTURAL CHANGE

The third story this study has told is about the nature of religious and, more broadly, cultural change. Religious traditions, like many other cultural objects, are not static but are constantly in flux. Most explanations of religious change start from the premise that rituals, theologies, or congregational cultures, like other forms of culture, are relatively stable and do not change until social structures or cultures outside the religious organization change. This is the fundamental premise of Swidler's classic article on culture, action, and change: ideologies and cultural repertoires do not change until the social world becomes unstable, and when this happens individuals and groups are compelled to rework their cultural repertoires or create new ideologies because the "unsettled times" or social crises have rendered the old meanings and practices obsolete.[23] This theoretical position informs studies of religious traditions, religious conflict, and congregational change.[24] While external social forces influence religious change, they do not necessarily catalyze change as directly as the literature suggests.

Traditions change in part because larger social forces outside the tradition impinge on our ways of thinking and acting outside the doors of the church. For example, the movement for women's equality, the gains of women in the workforce, and the broad politicization of women in the United States have pushed congregations to open up new leadership roles for women. However, changes in attitudes and roles for women in American society did not have the same effect on all congregations. Whether or not a denomination moved to ordain women depended on the nature of the networks and reference groups to which a denomination belongs. Chaves found that denominations took cues from other denominations that they perceived as sharing similar orientations to worship, scripture, and values and with whom they were connected via ecumenical relationships. Early adopters in liberal and mainline environments created pressures to follow suit and ordain women, while denominations connected by commitments to nonsacramentalism and biblical inerrancy chose not to ordain women. His work suggests that religious organizations must interpret the external context as important to their ongoing life if it is to become a catalyst for change.[25]

More relevant to this study has been a series of changes in the wider religious environment of American Protestantism: the growing popularity of less ceremonial, more enthusiastic worship styles from the pietist tradition, the widespread adoption of the value of choice and the anti-institutional, individualistic language of faith used within evangelicalism and seeker spirituality, and the domination of megachurches and the church growth movement within the Protestant market for religious goods and services. Religious entrepreneurs claim that the religious context of America has fundamentally changed and therefore urge congregations to respond to these shifts or face organizational decline. Yet changes in the religious context do not automatically lead congregations to alter their tradition. Contexts are important primarily for setting the preconditions or providing opportunities for change by making available new worship forms, theological ideas, and languages or organizational models and by discrediting those associated with the historic Lutheran tradition as outdated or inefficient. But contexts must be interpreted. Congregations must decide collectively that the new context is relevant and thus requires some response. In chapter 3, I showed how congregations interpreted the context in different ways, depending on the nature and depth of their embeddedness in particular congregational-problems arenas (e.g., evangelical and church growth networks), congregations' histories and cultures, and leaders' perceptions of the importance of the Lutheran tradition to members. Leaders at seven of the nine congregations constructed causal stories to make sense of the new religious context and mark it as significant for their churches, and these stories guided how they adopted or adapted the new worship forms, rituals, and languages to the Lutheran tradition.

The nature of embeddedness in a congregational-problems arena also helps us account for the timing of change. The various changes in the American religious landscape did not suddenly delegitimate the Lutheran tradition and thus cause a crisis of meaning and membership for the congregations. Clergy and lay leaders of the congregations began to notice and become concerned about the tradition the more they got involved in evangelical, church growth, or interfaith and ecumenical organizations, read the latest book about church growth, or attended a seminar on church marketing or spirituality. Not surprisingly, the congregations least enmeshed in these networks were the least likely to change the tradition (e.g., St. Luke's). In addition, the power dynamics within the congregations influenced the onset of change. Six of the nine congregations had new clergy (most arriving or taking on senior-pastor roles within three years of the study) who were eager to establish themselves and set their congregations on a new course. Clergy at most of these congregations recruited like-minded lay members into positions of formal and informal leadership positions. These new lay leaders tended to replace the old guard (often lifelong Lutherans and older members) and thus created a powerful base of support for changing the tradition.

As the congregations' leaders began to suspect that the many aspects of the Lutheran tradition were not important or salient to many members, they faced a new problem: what would hold the congregation together? Interpersonal relationships and those regular practices of fellowship that constitute much of a congregation's life (e.g., shared meals, belonging to a support group) may not be adequate, given the highly transient nature of church membership (recall that one-third of Resurrection's membership routinely changes every two to three years and that church switching in the United States is quite common) and the inability of congregational fellowship to provide a common theological language and worldview. Eliasoph and Lichterman note that groups rely on collective representations from the larger culture to bolster shared ground for meaningful interaction.[26] If the tradition once constituted one of the bases that make interaction meaningful and solidarity possible but no longer does this, then leaders of congregations may look to alternative traditions and the broader religious culture to find the values, languages, and practices to make the tradition fulfill this collective task or, failing that, to create a new tradition. The strategies of reframing and hybridization were attempts to make the tradition a more powerful source of meaning and solidarity in the congregations. Adopting the language and music of evangelicalism at Faith and Zion, for example, remade worship and encouraged longtime Lutherans to hear the tradition in new ways. The praise music services also served as the new shared culture for members of the congregations.

Thus, the approach to change I develop places less causal emphasis on external events and market forces and places more emphasis on the internal processes of meaning making in which external religious forces come to be understood as significant for the congregations and demanding an organizational response. In addition to offering a new window into religious and cultural change, the study also suggests an alternative way of conceptualizing the process of change. Extant explanations of the process of change often look at the internal dynamics of organizations that fuel change, and they tend to emphasize its incremental or evolutionary nature. While internal dynamics were important for understanding change at the study congregations, the congregations did not conform neatly to the incremental model. For example, Bass argues that religious traditions change as church members engage in a running argument or conversation about what constitutes the tradition, which elements should be preserved, which should be altered, and which should be abandoned, and how the congregation should accomplish these tasks.[27] Yet the congregations in this study exhibited little interest in arguing about the tradition (except Good Shepherd). More often than not, congregation leaders decided that the tradition was largely irrelevant and thus set off unimpeded in search of new traditions to graft onto Lutheranism (the hybridization model) or ways to translate the tradition into the current religious lingua franca and thus make the tradition relatively invisible in the congregations' daily lives (the reframing model).

Chaves offers an incremental explanation for changes in the worship repertoires within American Protestant congregations. He argues that new styles of worship are introduced by new religious entrepreneurs seeking to define themselves as different but not too different from other congregations within an established religious field. In other words, they need to cultivate differentiation and legitimation. As a result, new worship styles build on existing practices and introduce modest variations. Innovation signals to prospective members or attendees that the congregation has something new to offer, while continuity with older traditions lets prospective members know that they will find something familiar and meaningful at worship on Sunday morning. Too radical a change in worship elements means that prospective members might not be able to recognize or participate in worship.[28]

Although this process of change was evident in several of the study congregations (e.g., in the way that Zion and Faith placed evangelical praise music within the Lutheran order of worship), there was also a more radical process of change. The congregations borrowed music, ritual forms, and languages, not from nearby traditions such as Episcopalianism or Roman Catholicism, but from more distant traditions such as evangelicalism or Buddhism—traditions that did not share the same understanding of the sacramental nature of worship, the same theological worldview, or the same biblical hermeneutic. This type of borrowing represents a more radical type of change that was made possible by the loose coupling of congregations to the Lutheran tradition. This loose coupling existed at both the cultural and the organizational levels. First, because many of the congregations' members possessed limited knowledge or appreciation of the tradition and many had little interest in preserving the tradition in general, the congregations faced limited pressure to slowly modify the tradition. Instead, their loose ties to the tradition freed them to proceed more rapidly and radically. Apart from the minorities of traditionalists at Zion, Faith, and Good Shepherd, few members at these three congregations cared or fully realized that the tradition was being altered. Similarly, at the other congregations, as long as a few core aspects of the tradition were preserved (e.g., the emphasis on the sacraments at Grace, Emmanuel, and Resurrection), most members welcomed significant alterations to the tradition. Second, most of the congregations did not have strong ties to the local synod or the national church. They did not turn to these bodies for resources, nor did they express a sense that they were accountable to the synod or ELCA except to meet the basic requirements of administering the sacraments. Such loose ties freed up the congregations to experiment more daringly.

I also argued in chapters 4 and 5 that the process of change was shaped by the interaction of members and leaders. Change is highly experimental and once initiated can take on a life of its own. At Good Shepherd, for example, too many changes to worship created a firestorm of protest as it became unrecognizable to some of the older members. When older members demanded a return to the old way of worship, withheld their tithes, and mobilized protest, the church's leaders acquiesced to their demands. At Resurrection, a period of intense study of church growth advice literature and the congregation's ongoing conversations about the church's future helped the congregation identify its core commitments to Lutheran worship and theology. As a result, the congregation buffered worship from significant change but were willing to try some of the marketing and evangelism strategies advanced by church growth experts. At Christ Lutheran, the congregation struggled to balance two goals. They wanted to modify the tradition to make it more accessible and meaningful to the multiracial and multiethnic population that they hoped to bring into the church. At the same time, they saw the need to keep the tradition alive to the majority of members who were lifelong Lutherans. The congregation tried on a variety of worship styles, largely borrowing from the black church tradition. Some, like the Sunday evening gospel service, failed quickly. Others met quiet resistance or grudging acceptance (e.g., the call-and-response style of preaching). By the end of the field period, Christ still had not made any of the changes to the tradition permanent.

The example of Christ Lutheran is paradigmatic of the open-ended nature of change. There was no return to order and stability at the congregations once the tradition had been altered or created anew. Each congregation struggled to varying degrees with the task of reinstitutionalizing the new version of its operative tradition. In a sense, scholars of tradition are correct in claiming that it is never a finished product, but in the case at hand, the tradition at several of the congregations had been so radically changed that it was difficult to discern how the emergent traditions remain tied to Lutheranism. In this way, the process of changing the tradition is not so much an ongoing conversation as a new conversation with different conversation partners.

Perhaps the account of change I have offered is a riff on an older story about ongoing tension between orthodoxy and heterodoxy.[29] It is not the more common story of the forces of orthodoxy crushing the forces of a nascent heterodoxy (this was the story of nineteenth-century American Lutheranism). Rather, it is a story of how several new traditions were grounded in the older, orthodox tradition of Lutheranism but significantly departed from it in terms of liturgical form and theological content. At some congregations, orthodoxy and heterodoxy exist side by side, while at others heterodoxy (in the form of evangelicalized Lutheranism or the fusion of spirituality, Buddhism, and Protestantism) engulfs orthodoxy.

The twist in the story is that the expected outcome of the challenging heterodoxy becoming the new orthodoxy has not come to pass. That is, it appears that none of the new versions of the Lutheran tradition will become the dominant tradition within the synod or national church. The lack of consensus within and between the congregations about the content of the tradition and the expressed doubts about the desirability of maintaining an overarching orthodox Lutheran tradition may make it difficult to reestablish orthodoxy within American Lutheranism. Instead, Lutheranism may be headed toward a state of balkanization in which multiple versions of the tradition have limited and localized authority. And this might be a good thing for congregations and the denomination as a whole. By freeing themselves from an overly tight adherence to and preservation of one tradition, congregations may gain the flexibility to tailor the tradition to fit the religious interests and needs of people within particular markets. In doing so, they may be able to expand the boundaries of the tradition so that Lutheranism can remain relevant and competitive in an increasingly nondenominational religious world.

Appendix

A NOTE ON
DATA AND METHODS

I was hired in the fall of 1999 by Pacific Lutheran Theological Seminary to direct a new Lilly Endowment grant that was intended, in part, to fund a study of Lutheran congregations in the western United States. Because the grant did not provide funding for a survey of congregations across the West or significant travel to study congregations outside the San Francisco Bay Area, where the seminary is located, I decided to conduct an ethnographic study. I also came to this decision after my initial review of the literature. There is a large body of research describing and explaining the decline of mainline Protestant denominations in the United States, but few sources provide a detailed look at how this restructuring affects local congregations or explain how some congregations are able to thrive in a region of the country that has been relatively inhospitable to mainline Protestantism.

My colleagues at the seminary were very interested to learn how some Lutheran congregations became or remained vital in some way or another (i.e., those that were growing, serving some special niche, or trying to be Lutheran in new ways) and did not follow the typical pattern of stagnation and decline that characterized many Lutheran congregations in the West. Dr. Timothy Lull, the seminary's president, described two types of Lutheranism in the western United States and urged me to study congregations that were trying to move beyond them. The first type is composed of congregations that try to reproduce an ideal/typical version of midwestern Lutheranism that was lost during the move from the Great Plains to California. In practice, this usually is an attempt to preserve a particular version of the Lutheran tradition that was prominent in the one period of magical growth for the denomination in California following World War II. The other type of Lutheranism has abandoned all efforts to preserve the Lutheran tradition and identity in light of the rise of nondenominationalism and rampant church switching. This type operates on the assumption that most people in the West are unfamiliar with and uninterested in the Lutheran tradition, and thus these congregations jettison their distinctively Lutheran identity and practices. To make religion relevant to these people (and make their churches grow), they adopt the worship styles, theologies, and resources from successful churches of any stripe—in effect, reducing Lutheranism to a form of pietistic or revivalistic Protestantism that characterizes growing churches. Dr. Lull urged me to try to explain how some congregations were developing a third type of Lutheranism and thus a way out of the restorationist or reductionist traps.

Given the limitations and the complex nature of the question, I decided that an ethnographic study of a small number of congregations within the region would be the most feasible method for the project. After visiting congregations during my first six months and talking with clergy in the area and synodical officials, I narrowed my pool of congregations to those that area experts considered vital, growing, or innovative congregations or those that served a particular niche (such as gay/lesbian or racial and ethnic populations that historically have not been part of the Lutheran church). I selected nine of these allegedly vital congregations to study in depth. Although I sampled on the dependent variable, a number of other criteria guided my selection: geographic location, size, racial or ethnic composition, congregational culture, and political orientation. I wanted the congregations to reflect the diversity of Lutheran congregations in the region and to capitalize on some of the unique features of their location in the Bay Area, such as the gay/lesbian issue and the large high-tech industry in the Silicon Valley.

Ultimately, I selected three congregations in each of three geographic regions: Oakland, to represent urban and more racially or ethnically diverse congregations; the East Bay suburbs, to represent suburban, large, more socially and politically conservative, and primarily Anglo congregations; and Silicon Valley, to represent the unique high-tech corridor and congregations seeking to serve an ethnically and religiously pluralistic area in which work and rapid population shifts dominate the landscape. The congregations include three with over a thousand members (large for California Lutheranism), three medium-sized congregations (membership between three hundred and one thousand), and three small congregations (active membership under three hundred, with an average worship attendance of between thirty-five and ninety-five); one African American congregation and one mixed-race congregation; five liberal to moderate congregations, including two that officially welcomed gay, lesbian, bisexual, and transgendered persons, and four socially and politically conservative congregations.

From September 2000 through June 2003 I studied the nine congregations. I spent five to six months in each doing participant observation and interviewing clergy and lay leaders. I attended worship services, council meetings, Bible studies, new-member classes, and social events. In several congregations I taught classes on Sunday mornings, helped committees gather information from members about programs or ministries, listened to weary council members and clergy try to make sense of the conflict that accompanies organizational change, and even assisted in worship on occasion. After spending a month or two in a congregation, I conducted in-depth interviews with clergy and members who were among the most active in each congregation.[1] I generated lists of informed members through snowball sampling, cultivating one or two key informants in each congregation (i.e., the person who seems to know everyone and everything at a church), and identifying prospective respondents as I observed worship, classes, and meetings. I began by interviewing the clergy and council members in each congregation and asked them to identify members who could help me tell the congregation's story.

On average, I interviewed 20 members per congregation, with a high of 28 in the largest congregation and a low of 15 in the smallest. I used a semistructured format for the clergy interviews and a more structured one for the interviews with members (see the Interview Guide at the end of this appendix). All the lay members were asked the same set of core questions, and then I developed a set of specific questions tailored to each congregation's context and efforts at innovation and change. I interviewed 197 individuals, singly or in pairs, and an additional 56 people in eight focus groups at three of the congregations.

I made the congregation the focus of the interviews. I asked lay members to reflect on their experiences with worship and the tradition in the congregation, to reflect on the strengths and weakness of the church, to tell me about the importance and salience of the Lutheran tradition and identity for the church and themselves, and to relate how and why the congregation has changed. Along the way, my theoretical interest in the process of cultural change and the ways in which the tradition was being transformed came into focus as I participated in the lives of these nine churches and listened to the congregational stories of over two hundred members. I have used pseudonyms for the congregations, clergy, and members to protect identities, and this became even more important after several congregations experienced conflict during the field period.

THE INTERVIEW GUIDE

The following questions served as the basis for structured interviews with the lay leaders at all nine congregations. I scripted many of the questions to fit the language or issues of a given congregation. In addition, I developed a unique set of questions for each congregation based on their unique histories and cultures, as well as questions about topics the church councils of each congregation asked me to investigate. Usually these congregation-specific questions had to do with specific programs on which leaders wanted feedback, current and past conflicts, or past changes in worship, theology, or leadership. Interviews with clergy were less structured and focused on the congregation's relationship to the tradition, intentional efforts to alter the tradition, members' responses to such changes, and the congregation's mission.

I. General Questions about the Membership and Identity of the Congregation

How long have you been a member at . . . ?
How did you come to join . . . ?

What was it about the congregation that made you want to join?

Are these the things that keep you here, or are there other reasons why you are still a member? Have you thought about leaving? Why and what prevented you from leaving?

Was there ever a period of time when you stopped going to church or stopped practicing the religion in which you were raised? When was this? What was going on in your life at the time? Was leaving the church a conscious decision or something that just happened by itself? What were the reasons behind your decision? What led you back to church?

Is it important for you that this is a Lutheran congregation?

What do you like or appreciate about being Lutheran?

Why does/doesn't being Lutheran matter very much to you?

Describe the congregation to me as if I'm a first-time visitor.

In what ways has the congregation changed since you've been a member?

What makes you proud of this congregation?

What kinds of events or activities bring the church together? What kinds of events or activities create problems for the church?

How does this congregation take care of its members?

Would you say this congregation is liberal, conservative, or moderate? What do you think these words/labels mean to you and to people in the congregation?

Is the congregation involved in local politics or civic issues like education, homelessness, poverty, crime? National- or international-level issues? [Probe: Why or why not? What prevents the congregation from getting involved?]

II. Questions about Congregational Change

Please tell me about the vision of this church: What is it? Where is this church headed? [Refer to vision or mission documents if applicable.]

How has this vision developed?

What percentage of members understand and have ownership of this vision?

Why do you think some understand and buy it and others don't?

What do you think are the most important challenges and the best opportunities that will move the congregation toward achieving the vision?

Is there anything you wish the congregation did differently or is there something you'd like to change about the congregation?

How does this congregation handle change? Why do you think being in transition and developing a new vision and ministries haven't caused a lot of conflict and unrest in the congregation?

Have there been other serious disagreements or even conflicts in the church in the past five or ten years? When was the last conflict? What was it about? How was it resolved? Is this issue[s] still important or alive for members?

What makes this congregation different from other Lutheran churches? From other churches in [name of city or suburb]?

III. Questions about Individual's Worship, Faith, and Fellowship Experiences

Worship

What do you like best about worship at . . . ? What do you like least? Why?

What do you expect to hear, see, feel when you attend church?

Is there a common message you hear in the sermons at . . . ?

Religion and Spirituality

Do you think you need to go to church to be a Christian?

Do you consider yourself a spiritual person?

What does "spiritual" mean for you? Does being a member at . . . help you grow or develop spiritually? What kinds of things do you do to be spiritual?

Faith and Life and the Centrality of the Congregation in Respondent's Life

What are the two or three most important concerns or worries in your life right now?

In what ways does your faith help you address these concerns? [Probe: If not helpful, ask why not. Does the congregation help you integrate faith and life? In what ways?]

Do you think your personal faith is different because you live in the Bay Area?

Does your congregation help you cope with any of the unique challenges or dilemmas of being a Christian in the Bay Area? [Probes: unemployment, housing costs, recreation, unchurched or irreligious nature of the general population]

Do you think the congregation is influenced by its location in the Bay Area?

How many of your friends are from this congregation? [Probe: more than one-half, between one-fourth and one-half, less than one-fourth] Have you always had this many/this few friends from church? Why do you think that is?

What does this congregation offer or provide you that you can't get from any other organization, group of friends, or activities?

If you miss church on a Sunday, what are the usual reasons?

Activities and Leadership Roles

What offices or positions have you held?

What activities have you been involved with as a member? In what ways have these activities helped you make friends in the church or feel more connected to the community?

Individual Background/Identity

What is your level of education?

What is your age?

What is/was your occupation(s)?

How long have you lived in California? [Probe: If moved here as an adult: Where did you live before California?]

Anything else you'd like to tell me about?

NOTES

Chapter One

1. All names of congregations „and individuals are pseudonyms.
2. See Clifford Geertz, "Deep Play: Notes on the Balinese Cockfight," in *The Interpretation of Cultures,* by Clifford Geertz (New York: Basic Books, 1973), 412–53; Catherine Bell, *Ritual: Perspectives and Dimensions* (New York: Oxford University Press, 1997), 62–68.
3. Megachurches are congregations whose average weekly worship attendance is at least two thousand persons. But size alone does not define megachurches. They have a set of organizational characteristics that distinguish them from most mainline congregations. Megachurches tend to be loosely tied to denominations or are intentionally nondenominational (only 11 percent of megachurches are part of a mainline Protestant denomination). They self-identify as evangelical, charismatic, or Pentecostal and are theologically conservative. On megachurches see Scott Thumma, "Exploring the Megachurch Phenomena: Their Characteristics and Cultural Context," Hartford Institute for Religion Research, 2003, http://hirr.hartsem.edu/bookshelf/thumma_article2.html (accessed May 16, 2006); Scott Thumma and Jim Peterson, "Goliaths in Our Midst: Megachurches in the ELCA," in *Lutherans Today: American Lutheran Identity in the 21st Century,* ed. Richard Cimino (Grand Rapids, MI: Eerdmans, 2003), 102–24; Kimon Howland Sargeant, *Seeker Churches: Promoting Traditional Religion in a Non-traditional Way* (New Brunswick, NJ: Rutgers University Press, 2000); Stuart M. Hoover, "The Cross at Willow Creek: Seeker Religion and the Contemporary Marketplace," in *Religion and Popular Culture in America,* ed. Bruce David Forbes and Jeffrey H. Mahan (Berkeley and Los Angeles: University of California Press, 2000), 145–60.
4. Seeker spirituality refers to the search to find or connect with God or the sacred as part of a broader attempt to develop the self and make life meaningful. Such searches may take place within the walls of a church but are not confined to church. Seekers often combine elements from a variety of traditions, both Christian and non-Christian. This form of spirituality emerged in the 1970s with the baby boom generation and

has been institutionalized in many congregations, both mainline and evangelical. On seeker spirituality, see Robert Wuthnow, *After Heaven* (Berkeley and Los Angeles: University of California Press, 1998); Wade Clark Roof, *Spiritual Marketplace* (Princeton: Princeton University Press, 1999); Wade Clark Roof, *A Generation of Seekers* (San Francisco: HarperCollins, 1993).

5. On the concept of "unsettled times," see Ann Swidler, "Culture in Action: Symbols and Strategies," *American Sociological Review* 51 (1986): 273–86.

6. Robert N. Bellah, Richard Madsen, William M. Sullivan, Ann Swidler, and Steven M. Tipton, *Habits of the Heart*, 1st California pbk. ed. (Berkeley and Los Angeles: University of California Press, 1996); Wuthnow, *After Heaven*; Wade Clark Roof, *Spiritual Marketplace* (Princeton: Princeton University Press, 1999); Nancy L. Eiesland, *A Particular Place: Urban Restructuring and Religious Ecology in a Southern Suburb* (New Brunswick, NJ: Rutgers University Press, 2000); Michele Dillon, *Catholic Identity* (New York: Cambridge University Press, 1999); Lynn Davidman, *Tradition in a Rootless World* (New Brunswick, NJ: Rutgers University Press, 1991).

7. Robert Wuthnow, *The Restructuring of American Religion* (Princeton: Princeton University Press, 1988); Wade Clark Roof and William McKinney, *American Mainline Religion* (New Brunswick, NJ: Rutgers University Press, 1987); David A. Roozen and C. Kirk Hadaway, eds., *Church and Denominational Growth* (Nashville: Abingdon Press, 1993); Roof, *Generation of Seekers*; Roof, *Spiritual Marketplace*; Wuthnow, *After Heaven*.

8. See E. Cliford Nelson, ed., *The Lutherans in North America*, rev. ed. (Philadelphia: Fortress Press, 1980), 453–541.

9. C. Kirk Hadaway and Pennly Long Marler, "All in the Family: Religious Mobility in America," *Review of Religious Research* 35, no. 2 (1993): 97–117.

10. Roof, *Generation of Seekers*; Roof, *Spiritual Marketplace*; Wuthnow, *After Heaven*.

11. See Roof, *Spiritual Marketplace*; Penny Edgel Becker, "Making Inclusive Communities: Congregations and the 'Problem of Race,'" *Social Problems* 45 (1998): 451–72.

12. Nancy Ammerman, *Pillars of Faith: American Congregations and Their Partners* (Berkeley and Los Angeles: University of California Press, 2005), 422; see also ibid., 206–53. Ammerman shows how denominational identities and the preservation of tradition are most precarious among mainline Protestant congregations, especially those that do not use denominational educational curricula, hymnals, and/or orders of worship.

13. Thumma, "Exploring the Megachurch Phenomena," 22–24; Sargeant, *Seeker Churches*, 22.

14. See Donald E. Miller, *Reinventing American Protestantism: Christianity in the New Millennium* (Berkeley and Los Angeles: University of California Press, 1997); Darryl G. Hart, *The Lost Soul of American Protestantism* (Oxford: Rowman and Littlefield Publishers, 2002); Thumma, "Exploring the Megachurch Phenomena"; and Sargeant, *Seeker Churches*.

15. Donald E. Miller, *Reinventing American Protestantism*.

16. For example, Eiseland, *Particular Place*; and Nancy Ammerman, *Congregation and Community* (New Brunswick, NJ: Rutgers University Press, 1997), focus on local

religious ecologies and how congregations adapt as the ecology or environment changes. One exception is Warner's exemplary study of one congregation in Mendocino, California: R. Stephen Warner, *New Wine in Old Wineskins: Evangelicals and Liberals in a Small-Town Church* (Berkeley and Los Angeles: University of California Press, 1988).

17. Roof, *Generation of Seekers*; Roof, *Spiritual Marketplace*; Roof and McKinney, *American Mainline Religion*; Dean R. Hoge, Benton Johnson, and Donald A. Luidens, *Vanishing Boundaries: The Religion of Mainline Protestant Baby Boomers* (Louisville, KY: Westminster/John Knox Press, 1994).

18. Dorothy C. Bass, "Congregations and the Bearing of Tradition," in *American Congregations*, vol. 2, ed. James P. Wind and James W. Lewis (Chicago: University of Chicago Press, 1994), 172.

19. This is not an exhaustive review of the three theoretical approaches. I discuss exemplary studies within each school of thought. Secularization theory is the fourth major explanation of religious change; however, I am excluding it from this study because the nine congregations that I investigated show little evidence of becoming less religious. While secular forces such as marketing practices influence the strategies of change, the overall tendency in these congregations is to become more devout Christian communities.

20. Roof, *Spiritual Marketplace*, 26–29, 191–203.

21. Becker, "Making Inclusive Communities"; Penny Edgel Becker, *Congregations in Conflict* (London and New York: Cambridge University Press, 1999).

22. At least two congregations were faced with dwindling membership as the neighborhood shifted from predominantly white to predominantly African American. The congregations tried to become more racially inclusive by changing their worship practices and power structures.

23. See Becker, *Congregations in Conflict*, 180–94.

24. However, four of the congregations that Becker studied followed multiple cultural models, and in those cases the models could not contain the conflict. The conflicts in these churches either went unresolved or led to the exit of large groups of members.

25. Robert Wuthnow, *Meaning and Moral Order: Explorations in Cultural Analysis* (Berkeley and Los Angeles: University of California Press, 1987); Ammermann, *Congregation and Community*. Eiesland's study of religious change in an exurban area outside Atlanta, Georgia, also falls into the ecological camp. She contends that "change happens less through adaptation and more by organizational replacement," although her rich cases studies provide support for adaptation as well (*Particular Place*, 14).

26. Chaves's neoinstitutionalist account of the shift to embrace women's ordination within American Protestantism tests both internal and external catalysts and finds that the internal denominational processes are much weaker than the external forces pushing toward women's ordination. See Mark Chaves, "Ordaining Women and Organizational Innovation," *American Journal of Sociology* 101 (1997): 840–73.

27. Ammermann, *Congregation and Community*, 215–17.

28. Church-sect theory rests on the premise that religious organizations exist in some degree of tension with their sociocultural environments. Sects exist at a relatively high

rate of tension with society, while churches exist at a low rate of tension. Historically, sects tend to become churches or churchlike and are often a source of religious innovation and change. See Benton Johnson, "On Church and Sect," *American Sociological Review* 28 (1963): 539–49; Roger Finke and Rodney Stark, *The Churching of America, 1776–1990: Winners and Losers in Our Religious Economy* (New Brunswick, NJ: Rutgers University Press, 1992); Roger Finke and Rodney Stark, "The New Holy Clubs: Testing Church-to-Sect Propositions," *Sociology of Religion* 62 (2001): 175–89.

29. See Roger Finke, "The Consequences of Religious Competition: Supply-Side Explanations for Religious Change," in *Rational Choice Theory and Religion: Summary and Assessment,* ed. Lawrence R. Young (New Brunswick, NJ: Rutgers University Press, 1997), 45–64; Finke and Stark, *Churching of America.*

30. On the concept of the "negotiated order," see Gary Alan Fine, "Negotiated Orders and Organizational Cultures," *Annual Review of Sociology* 10 (1984): 239–62.

31. Swidler, "Culture in Action."

32. Paul Ingram and Karen Clay, "The Choice-within-Constraints New Institutionalism and Implications for Sociology," *Annual Review of Sociology* 26 (2000): 540. See also Matthew S. Kraatz and Edward J. Zajac, "Exploring the Limits of the New Institutionalism: The Causes and Consequences of Illegitimate Organizational Change," *American Sociological Review* 61 (1996): 812–36; Paul J. DiMaggio and Walter W. Powell, "The Iron Cage Revisited: Institutional Isomorphism and Collective Rationality," in *The New Institutionalism in Organizational Analysis,* ed. Walter W. Powell and Paul S. DiMaggio (Chicago: University of Chicago Press, 1991), 63–82.

33. Neil Fligstein, "The Structural Transformation of American Industry: An Institutional Account of the Causes of Diversification in the Largest Firms, 1919–1979," in *The New Institutionalism in Organizational Analysis,* ed. Walter W. Powell and Paul S. DiMaggio (Chicago: University of Chicago Press, 1991), 311–36.

34. Emerson and Kim also emphasize internal sources of change in their study of multiracial congregations. In particular, they find that a congregation's mission ("its theological, cultural, and/or symbolic orientation") and resources were critical determinants of whether or not a congregation attempted to become multiracial. At the same time, external shifts in the population often were the catalysts for congregational change. See Michael O. Emerson and Karen Chai Kim, "Multiracial Congregations: An Analysis of Their Development and a Typology," *Journal for the Scientific Study of Religion* 42 (2003): 220.

35. Roof, *Spiritual Marketplace,* 167–71; Becker, "Making Inclusive Communities."

36. On "codes," see Ann Swidler, *Talk of Love* (Chicago: University of Chicago Press, 2001), 162–76.

37. See Fine, "Negotiated Orders and Organizational Cultures," 241.

38. John B. Thompson, "Tradition and the Self in a Mediated World," in *Detraditionalization,* ed. Paul Heelas, Scott Lash, and Paul Morris (Cambridge, MA: Blackwell, 1996), 92.

39. Jackson W. Carroll, *Mainline to the Future: Congregations for the 21st Century* (Louisville, KY: Westminster John Knox Press, 2000), 12–13.

40. Carroll, *Mainline to the Future;* Roof, *Spiritual Marketplace.*

41. Bellah et al., *Habits of the Heart*, 152–55. See also Bass, "Congregations and the Bearing of Tradition."

42. Although pietism's contemporary incarnation in evangelicalism has a strong intellectual infrastructure in its network of colleges, seminaries, and think tanks, in practice, especially in terms of worship, it has emphasized emotion and practical knowledge (e.g., how the Bible can help solve personal dilemmas). On pietism and evangelicalism, see Nathan O. Hatch, "The Appeal of American Evangelicalism," in *The Appeal of American Evangelicalism*, Concordia Seminary Monograph Series, Symposium Papers (St. Louis: Concordia Seminary, 1993), 9–20; Mark A. Shibley, "Contemporary Evangelicals: Born-Again and World Affirming," *Annals of the American Academy of the Political and Social Sciences* 558 (1998): 67–87; Robert Wuthnow, *Communities of Discourse: Ideology and Social Structure in the Reformation, the Enlightenment, and European Socialism* (Cambridge, MA: Harvard University Press, 1989), 173–81, 191–97; Donald E. Miller, *Reinventing American Protestantism;* Sargeant, *Seeker Churches.*

43. Hart, *Lost Soul,* 31. Historically there has been a strain of pietism within American Lutheranism. Although it shared some of the same features of American revivalism, it was more strongly influenced by European pietism. Lutheran pietism minimized the primacy of doctrine and an intellectualized faith and emphasized a more affective faith in which the experience of a heartfelt conversion pushed individuals toward ethical action. It shared many features of nineteenth-century revivalism but avoided the radical individualism and nondogmatic, anticlerical, and antichurch positions of revivalism. One of the founders of American Lutheranism and the pietistic strain in the United States, Henry Muhlenberg, "embraced revivalism and spoke positively of its benefits but insisted that it be kept within a churchly or liturgical framework. He believed in the expression of emotion, as long as it was not pursued as an end in itself and good order was maintained" (Paul P. Kuenning, *The Rise and Fall of American Lutheran Pietism: The Rejection of an Activist Heritage* [Macon, GA: Mercer University Press, 1988], 38). See also Mark A. Noll, "The Lutheran Difference," *First Things* 20 (February 1992): 31–40; Robert F. Scholz, "Henry Melchior Muhlenberg's Relation to the Ongoing Pietist Tradition," in *Lutheranism and Pietism: Essays and Reports,* vol. 14, ed. Aug R. Seulflow (St. Louis: Lutheran Historical Conference, 1992), 40–66; L. DeAnne Lagerquist, *The Lutherans* (Westport, CT: Greenwood Press, 1999), 65–88.

44. Hart places Lutheranism, Anglicanism, Presbyterianism, and the Reformed churches in the confessionalism camp due to their shared commitment to creeds and doctrines, liturgical forms of worship, and an understanding of the Christian life as fundamentally about "participation in the forms and rites of the church as opposed to the convert's solitary quest to lead an earnest moral life" (*Lost Soul,* 47).

45. Ibid., 50.

46. The terms "communities of memory" and "communities of interest" come from Bellah et al., *Habits of the Heart.* The former refers to communities that are "constituted by their past" by retelling their stories or passing along their inherited traditions (153). The latter refers to a thinner version of community in which "self-interested individuals join together to maximize individual good" (134). The authors of that seminal

work argue that churches have been affected by the society-wide shift from communities of memory to communities of interest (239).

47. The argument about the causal power of cultural forms and the interdependence of form and content is grounded in the work of Frye and Burke and more recently in studies of social movements and politics. See Northrup Frye, *Anatomy of Criticism* (Princeton: Princeton University Press, 1957); Kenneth Burke, *A Rhetoric of Motives* (Berkeley and Los Angeles: University of California Press, 1969). See also Gary Alan Fine, "Public Narration and Group Culture: Discerning Discourse in Social Movements," in *Social Movements and Culture*, ed. Hank Johnston and Bert Klandermans (Minneapolis: University of Minnesota Press, 1995), 127–43; Francesca Polletta, "'It Was Like a Fever . . .': Narrative and Identity in Social Protest," *Social Problems* 45 (1998): 137–59; Mabel Berezin, "Cultural Form and Political Meaning: State-Subsidized Theater, Ideology, and the Language of Style in Fascist Italy," *American Journal of Sociology* 99 (1994): 1237–86.

48. Roof, *Spiritual Marketplace*.

49. I grew up Lutheran and witnessed many of the changes in American Lutheranism that have profoundly shaped the nature of the tradition: the adoption of the current hymnal, the rise of "contemporary worship" or folk masses, the merger of three independent church bodies in 1987 that formed the ELCA, and the move toward high-church worship styles after the merger among mid-Atlantic and midwestern Lutheran congregations. Although I had not been active in a congregation for most of my graduate school career, and was somewhat alienated from the institutional church, I still carried a set of preconceptions about what constitutes authentic Lutheran theology and worship and quickly realized (with some helpful prodding from my partner, Jennifer) that those preconceptions were acting as blinders and were preventing me from seeing how the churches I was studying understood the tradition, used it, and attempted to modify it. At the same time, my past experiences in the Lutheran church helped me identify when the tradition was being accessed, whether in a reference to Luther's writing or in some Scandinavian joke, and they helped me connect with some of the longtime Lutherans whom I interviewed.

Chapter Two

1. Willow Creek Community Church was a pioneer in the development of many of the worship and small-group practices designed to attract "religious seekers." See Sargeant, *Seeker Churches;* Gordon Lathrop, "The Shape of the Liturgy: A Framework for Contextualization," in *Christian Worship: Unity in Cultural Diversity*, ed. S. Anita Stauffer, LWF Studies (Geneva, Switzerland: Department for Theology and Studies, Lutheran World Federation, 1996), 67–75.

2. Edward Shils, *Tradition* (Chicago: University of Chicago Press, 1981), 13.

3. Carroll, *Mainline to the Future*, 10, 11. The notion of tradition as encompassing both archive and activity is derived from Griswold's discussion of cultural objects: Wendy Griswold, *Renaissance Revivals* (Chicago: University of Chicago Press, 1986).

4. This is the basic claim in H. Richard Niebuhr's classic account of American Protestantism: H. Richard Niebuhr, *Christ and Culture* (New York: Harper and Row, 1951).

5. Both Roof (*Spiritual Marketplace,* 164–65) and Carroll (*Mainline to the Future,* 15–16) argue that the United States has always existed in a state of posttraditionalism, given the country's history of anticolonialism, democracy, and immigration. However, both acknowledge that people relate to and understand the role of tradition differently today than in previous time periods.

6. Roof, *Spiritual Marketplace,* 74.

7. Carroll, *Mainline to the Future,* 10.

8. Roof, *Spiritual Marketplace,* 75.

9. The clergy at Faith Lutheran Church often used the term "dysfunction" in place of "sin" and in doing so changed the theological meaning. The understanding of sin either as an inherent human condition of separation from God or as immoral acts of individuals is lost when "sin" is replaced by "dysfunction" because the latter term refers to a flawed but ultimately correctable problem in human social relationships or to an illness that can be treated. On the shift to therapeutic religion, see Bellah et al., *Habits of the Heart;* Marsha Witten, *All Is Forgiven* (Princeton: Princeton University Press, 1993); Wuthnow, *After Heaven;* Roof, *Spiritual Marketplace.*

10. Shils, *Tradition,* 14.

11. Thompson, "Tradition and the Self in a Mediated World," 92.

12. On this shift in authority, see Anthony Giddens, *Modernity and Self-Identity* (Stanford: Stanford University Press, 1991); Zygmunt Bauman, *Life in Fragments: Essays in Postmodern Morality* (Cambridge, MA: Blackwell, 1995), 72–104; Adam B. Seligman, *Authority, the Self, and Transcendence* (Princeton: Princeton University Press, 2000).

13. Thompson, "Tradition and the Self in a Mediated World," 90.

14. In this they are similar to the churchgoers reported on in the Evangelical Identity and Influence Study. See David Sikkink, "'I Just Say I'm Christian': Symbolic Boundaries and Identity Formation among Church-going Protestants," in *Re-forming the Center: American Protestantism, 1900 to the Present,* ed. Douglas Jacobsen and William Vance Trollinger Jr. (Grand Rapids, MI: Eerdmans, 1998), 49–71.

15. E.g., Roof, *Spiritual Marketplace,* 164–72; Bass, "Congregations and the Bearing of Tradition."

16. Bass, "Congregations and the Bearing of Tradition," 184; Alasdair MacIntyre, *After Virtue,* 2d ed. (Notre Dame, IN: University of Notre Dame Press, 1984).

17. Bass, "Congregations and the Bearing of Tradition," 182.

18. On membership numbers, see Nelson, *Lutherans in North America,* 40, 147; and Noll, "Lutheran Difference," 32).

19. Nelson, *Lutherans in North America,* 175.

20. On the principle of *adiaphora,* see Erwin L. Lueker, ed., *Lutheran Cyclopedia* (St. Louis: Concordia Publishing House, 1954), 5; Leigh D. Jordahl, "Schmucker and Walther: A Study of Christian Response to American Culture," in *The Future of the American Church,* ed. Philip J. Hefner (Philadelphia: Fortress Press, 1968), 71–90.

21. Cited in Theodore E. Schmauk and C. Theodore Benze, *The Confessional Principle and the Confessions of the Lutheran Church as Embodying the Evangelical Confession of the Christian Church* (Philadelphia: General Council Publications Board, 1911).

22. Christa Resmeyer Klein, "Lutherans, Merger and the Loss of History," *Christian Century*, January 2–9, 1985, 20.

23. Jordahl, "Schmucker and Walther."

24. On pietism in Europe and the American colonies, see Nelson, *Lutherans in North America*, 39–77; Kuenning, *Rise and Fall*, 7–96.

25. The new measures included meetings that lasted from several hours to several weeks; all-night prayer meetings; praying for sinners by name; allowing women to pray or speak in public; and using the "anxious bench," that is, a seat "at the front of the congregation at which awakening sinners were asked to come for special prayers and exhortations by the revivalist" (William G. McLoughlin, *Revivals, Awakenings, and Reform* [Chicago: University of Chicago Press, 1978], 124).

26. Kuenning, *Rise and Fall*, 76; see also Rhoda Schuler, "Worship among American Lutherans: A House Divided," *Studia Liturgica* 25 (1995): 174–91; Nelson, *Lutherans in North America*, 135–44; Abdel Ross Wentz, *The Lutheran Church in American History* (Philadelphia: United Lutheran Publication House, 1923), 66–78.

27. It is generally accepted that the confessionalists' claims about the pietists were exaggerated. In reality, pietists had simply put greater stress on the Lutheran doctrine of sanctification (i.e., beliefs about how a Christian should live after experiencing God's forgiveness) while adopting postmillennialism (see Nelson, *Lutherans in North America*, 210–27; Kuenning, *Rise and Fall*).

28. Church organization is discussed in article VII. See *The Augsburg Confession* (St. Louis: Concordia Publishing House, 1906).

29. On the fight between confessionalists and pietists, see Nelson, *Lutherans in North America*, 210–27; Kuenning, *Rise and Fall*, 163–75.

30. Jordahl, "Schmucker and Walther," 84.

31. I reconstructed the American Lutheran tradition based on my reading of several Lutheran histories, especially Lagerquist, *Lutherans*, 3–19; and Nelson, *Lutherans in North America*.

32. Paul J. Graverock, "Liturgy for Life: The Liturgy and Adult Instruction for Lutheran Congregations" (DMin diss., San Francisco Theological Seminary, 1990), 20. This worship style followed the order of service set out in Luther's *Formula missae* and *Deutsche missae*, both of which follow the structure and content of the Roman Catholic Mass but allow greater lay participation by using the vernacular rather than Latin.

33. Carl F. Schalk, "Sketches of Lutheran Worship," in *A Handbook of Church Music*, ed. Carl Halter and Carl F. Schalk (St. Louis: Concordia Publishing House, 1978), 103.

34. Robert D. Hawkins, "Whither Now Lutherans?" *Alleluia, Worship Newsletter* (North Carolina Synod, ELCA), Spring 1993, 5.

35. The more accurate phraseology combines a different three statements: *sola gratia* (by grace alone), *sola fide* (by faith alone), and *sola Christus* (for the sake of Christ alone). *Sola scriptura* (the Bible alone) stood apart from the other three but has taken the place of Christ Alone in popular usage among Lutherans. An excellent summary of the Lutheran tradition written for a non-Lutheran audience is Daniel Erlander's *Baptized We Live: Lutheranism as a Way of Life* (self-published, 1981). See also Lowell G. Almen, *One Great Cloud of Witnesses* (Minneapolis: Augsburg Fortress, 1997).

36. On the twentieth-century pattern of diversity in belief and practice among Lutherans, see Robert Wuthnow, "Sources of Doctrinal Unity and Diversity," in *Views from the Pews,* ed. Roger A. Johnson (Philadelphia: Fortress Press, 1983), 33–56; Kenneth W. Inskeep, "Denominational Identity in the Evangelical Lutheran Church in America" (Department for Research and Evaluation, Evangelical Lutheran Church in America, Chicago, 2001, unpublished paper).

37. Ironically, Lutherans have fought as much about worship practices, despite their confessional principles that allow diversity of practice, as churches that struggle to maintain liturgical unity and allow for wider theological diversity (e.g., the American Episcopal Church).

38. Lagerquist, *Lutherans,* 78.

39. This anonymous quotation can be found in Richard O. Johnson, "Sierra Pacific Synod: Looking Back," p. 3, 1997, Sierra Pacific Synod Archives, Berkeley, CA.

40. Statistics and quotation from D. Michael Quinn, "Religion in the American West," in *Under Open Sky: Rethinking America's Western Past,* ed. George Miles and Jay Gitlin (New York and London: W. W. Norton and Co., 1992), 158.

41. Ferenc M. Szasz, *Religion in the Modern American West* (Tucson: University of Arizona Press, 2000), 99.

42. For the 1990 data, see Barry A. Kosmin and Seymour P. Lachman, *One Nation under God: Religion in Contemporary American Society* (New York: Harmony Books, 1993), 88. The last survey also found a sizable gap between religious identification and church membership, such that nearly 40 percent of the national sample who identify with a religion report that they or someone in their household does not belong to an organized religious group.

43. Szasz, *Religion in the Modern American West,* 24–26; Ferenc M. Szasz, "'New Thought' and the American West," in *Religion in the West,* ed. Ferenc M. Szasz (Manhattan, KS: Sunflower University Press, 1984), 83–90; Kosmin and Lachman, *One Nation under God,* 77–80; Sandra Sizer Frankiel, *California's Spiritual Frontiers: Religious Alternatives in Anglo-Protestantism, 1850–1910* (Berkeley and Los Angeles: University of California Press, 1988).

44. See Szasz, *Religion in the Modern American West,* 3–5; Quinn, "Religion in the American West," 153–54.

45. Quinn, "Religion in the American West," 154.

46. These numbers do not include the Lutheran Church—Missouri Synod, which has remained separate from the rest of American Lutheranism in the twentieth and twenty-first centuries. Membership numbers are from the following sources: *1964 Yearbook of the American Lutheran Church* (Minneapolis: Augsburg Publishing House, 1963); *1964 Yearbook of the Lutheran Church in America* (Philadelphia, 1963); *2002 Yearbook of the Evangelical Lutheran Church of America* (Minneapolis: Augsburg/Fortress, 2001).

47. For 2001 numbers, see Barry A. Kosmin, Egon Mayer, and Ariela Keysar, "Religious Identification Survey, 2001," Graduate Center of the City University of New York, December 19, 2001, http://www.gc.cuny.edu/faculty/research_studies/aris.pdf (accessed March 5, 2006). For 1990 numbers, see Kosmin and Lachman, *One Nation under God,* 88–92.

48. Kosmin and Lachman, *One Nation under God*, 84–85. A common joke I heard among clergy and longtime West Coast Lutherans is that many Lutherans left their faith behind when they crossed the Rockies.

49. See Philip A. Nordquist, "Lutherans in the West and Northwest," in *New Partners, Old Roots: A History of Merging Lutheran Churches in the Pacific Northwest*, ed. Heidi Emerson, Milton Nesvig, Philip A. Nordquist, and Roland Swanson (Tacoma, WA: North Pacific and Rocky Mountain Districts of the American Lutheran Church, the Pacific Northwest Synod of the Lutheran Church in American, and the Pacific Regional Synod of the Association of Evangelical Lutheran Churches, 1986), 3–18; Jon F. Dechow, "Mission West: A History of the Association of Evangelical Lutheran Churches (AELC) in the West," 1988, Sierra Pacific Synod Archives, Berkeley, CA; Patricia Killen, "Christianity in the Western United States," *Span*, Summer 2002, 6–7, 25, 28.

50. Eldon Ernst, "American Religious History from a Pacific Coast Perspective," in *Religion and Society in the American West: Historical Essays*, ed. Carl Guarneri and David Alvarez (Lanham, MD: University Press of America, 1987), 21.

51. See Killen, "Christianity in the Western United States," 7.

52. The predecessor church bodies included the Augustana Synod, the Finnish Evangelical Lutheran Church, the American Evangelical Lutheran Church, and the United Lutheran Church in America, which merged in 1962 to form the Lutheran Church in America (LCA). The American Lutheran Church (ALC) formed in a series of mergers from 1960 to 1963 with the union of the old American Lutheran Church, the United Evangelical Lutheran Church, the Lutheran Free Church, and the Evangelical Lutheran Church. By the mid-1960s, the majority of Lutherans belonged to one of three bodies—the ALC, LCA, and the Lutheran Church—Missouri Synod. The ALC and LCA, along with the American Evangelical Lutheran Church, merged in 1987 to form the Evangelical Lutheran Church in America (ELCA). See Todd Nichol, *All These Lutherans: Three Paths toward a New Lutheran Church* (Minneapolis: Augsburg Publishing House, 1986), for a brief history of these predecessor church bodies and the mergers out of which came the ELCA.

53. Ansle Severton, "South Pacific District, the American Lutheran Church" (Berkeley, 1989, unpublished paper), 3; Dr. George Muedeking, interview by Ray F. Kibbler III, July 14, 1981, transcript, Sierra Pacific Synod Archive, Berkeley, CA. The South Pacific District included California, Utah, Nevada, Arizona, New Mexico, and Colorado.

54. Dr. Gaylerd Falde (South Pacific District of the American Lutheran Church), interview by Ansle Severton, July 26, 1983, transcript, Sierra Pacific Synod Archive, Berkeley, CA. See also Ansle Severton, "Norwegian Lutherans in the Pacific Southwest" (Berkeley, 1987, unpublished paper).

55. Dr. R. Dale Lechleitner, interview by Ray F. Kibbler III, July 15, 1981, transcript, Sierra Pacific Synod Archive, Berkeley, CA; Dr. George H. Muedeking, interview by Ray F. Kibbler III, July 15, 1981, transcript, Sierra Pacific Synod Archive, Berkeley, CA.

56. To orient myself to the recent history of California Lutheranism, I interviewed ten retired clergy during 1999 and 2000 as I developed the research design. This is not a representative sample but their comments about the church mirror those made by other church leaders whose papers are in the ELCA archives in Berkeley.

57. Kosmin and Lachmann, *One Nation under God*, 111.
58. The ELCA has membership data extending back only to 1994 and forward to 2000. See Evangelical Lutheran Church in America, "Synod Statistics," 2006, http://www.elca.org/re/synod_stats.html (accessed March 5, 2006).
59. Median household income in California is $47,493. See U.S. Census Bureau, "State and County QuickFacts: California," January 12, 2006, http://quickfacts.census.gov/qfd/states/06000.html (accessed March 5, 2006).
60. Good Shepherd lost about 150 members at the end of a long conflict over the tradition and pastoral authority. The remainder of the loss was a result of the church finally updating its membership list.
61. PFLAG, or Parents, Families, and Friends of Lesbians and Gays, is a national, chapter-based organization that promotes the well-being of gay, lesbian, bisexual, and transgendered persons and their families.
62. The Lutheran Confessions are a set of documents written during the Protestant Reformation that contain the core teachings of Lutheranism regarding the nature of God, sin and justification by faith, the sacraments, worship, and church order. These documents represent the beliefs that Lutherans confess, or declare their faith in, and as such are the theological markers of Lutheran distinctiveness. The documents are collected in *The Book of Concord* and include the three ecumenical creeds (the Apostles' Creed, the Nicene Creed, and the Athanasian Creed), the Augsburg Confession and the Defense of the Augsburg Confession, Luther's Large and Small Catechisms, the Smalcald Articles, the Treatise on the Power and Primacy of the Pope, the Epitome of the Formula of Concord, and the Thorough Declaration of the Formula of Concord.
63. On this trend within Lutheranism, see Scott Thumma and Jim Petersen, "Goliaths in Our Midst," 102–12; Noll, "Lutheran Difference."

Chapter Three

1. Statistics are from the 1990 and 2000 U.S. census; see U.S. Census Bureau, "American Factfinder," January 12, 2006, http://factfinder.census.gov (accessed March 5, 2006). Similarly, the suburbs east of Oakland and Berkeley experienced modest population growth between 1990 and 2000 but very little overall change in the racial or ethnic composition of the population. The three suburbs on average increased their total population by 18 percent between 1990 and 2000, with an average decrease in the white population of 6 percent and an average increase in the Asian population of 3.6 percent. For populations see the 1990 and 2000 U.S. censuses at U.S. Census Bureau, "Summary Tape File 1," January 12, 2006, http://factfinder.census.gov (accessed March 5, 2006).
2. On niche congregations, see Ammerman, *Congregation and Community*, 130–60.
3. Some ecological and cultural explanations draw on organizational theories that stress how conflict, membership loss, an infusion of new members, or leadership changes are among the organizational characteristics that might serve as catalysts for change. See, e.g., Ammerman, *Congregation and Community*; Becker, *Congregations in Conflict*. However, in the nine study congregations, few of these internal features led to change. There were no precipitating conflicts that moved a congregation to change

its tradition (although conflict often emerged during the process of altering the tradi-tion). Several congregations experienced membership loss or turnover, but this loss alone cannot explain the timing of change efforts. The Oakland congregations had been experiencing membership loss for years before beginning the change process, and two of the suburban parishes experienced regular membership turnover due to the high mobility of the population they served.

4. Two congregations, Grace and St. Luke's, did not see themselves facing a crisis of mean-ing or membership and I exclude them from this chapter. While they were engaged in efforts to change the congregation and its inherited tradition, this process had a longer history and took a more evolutionary course. I will discuss Grace in chapters 4 and 6, and St. Luke's in chapter 5. A third congregation, St. Peter's Lutheran Church in the Silicon Valley, had created a new vision/mission plan and implemented cultural and structural changes before the field period. Unfortunately, I do not have very complete data about what triggered change for this congregation. The retrospective accounts members gave provided tantalizing clues but few details about the rationale, motiva-tions, or presence of a felt crisis driving change. For these reasons, I have excluded St. Peter's from this chapter, but I will draw on the data in chapters 5 and 6.

5. On "causal stories" see Deborah A. Stone, "Causal Stories and the Formation of Policy Agendas," *Political Science Quarterly* 104 (1989): 281–300; Paul Burstein and Marie Bricher, "Problem Definition and Public Policy: Congressional Committees Confront Work, Family, and Gender, 1945–1990," *Social Forces* 75, no. 4 (1997): 135–69.

6. See Stone, "Causal Stories."

7. Saddleback Community Church is a megachurch in southern California that is led by Pastor Rick Warren, the author of a best-selling church growth book, *The Pur-pose-Driven Church* (Grand Rapids, MI: Zondervan, 1995), that many leaders of the congregations in this study had read and whose ideas they were trying to implement.

8. Quotations are from the pastors' letters to the congregation in the January 8, 2002, August 22, 2000, and August 21, 2001 newsletters.

9. See Wuthnow *After Heaven*, 19–84, on the 1950s pattern and the rise of seeker spirituality.

10. I will discuss the conflict over spirituality and worship at Good Shepherd in chapter 6.

11. The term "millennialists" refers to the generation who grew up with the Internet.

12. Christ Lutheran was intentionally following the organizing strategy taught by the Ga-maliel Foundation. It stresses the use of "one-on-one meetings" to identify common interests among different parties and to build community both within the congrega-tion (the foundation calls this the "in-reach" process) and with individuals outside the congregation (the process of "out-reach" whereby members of the congregation meet with members of the community to hear their concerns about local problems and learn how the church could help solve those problems). See Mark I. Wegener, "Congre-gation-Centered Organizing: A Strategy for Growing Stronger Communities," 2003, http://gamaliel.org/Library/congregationCenteredOrganizing.htm (accessed March 5, 2006).

13. Cheryl Townsend Gilkes, "Plenty Good Room: Adaptation in a Changing Black Church," *Annals of the American Academy of Political and Social Sciences* 558 (1998):

107–10. See also Andrew Billingsley, *Mighty Like a River: The Black Church and Social Reform* (New York: Oxford University Press, 1999); Omar M. McRoberts, "Understanding the 'New' Black Pentecostal Activism: Lessons from Ecumenical Urban Ministries in Boston," *Sociology of Religion* 60, no. 1 (1999): 47–70.

14. Resurrection had a change in pastors in 2001 and the debt from the sanctuary remodel to retire; Christ had new pastors and the momentum for change that followed the merger; Emmanuel's commuter population largely ceded decision-making power to its pastor.

15. The term "claims makers" comes from the social-problems literature and refers to the individuals, such as reporters, government and elected officials, and employees of nonprofit organizations, who work in a given social-problem arena and actively seek to define what is a public problem, win support for their definition, and implement their desired solution to the problem. See Stephen Hilgartner and Charles L. Bosk, "The Rise and Fall of Social Problems: A Public Arenas Model," *American Journal of Sociology* 94 (1988): 53–78.

16. Ibid.; Stone, "Causal Stories." For constructivist accounts of problems, see also Joseph R. Gusfield, *The Culture of Public Problems: Drinking-Driving and the Symbolic Order* (Chicago: University of Chicago Press, 1981); Joel Best, *Threatened Children: Rhetoric and Concern about Child-Victims* (Chicago: University of Chicago Press, 1990); Burstein and Bricher, "Problem Definition and Public Policy."

17. Stone, "Causal Stories," 282.

18. The public-arenas model stresses the institutional spheres or arenas in which competing claims makers vie to win support and resources for a given definition of a social problem. The model is not wholly applicable to the case of constructing the problems and rationales for congregational change insofar as the arena is quite small and confined to the sphere of religion, competition is muted, and there is considerably less variability or change in the universe of potential problems than in other policy arenas.

19. See Net Results: New Ideas in Church Vitality, http://www.netresults.org (accessed March 5, 2006). See also Easum Bandy Associates, 2006, http://www.easumbandy .com (accessed March 5, 2006); Church Doctor: A Ministry of Church Growth Center, http://www.churchdr.com (accessed March 5, 2006); McIntosh Church Growth Network, 2004, http://www.churchgrowthnetwork.com (accessed March 5, 2006); Church Growth Incorporated, 2005, http://www.churchgrowth.net (accessed March 5, 2006); American Society for Church Growth, affiliated with Fuller Seminary, February 16, 2006, http://www.ascg.org (accessed March 5, 2006). Many of these Web sites have links to one another, and some megachurch Web sites also have links to these organizations (among others) as well as offering church growth publications and consulting services of their own. For example, see the Web site of Community Church of Joy, 2006, http://www.joyonline.org (accessed March 5, 2006).

20. I reviewed the books clergy and lay people in the different congregations were reading or recommended, as well as texts from key figures in the church growth industry, including Gary McIntosh, Rick Warren, Lyle Schaller, Thomas Bandy, William Easum, George Barna, Norman Sawchuck, Leonard Sweet, and John Spong.

21. E.g., see John Shelby Spong, *Why Christianity Must Change or Die* (San Francisco: Harper, 1999); Leonard Sweet, *AquaChurch* (Loveland, CO: Group, 1999).

22. On the way in which cultural production is constrained and channeled toward certain outcomes, see Lynn Spillman, "Culture, Social Structures, and Discursive Fields," in *Current Perspectives in Social Theory*, vol. 15, ed. Ben Agger (Greenwich, CT: JAI Press, 1995), 129–54; Wuthnow, *Communities of Discourse*; Wendy Griswold, "Formulaic Fiction: The Author as Agent of Elective Affinity," in *Comparative Social Research*, vol. 11, ed. Craig Calhoun (Greenwich, CT: JAI Press, 1989): 75–130; Richard A. Peterson, "Six Constraints on the Production of Literary Works," *Poetics* 14 (1985): 45–67.

23. William M. Easum and Thomas G. Bandy, *Growing Spiritual Redwoods* (Nashville: Abingdon Press, 1997); Gary McIntosh, *One Size Doesn't Fit All* (Grand Rapids, MI: Revell Books, 1999); Warren, *Purpose-Driven Church*.

24. The video seminars at Faith Lutheran (to which all congregations in the synod are invited to send clergy or lay leaders) included "Churches That Change Lives" (led by George Barna); "A Motivating, Encouraging, Proven-Effective Way to Equip Your Laity to Become Active Participants"; "Developing Effective Children's Ministries" (led by leaders from San Diego First Assembly of God); and "Spiritual Gifts."

25. Warren, *Purpose-Driven Church*, 243, 189, 199. At one point in the book Warren notes that when he learned that many unchurched southern Californians would never consider visiting a Southern Baptist church, he intentionally downplayed the church's Southern Baptist connections and heritage until visitors had become members.

26. Quotations are from the church's mission document "Upon This Rock" published by the church in 1999.

27. See the discussion of pietism and confessionalism in chapter 1. See also Leigh D. Jordahl, "Folk Church, Liturgy, and Ceremony: Or Can We Avoid Disaster?" *Dialog* 14 (1975): 116; Michael B. Aune, "The Corporate and Confessional Character of Worship: The Common Service Debate," *Word and World* 8 (Winter 1988): 32–41. On how worship is organized in megachurches, especially Willow Creek Community Church, to facilitate individuals' conversion, see Sargeant, *Seeker Churches*, chaps. 3–4.

28. Warren, *Purpose-Driven Church*, 144.

29. I've omitted Emmanuel Lutheran from this discussion because it has relied more on its own experiences as an innovative black church in a white denomination and the models of worship and change from the historic black denominations rather than on the expert advice of church growth consultants.

30. The quotation and the information about the seminar come from the detailed outline "Leadership in the 21st Century" (2000), by William Easum and Thomas Bandy. I have the official outlines from their seminar that members of Good Shepherd attended in 2000 and members of Christ Lutheran attended in 2002, and they are nearly identical in terms of content.

31. On cultural reception theory, see Andrea Press, "The Sociology of Cultural Reception: Notes toward an Emerging Paradigm," in *The Sociology of Culture*, ed. Diana Crane (Cambridge, MA: Blackstone, 1994), 221–46; John Fiske, "Audiencing: A Cultural Studies Approach to Watching Television," *Poetics* 21 (1992): 345–59; Elizabeth Long, "Women, Reading, and Cultural Authority: Some Implications of the Audi-

ence Perspective in Cultural Studies," *American Quarterly* 38 (1986): 591–612; Stuart Hall, "Encoding/Decoding," in *Popular Culture: Production and Consumption,* ed. Lee C. Harrington and Denise D. Bielby (Malden, MA: Blackwell Publishers, 2000), 123–32.

32. See the example of how the church weaves Easum's material into its authenticity causal story above.

33. Civic congregations "focus on the here and now as the main arena of God's redemptive activity. They express their concern for public life through the education of their members and secondarily through funding or sponsoring social service activities" (David A. Roozen, William McKinney, and Jackson W. Carroll, *Varieties of Religious Presence* [New York: Pilgrim Press, 1988], 100).

34. It is a national market because the entrepreneurs (many of the experts self-identify as entrepreneurial) come from Maryland, Illinois, Kentucky, Texas, Florida, Arizona, and southern California. I was unable to identify any expert or congregation from the San Francisco Bay Area from whom the congregations in the study purchased materials or borrowed ideas.

35. See ARDA: The Association for Religious Archives, "County Membership Report: Contra Costa County, California," 2006, http://www.thearda.com/mapsReports/reports/counties/06013_2000.asp (accessed March 5, 2006).

36. I am grateful to one anonymous referee for this insight about the mediating role of religious entrepreneurs, consultants, and denominational officials.

Chapter Four

1. Roof, *Spiritual Marketplace,* 171.

2. Sargeant, *Seeker Churches,* 180–84.

3. Roof, *Spiritual Marketplace,* 167.

4. Swidler, "Culture in Action." Similarly, Dillon shows how progressive Roman Catholics interrogate their own tradition for "clues, symbols and ideas that might legitimate an emancipatory agenda" (Dillon, *Catholic Identity,* 25). Progressive Catholic groups use the tradition, she argues, to criticize official church doctrines and policies regarding women's ordination, abortion, and the inclusion of gay and lesbian persons in the life of the church. The process of selectively drawing on, reinterpreting, or arguing with the tradition is also identified in Ammerman's 1997 study, *Congregation and Community,* and in work on immigrant religions; see, e.g., Fenggang Yang and Helen Rose Ebaugh, "Transformations in New Immigrant Religions and Their Global Implications," *American Sociological Review* 66, no. 2 (2001): 278–81.

5. Becker, "Making Inclusive Communities," 462.

6. See chapter 2.

7. Reframing thus operates much like institutional isomorphism insofar as it refers to a generic and overarching practice of organizational change or innovation. See DiMaggio and Powell, "Iron Cage Revisited."

8. Goffman even refers to primary frameworks as a group's "belief system" or "cosmology," thus suggesting the connections between frames and religious traditions; see Erving Goffman, *Frame Analysis* (Boston: Northeastern University Press, 1986), 27.

9. Goffman argues that one way of changing a frame is by "keying," a process in which "a given activity, already meaningful in terms of some primary framework, is transformed into something patterned on this activity but seen by participants to be something quite else" (ibid., 44–45). Goffman's analysis of keying or changing a frame is more situational and limited in scope than the reframing work I observed at the churches in my study. Moreover, keying presumes all people involved fully understand the frame that is being altered, whereas in the churches I studied, most people had at best a rudimentary knowledge of the tradition.

10. On the decline of the importance and knowledge of doctrine among American Protestants, especially mainline and liberal Protestants, see Alan Wolfe, *The Transformation of American Religion* (New York: Free Press, 2003); Roof, *Spiritual Marketplace*, 56; Christian Smith, *American Evangelicalism: Embattled and Thriving* (Chicago: University of Chicago Press, 1998), 51–63; Donald E. Miller, *Reinventing American Protestantism*, 127–29.

11. My concept of "translation" is similar to Roof's more narrow use of the term (Roof, *Spiritual Marketplace*). Liebman calls a similar process "transvaluation," in which a congregation retains "the forms of traditional symbols while imposing new meanings on the traditional symbols"; see Charles S. Liebman, "The Reappropriation of Jewish Tradition in the Modern Era," in *The Uses of Tradition*, ed. Jack Wertheimer (Cambridge, MA: Harvard University Press, 1992), 476.

12. Roof identifies this strategy and argues that reconnecting often happens when individuals are facing existential life crises such as death, illness and suffering, or aging (Roof, *Spiritual Marketplace*, 167–69). The congregations in my study used the strategy, not to help people find religious ways to cope with personal struggles, but for larger organizational purposes.

13. Wolfe, *Transformation of American Religion*, 17.

14. The only time I heard widespread dissent about retraditioning came after a service in which the mystical experiences and ideas of St. Julian of Norwich were dramatically presented in a play. This service became known as "the vampire service" because the play transformed Julian into a vampire who had to give her own blood to stay alive rather that take others' blood as in the common vampire myth. Members reported having a hard time "hearing the gospel" or finding much of redeeming value in the service, although it did provoke one member to reflect on the meaning of Communion and God's sacrifice through the death of Jesus.

15. On the Lutheran doctrine of atonement and salvation, see Carl Braaten, *Principles of Lutheran Theology* (Philadelphia: Fortress Press, 1983); Eric W. Gritsch and Robert W. Jenson, *Lutheranism: The Theological Movement and Its Confessional Writings* (Philadelphia: Fortress Press, 1976); Robert Kolb, *The Christian Faith: A Lutheran Exposition* (St. Louis: Concordia Publishing House, 1993).

16. In this excerpt the pastor is referring to the processional cross that usually sits in a wooden holder near the altar. The holder was damaged by some children, and the cross was removed from the sanctuary for several weeks.

17. See Sargeant, *Seeker Churches;* Wolfe, *Transformation of American Religion.* Witten has shown how the language of psychology was routinely used in the sermons of Pres-

byterian and Baptist ministers to convey a more optimistic, less judgmental view of the Christian faith (Witten, *All Is Forgiven*).

18. See James William Coleman, *The New Buddhism: The Western Transformation of an Ancient Tradition* (New York: Oxford University Press, 2001), 88–119.

19. See Aune, "Corporate and Confessional Character of Worship"; Gordon Lathrop, "A Contemporary Lutheran Approach to Worship and Culture: Sorting Out Critical Principles," in *Worship and Culture in Dialogue*, ed. S. Anita Stauffer, LWF Studies (Geneva, Switzerland: Department for Theology and Studies, Lutheran World Federation, 1994), 137–51; Lathrop, "Shape of the Liturgy."

20. For example, at a focus group interview a week after this service, one woman, in tears, complained that the service was not Christian because it did not include the Apostles' Creed.

21. Lagerquist, a Lutheran historian, writes that "in contrast to the gathered ecclesiology of revival-influenced American churches, it is not the coming together of the congregation that makes the church. Rather, in Lutheran teaching the preaching and the sacraments make the church, drawing people and giving them access to divine forgiveness and grace." See L. DeAnne Lagerquist, *In America the Men Milk the Cows: Factors of Gender, Ethnicity, and Religion in the Americanization of Norwegian-American Women* (Brooklyn: Carlson Publishing, 1991), 12.

22. Although the congregation did not provide me with demographic statistics of its membership, my interviews and casual conversations with members suggest that the average age of the members was at least midsixties (the youngest active members were in their midforties during the field period). One of the pastors and several council members mentioned to me that, in the two years after the merger, attendance dropped off because aging members in poor health could no longer travel to church.

23. *Sola gratia* (grace alone) was a watchword of the Lutheran Reformation that continues to be used by many contemporary Lutherans in the United States. In interviews with many members of the nine congregations, the Lutheran emphasis on grace was the one distinguishing characteristic of the tradition they could identify and often was the one part of the tradition they appreciated and wished to preserve.

24. Grace was one of the first Lutheran congregations in the area (and the first in the East Bay suburbs) to officially welcome gay and lesbian persons. It also had supported such endeavors as the Central American peace/sanctuary movement, antiwar movements, and the antiapartheid movement. Christ Lutheran and some of its members had been involved in local political reform projects and promoted racial equality. However, its pastor noted that, although members would vote for a nonwhite candidate, few would actually work for any political candidate. He was trying to push the congregation to adopt a more activist identity.

25. See Swidler, *Talk of Love*, 162–65; William H. Sewell Jr., "A Theory of Structure: Duality, Agency, and Transformation," *American Journal of Sociology* 98, no. 1 (1992): 6–8.

26. See Theodore Caplow, "Rule Enforcement without Visible Means: Christmas Gift Giving in Middletown," *American Journal of Sociology* 89, no. 6 (1984): 1306–23; Swidler, *Talk of Love*, 162–63.

27. See Sargeant, *Seeker Churches;* David Lyon, *Jesus in Disneyland* (Cambridge, UK: Polity Press, 2000); R. Laurence Moore, *Selling God* (New York: Oxford University Press, 1994.)

28. On church-sect theory, see Johnson, "On Church and Sect," 539–49; Rodney Stark and William Sims Bainbridge, "Of Churches, Sects, and Cults: Preliminary Concepts for a Theory of Religious Movements," *Journal for the Scientific Study of Religion* 18, no. 2 (1979): 117–33; Finke and Stark, *Churching of America,* 40–46; Donald E. Miller, *Reinventing American Protestantism,* 153–55; Philip E. Hammond, "The Market Paradigm and the Future of Religious Organizations," in *The Dynamics of Religious Organizations* (New York: Oxford University Press, 2000), 32–47.

29. Donald E. Miller, *Reinventing American Protestantism.*

30. Mark Chaves, *Congregations in America* (Cambridge, MA: Harvard University Press, 2004), 146–52.

Chapter Five

1. The term "traditional liturgy" refers to any of the three liturgies that are based on the Common Rite in *The Lutheran Book of Worship.* Nearly all of my interviewees in all nine churches called *LBW*-based liturgies "traditional."

2. This was part of a twelve-week sermon series, "Plugged into . . . " A giant electrical outlet behind the altar reminded members about the series.

3. *The Lectionary for the Common Mass* (*Lectionary for Mass*) (Collegeville, MN: Liturgical Press, 1970) and *The Common Worship Lectionary: New Revised Standard Version, Anglicized Edition,* Desk Edition, ed. Martin Manser, Kenneth Stevenson, and Martin Kitchen (Oxford: Oxford University Press, 1999), assign scripture lessons for each Sunday of the year that include a lesson from the Old Testament, the Psalms, the Epistles, and the Gospels. The first lectionary was developed by the Roman Catholic Church as part of its liturgical reform movement, and it was adopted in 1970 by the Presbyterians, Lutherans, and Episcopalians. Today it is used in many Protestant denominations.

4. DiMaggio and Powell ("Iron Cage Revisited") identify three types of isomorphism—coercive, mimetic, and normative—but do not discuss the differing degrees to which organizations adopt certain practices, myths, or decision-making structures from successful organizations or how such selective adoption changes the organization.

5. See Finke and Stark, *Churching of America;* Eiseland, *Particular Place.*

6. Roger Finke, "Innovative Returns to Tradition: Using Core Teachings as the Foundation for Innovative Accommodation," *Journal for the Scientific Study of Religion* 43, no. 1 (2004): 19–34.

7. Chaves, *Congregations in America,* 157.

8. The contemporary evangelical worship tradition is based on the nineteenth-century practices and forms developed on the American frontier during the revivals of the Second Great Awakening. Among scholars of Christian worship, the term "frontier tradition" is sometimes used when discussing evangelical worship practices. See Schuler, "Worship among American Lutherans"; James F. White, *Christian Worship in North America* (Collegeville, MN: Liturgical Press, 1997); and James F. White, *Protestant Worship* (Louisville, KY: Westminster/John Knox Press, 1989).

9. On the historical variety of worship in American Lutheranism, see Klein, "Lutherans, Merger and the Loss of History"; Aune, "Corporate and Confessional Character of Worship"; Jordahl, "Folk Church, Liturgy, and Ceremony." For the ELCA, the common and normative practice of worship is enshrined in the *Lutheran Book of Worship*, 10th ed. (Minneapolis: Augsburg Publishing House; Philadelphia: Board of Publication, Lutheran Church in America, 1990).

10. Aune, "Corporate and Confessional Character of Worship," 32.

11. The Augsburg Confession defines church and worship as "the assembly of believers among whom the Gospel is preached in its purity and the holy sacraments are administered according to the Gospel" (quoted in Lathrop, "Shape of the Liturgy," 68). On the Common Rite and Lutheran worship, see Michael B. Aune, "*Lutheran Book of Worship*: Relic or Resource?" *Dialog* 33, no. 3 (1994): 174–82; Lathrop, "Contemporary Lutheran Approach to Worship and Culture"; Gordon Lathrop, *What Are the Essentials of Christian Worship?* (Minneapolis: Augsburg Fortress Press, 1994); Lathrop, "Shape of the Liturgy."

12. *Lutheran Book of Worship*, 8.

13. See ibid., in which each element of the liturgy is explained and defined either as optional or as essential and, by implication, mandatory.

14. James F. White, *Christian Worship in North America*, 165.

15. James F. White, *Protestant Worship*, 171.

16. James F. White, *Christian Worship in North America*, 106.

17. This stepwise approach is much like the purpose-driven church model described in chapter 3. See Gordon Lathrop, "New Pentecost or Joseph's Britches? Reflections on the History and Meaning of the Worship Ordo in the Megachurches," *Worship* 76, no. 6 (2001): 521–38; Sargeant, *Seeker Churches*, 79.

18. See Sargeant, *Seeker Churches*, 77–105; Schuler, "Worship among American Lutherans," 183; Philip Reiff, *The Triumph of the Therapeutic* (New York: Harper Torchbooks, 1966).

19. See James F. White, *Christian Worship in North America*, 103–13, 155–72; Sargeant, *Seeker Churches*, 54–76; Lathrop, "New Pentecost or Joseph's Britches?"; Schuler, "Worship among American Lutherans."

20. Schuler, "Worship among American Lutherans," 181.

21. Sargeant, *Seeker Churches*, 65–68.

22. See Frank C. Senn, "'Worship Alive': An Analysis and Critique of 'Alternative Worship Services,'" *Worship* 69, no. 3 (1995): 195; Sargeant, *Seeker Churches*, 65–66; Warren, *Purpose-Driven Church*, 279–92.

23. See Senn, "'Worship Alive,'" 208.

24. The pastor for youth and family ministry also spoke about the intentional evangelical turn of worship at Faith. Like Pastor Lincoln, he claimed that "altar calls are a part of the traditional Lutheran church, when we make a public profession that we accept Jesus Christ as Lord and savior." While he never specified in which part of the service this profession occurs, he could have been referring to the recitation of the creed or the "Confession." However, the historic liturgy does not use the evangelical language of accepting Jesus as one's personal savior. The pastor continued by noting that the

congregation appears to have embraced the "decisional theology" of the American Baptist tradition (a theology that emphasizes the necessity and ability of individuals to make a decision to convert and become Christian). Then he cited a classic theological text in the Lutheran tradition (Carl E. Braaten and Robert W. Jenson, eds., *Christian Dogmatics,* 2 vols. [Philadelphia: Fortress Press, 1984]) to argue that Lutherans "believe the Holy Spirit leads people to this decision and helps us make it."

25. This "prayer" is not really a prayer at all. It is the first sentence in Luther's explanation of the third article of the "Apostles' Creed" in Luther's *Small Catechism* (Minneapolis: Augsburg Publishing House; Philadelphia: Fortress Press, 1968). The phrase "sinner's prayer" comes from Protestant revivalism, and such a prayer often appears at the end of tracts passed out by churches or individuals to so-called unbelievers. There are a number of variations but most include a recognition by the individual of her or his sin and need to be saved (e.g., "Heavenly Father, I know that I am a sinner and that I deserve to go to hell. I believe that Jesus died on the cross for my sins. I do now receive him as my personal Lord and Savior. I promise to serve you the best I can. Please save me. In Jesus' name, amen."). Pastor's Lincoln's equation of Luther's explanation that forms the basis of the Lutheran doctrine of justification with the evangelical tradition's "sinner's prayer" may be seen as one indication of how the latter tradition has impacted his own theological understandings.

26. The senior pastor and the lay leader in charge of new-member classes reported that nearly one-third of new members were coming from Baptist or evangelical backgrounds.

27. At the end of the field period at Zion, the congregation had voted to install video screens in the sanctuary.

28. Senn ("'Worship Alive,'" 201) notes that hundreds of Lutheran congregations use a praise-music-based service that follows the evangelical three-part structure.

29. On the way in which religious symbols and rituals create moods and motivations for action, see Geertz, *Interpretation of Cultures,* 94–98. When I attended the contemporary services at Zion and Faith, I commonly saw anywhere from one-third to one-half of the people sitting in my section of the sanctuary (both churches have large sanctuaries) not singing.

30. Lutheran liturgical scholar Michael Aune argues that the fundamental structure of the Common Rite and hence the Lutheran service as it currently exists in the *LBW* is one in which God speaks first and then the people respond (*"Lutheran Book of Worship:* Relic or Resource?" 181–82). (The Lutheran understanding of call and response should not be confused with the emotional and demonstrative call-and-response preaching style of the historic black church.) In the evangelical tradition, there is plenty of opportunity for God to speak (in songs and the sermon) but fewer opportunities to respond, and then the response mandated is one of conversion or recommitment.

31. Sargeant, *Seeker Churches;* Senn, "'Worship Alive.'"

32. Sargeant (*Seeker Churches*) argues that seeker churches, as exemplified by Willow Creek Community Church, rely on music and preaching to promote an inoffensive, personalistic faith and to persuade visitors to convert based on the psychological

benefits of faith presented in the service. Wuthnow (*After Heaven*) makes a similar argument about the inoffensive and nonsacrificial nature of the various types of spirituality practiced by American evangelicals.

33. At one Faith Lutheran service during Lenten season of 2000, two of the three praise songs were celebratory in content—the verses spoke about dancing and celebrating, singing and shouting, and clapping in joy—which created an odd disjuncture between the somber mood of the season as reflected in the sermon and the choir anthem, both of which spoke directly about Jesus' coming death and sacrifice.

34. See Senn, "'Worship Alive,'" 221. See also Linda Clark, "'Songs That My Mother Taught Me': Hymns as Transmitters of Faith," in *Beyond Establishment: Protestant Identity in a Post-Protestant Age,* ed. Paul F. Bradshaw and Lawrence A. Hoffman (South Bend, IN: University of Notre Dame Press, 1993), 99–105.

35. Griswold identifies the importance of examining the "generic logic and necessity" of literary forms "to understand how they work in their representational capacities" ("Formulaic Fiction," 83). The notion of culture's internal logic is grounded in Simmel's ideas about the autonomy of forms of sociation (Georg Simmel, *The Sociology of Georg Simmel,* trans., ed., and with an introduction by Kurt H. Wolff [New York: Free Press, 1964], 40–57), structuralism, and more recently in the work of Jeffrey Alexander; see Jeffrey Alexander, "Citizen and Enemy as Symbolic Classification: On the Polarizing Discourse of Civil Society," in *Cultivating Differences,* ed. Michèlle Lamont and Marcel Fournier (Chicago: University of Chicago Press, 1992), 289–308; Jeffrey C. Alexander and Philip Smith, "The Discourse of American Civil Society: A New Proposal for Cultural Studies," *Theory and Society* 22 (1993): 151–207.

36. Hayden V. White, *Metahistory* (Baltimore: Johns Hopkins University Press, 1973), 7–11; Frye, *Anatomy of Criticism,* 186–206.

37. Michael Blain, "Fighting Words: What We Can Learn from Hitler's Hyperbole," *Symbolic Interaction* 11 (1988): 257–76. See also Patricia Ewick and Susan S. Silbey, "Subversive Stories and Hegemonic Tales: Toward a Sociology of Narrative," *Law and Society Review* 29 (1995): 197–226; Griswold, "Formulaic Fiction."

38. Michael B. Aune, "Liturgy Interest Group," in *Guide to Introducing the "Lutheran Book of Worship,"* ed. Henry J. Ehlen et al. (Minneapolis: Augsburg Publishing House; Philadelphia: Board of Publications, Lutheran Church in America, 1978), 21–22. See also Sergeant, *Seeker Churches,* 57.

39. On this point about form creating audience expectations, see Burke, *Rhetoric of Motives;* Thomas M. Leitch, *What Stories Are* (University Park, PA: Pennsylvania State University Press, 1986); Robin Wagner-Pacifici, *The Moro Morality Play* (Chicago: University of Chicago Press, 1986).

40. In the Lutheran tradition, the confession is done collectively during the worship service, whereas in Roman Catholicism, the confession tends to be done individually and not incorporated into the worship service.

41. See Aune, "Liturgy Interest Group," 21; James F. White, *Christian Worship in North America,* 164–65.

42. Roof, *Spiritual Marketplace,* 192.

43. See note 24.

44. On the importance of emotion and experience in worship for younger Americans, see Donald E. Miller, *Reinventing American Protestantism*.

45. While Pastor Andersen did not directly name evangelicals as backing down on sin, his comment about "church growth experts" refers to a variety of evangelical consultants he encountered in his studies at the conservative Beeson Institute, at Asbury Theological Seminary, and in his regular reading. During three conversations, he provided me with lists of the church growth experts he had read, and in all cases, they are aligned with evangelicalism or nondenominational megachurches.

46. Sargeant, *Seeker Churches*, 95. See also Witten, *All Is Forgiven*.

47. Compare this to the confession and absolution most commonly used in the *LBW*. Confession: "We confess that we are in bondage to sin and cannot free ourselves. We have sinned against you in thought, word, and deed, by what we have done and by what we have left undone. We have not loved you with our whole heart; we have not loved our neighbors as ourselves. For the sake of your Son, Jesus Christ, have mercy on us. Forgive us, renew us, and lead us, so that we delight in your will and walk in your ways, to the glory of your holy name. Amen." Absolution: "Almighty God, in his mercy, has given his Son to die for us and, for his sake, forgives us all our sins. As a called and ordained minister of the Church of Christ, and by his authority, I therefore declare to you the entire forgiveness of all your sins."

48. See the discussion of Saddleback in chapter 3.

49. In nineteen of the twenty-eight interviews with members of Faith, I specifically asked them about their experiences in the church's small groups (this was one of the topics the congregation's leaders asked me to focus on as part of their agreement to participate in the study). I also attended a weekly men's small group for three months and a four-week study on the world of the Old Testament at Zion that used a video and study guide from Willow Creek.

50. Not all members of these congregations used the language of evangelicalism to describe their faith. Some used the language of Lutheranism, and others sounded more like Ammerman's "golden rule Christians," who were not able to speak in great detail or depth about their faith during our interviews; see Nancy Ammerman, "Golden Rule Christianity: Lived Religion in the American Mainstream," in *Lived Religion in America: Toward a History of Practice*, ed. David Hall (Princeton: Princeton University Press, 1997), 196–216. Since I used snowball sampling rather than random sampling to select people to be interviewed, it is possible that I interviewed a disproportionate number of evangelically oriented individuals.

51. On the gendered language of Promise Keepers and, more generally, of evangelical and conservative Christianity, see Jon Bloch, "The New and Improved Clint Eastwood: Change and Persistence in Promise Keepers Self-Help Literature," *Sociology of Religion* 61, no. 1 (2000): 11–32; John P. Bartkowski, "Breaking Walls, Raising Fences: Masculinity, Intimacy, and Accountability among the Promise Keepers," *Sociology of Religion* 61, no. 1 (2000): 33–54; John P. Bartkowski, *Remaking the Godly Marriage: Gender Negotiation in Evangelical Families* (New Brunswick, NJ: Rutgers University Press, 2001).

52. Christian Smith, *American Evangelicalism*.

53. Because I was more interested in gathering information about the congregation than about individuals' personal religious lives, the friendship question tended to get dropped during interviews when the person had a great deal to say about the congregation or when the interview was running long and needed to be ended. Ten of the twenty-eight members interviewed at Faith answered the question, and thirteen of the nineteen members interviewed at Zion answered it. In both congregations, none of the respondents reported that less than half of their friends were also members of the congregation or Christians.

54. Information about the Word Alone Network can be found at their Web site: http://www.wordalone.org (accessed March 5, 2006). The network has just over three hundred member churches (roughly 3 percent of all ELCA congregations).

55. The 1996 agreement allowed clergy to serve either Episcopal or Lutheran congregations, as it required that the ELCA recognize the "historic episcopate," or more generally a polity in which bishops exercise real power. In the ELCA, bishops are more administrative officers than policy makers and cannot compel congregations to call specific clergy or take specific actions. Word Alone Network supporters argued that the imposition of the historic episcopate violated the governance and theological principles of the Lutheran confessional documents.

56. See R. Stephen Warner, "The Place of the Congregation in the Contemporary American Religious Configuration," in *American Congregations,* vol. 2, ed. James P. Wind and James W. Lewis (Chicago: University of Chicago Press, 1994), 54–99.

57. See the discussion in chapter 4.

58. After an official trial, the national church ruled that the congregation could remain in the ELCA but that the openly gay pastor was no longer recognized as a pastor in good standing within the Lutheran church. Officially, the congregation remains without a pastor, while unofficially it has continued to operate with its gay pastor.

59. Roof, *Spiritual Marketplace*, 185.

60. Sargeant, *Seeker Churches*, 57.

61. Clergy and lay leaders at both congregations dismissed the helpfulness of the local synod and the ELCA when looking for educational materials, inspiration for growth, new ideas for worship, or new pastors. Faith had significantly decreased the amount of money it sent to the ELCA and instead chose to give money to non-Lutheran, primarily evangelical, organizations that promoted foreign and domestic missions.

62. At Faith, Pastor Lincoln periodically attacked the ELCA as an irrelevant, outdated, antigrowth organization in newsletter columns, sermons, and our conversations.

63. The tradition's relative unimportance at Faith and Zion was reflected in the new-member and adult-education classes, where little attention were given to teaching about Lutheran theology and beliefs, Luther's *Small Catechism*, or the confessional documents. At St. Peter's, classes often had a distinctively Lutheran emphasis.

Chapter Six

1. Finke, "Innovative Returns to Tradition." See also Donald E. Miller, *Reinventing American Protestantism;* Kent D. Miller, "Competitive Strategies for Religious

Organizations," *Strategic Management Journal* 23 (2002): 435–56; Carroll, *Mainline to the Future*.

2. Becker, *Congregations in Conflict*.

3. Benford raises this critique in his discussion of empirical studies of social movement framing. He notes that "we tend to work backward from successful mobilization to the framings activists proffered and then posit a causal linkage between the two," in short, demonstrating that a set of meanings resonated with an audience but unable to demonstrate how or why. See Robert D. Benford, "An Insider's Critique of the Social Movement Framing Perspective," *Sociological Inquiry* 67 (1997): 412.

4. See Michael Schudson, "How Culture Works: Perspectives from Media Studies on the Efficacy of Symbols," *Theory and Society* 18 (1989): 153–80.

5. See Wuthnow, *Communities of Discourse*, 1–18; Griswold, *Renaissance Revivals*, 187–211.

6. On the concept of the "negotiated order," see Fine's review essay "Negotiated Orders and Organizational Cultures." The quotation is from a definition provided by Anselm Strauss in his book *Negotiations* (San Francisco: Jossey-Bass, 1978), 5.

7. The group spent several minutes discussing the pay of the three clergy and the prospect of forcing the council to cut their pay and benefits in order to force the clergy to follow the wishes of the majority of members and return the worship services to their original form. In addition, a council member who claimed to represent the unhappy members periodically raised the threat of cutting the pastors' salaries during council meetings in 2000 and 2001.

8. See Fine, "Negotiated Orders and Organizational Cultures," 241.

9. See chapter 4.

10. Wuthnow writes: "A spirituality of dwelling emphasizes *habitation:* God occupies a definitive place in the universe and creates a sacred space in which humans too can dwell; to inhabit sacred space is to know its territory and to feel secure. A spirituality of seeking emphasizes *negotiation:* individuals search for sacred moments that reinforce their conviction that the divine exists, but these moments are fleeting; rather than knowing the territory, people explore new spiritual vistas, and they may have to negotiate among complex and confusing meanings of spirituality" (Wuthnow, *After Heaven*, 3–4).

11. At Good Shepherd, this group was known as "The Letter Writing Committee." I renamed them to emphasize their goal of restoring the Lutheran tradition as they understood it.

12. The ELCA's ordination vows include an agreement "to teach and preach in accordance with the Holy Scriptures and the confessions of the Lutheran Church."

13. The evidence largely consisted of short statements made by the senior pastor in response to questions posed by a small group of members at an impromptu meeting after church one Sunday, at which one of the members secretly recorded the pastor's responses.

14. On "lay liberalism, see Hoge, Johnson, and Luidens, *Vanishing Boundaries*, 112–15; on golden rule Christianity, see Ammerman, "Golden Rule Christianity."

15. On the culture of literalism in the United States, see Vincent Crapanzano, *Serving the Word: Literalism in America from the Pulpit to the Bench* (New York: New Press, 2000). In the introduction, Crapanzano identifies several key elements of literalism that were shared by Good Shepherd's literalists: the denial that a sacred text can have more than one meaning; the absolute belief that the literal meaning in a text is eternal; and a refusal to acknowledge that meaning is socially constructed.

16. I was unable to learn the details about the decision-making process regarding the organ. Instead, I heard multiple and conflicting accounts. In one, the pro-organ party was excluded from planning the new building; in another, no one even asked the planning committee to consider a pipe organ; and in a third, the organ issue was delayed because of limited funds. It was difficult to reconstruct the history and process of this conflict because the congregation's leaders asked me not to ask members to speak about it during our interviews (I was allowed to let members raise the issue themselves) as a way of defusing the conflict and letting the congregation heal.

17. On "worship wars," see Thomas G. Long, *Beyond the Worship Wars: Building Vital and Faithful Worship* (Bethesda, MD: Alban Institute, 2001).

18. Several interviewees claimed that the pastors had not managed the change process very well. They complained that they lacked communication skills, "organizational savvy," and the experience to defuse conflict.

19. Finke, "Innovative Returns to Tradition."

20. "High Q" could refer to high IQ or high quality, but I am not sure what he meant, and I did not ask him to define the term during the interview.

21. At Faith, the plan formally to abolish the old committee system and shift power from the congregation to small, independent, ad hoc teams met some resistance from older members, but they were not able to gain widespread support. When I asked younger members for their reaction to the resistance, many of them seemed at a loss to explain it. "Delegating decisions to small working groups just makes sense. It's how we operate at work," said one, and his comment reflected the general agreement among members under the age of fifty-five that preserving a strong role for congregational governance in church matters was not very important.

22. St. Peter's also preserved religious choice when they replaced one *LBW* service with a praise music service. During the congregational meeting when church leaders explained why they were making this change in music, the senior pastor spoke about the need to offer a different style of worship that would appeal to non-Lutherans, but he then made two promises: first, that the theology of the service would remain Lutheran and, second, that St. Peter's "would always, always offer a traditional, liturgical service." Thus, at St. Peter's, in contradistinction to Grace and Good Shepherd, the process was defined in "win-win," rather than "zero sum," terms.

23. On the issue of authority in modernity and postmodernity, see Giddens, *Modernity and Self-Identity;* Bauman, *Life in Fragments;* Carroll, *Mainline to the Future;* Lyon, *Jesus in Disneyland.* On the culture of pragmatism or utilitarianism, see Bellah et al., *Habits of the Heart;* Paul Lichterman, "Self-Help Reading as a Thin Culture," *Media, Culture, and Society* 14 (1992): 421–47.

24. Donald E. Miller claims that congregations affiliated with Vineyard Fellowship, Hope Chapel, and Calvary Chapel represent a new type of congregational form in American Protestantism. He claims that such congregations are creating a new genre of worship, reorganizing church administration by following the model of the early church described in the New Testament, and "democratizing access to the sacred by radicalizing the Protestant principle of the priesthood of all believers" (*Reinventing American Protestantism,* 1). He identifies twelve "trademark qualities" of new-paradigm churches: "1. they were started in the mid-1960s; 2. the majority of congregation members were born after 1945; 3. seminary training of clergy is optional; 4. worship is contemporary; 5. lay leadership is highly valued; 6. they have extensive small group ministries; 7. clergy and congregants usually dress informally; 8. tolerance of different personal styles is prized; 9. pastors tend to be understated, humble, and self-revealing; 10. bodily, rather than mere cognitive, participation in worship is the norm; 11. the 'gifts of the Holy Spirit' are affirmed; 12. Bible-centered teaching predominates over topical sermonizing" (ibid., 20).
25. Moore, *Selling God,* 271.

Chapter 7

1. See Roof, *Spiritual Marketplace;* Wolfe, *Transformation of American Religion;* Richard Cimino and Don Lattin, *Shopping for Faith: American Religion in the New Millennium* (San Francisco: Jossey-Bass, 1998).
2. Roof, *Spiritual Marketplace.*
3. Popular theology in the pietist tradition tends to make human beings rather than God the central actors in the story of faith and frames the world and faith in a relatively simple and straightforward manner (e.g., the world is divided into the saved and the lost; good and evil). It is a system in which moral absolutes, determinism, and certitude do not allow much room for doubt or the possibility that God is not in control (e.g., see Christian Smith, *American Evangelicalism,* 20–66). Lutheran theology and its expression in worship make God the primary actor, allow greater room for doubt, and recognize that the ongoing tension between sin and righteousness within the individual and the contradictory pulls of this world and the kingdom of God make the life of faith a daily challenge.
4. On the codes and logics, see Swidler, *Talk of Love,* 160–80.
5. See James F. White, *Christian Worship in North America.*
6. On the role of tradition and church in the confessional tradition, see ibid.; Aune, "Corporate and Confessional Character of Worship"; Aune, *"Lutheran Book of Worship:* Relic or Resource?"
7. I am indebted to one of the anonymous reviewers for this idea about the information-brokering role of church growth experts.
8. These specialized services often used the pietist three-part worship structure rather than the Lutheran liturgical order. Some emphasized spirituality and practices such as meditation to help attendees experience the sacred.
9. See Roof, *Spiritual Marketplace,* 172–79.

10. In her study of an evangelical seminary, Wheeler notes that, in comparison to evangelicals' mass production of material religious culture, "the mainline Protestant inventory of symbols, manners, iconic leaders, images of leadership, distinctive language, decorations and sounds is very low indeed." She concludes that "a religious tradition that has little or nothing to look at, listen to, and touch cannot sustain us very long." See Barbara Wheeler, "We Who Were Far Off" (paper presented to the Religious Research Association, St. Louis, November 1994); cited in Hoover, "The Cross at Willow Creek," 151.

11. See Donald E. Miller, *Reinventing American Protestantism;* Wolfe, *Transformation of American Religion.*

12. See Ammerman, *Pillars of Faith,* 206–53; Eiseland, *Particular Place;* Dillon, *Catholic Identity;* Roof, *Spiritual Marketplace;* Becker, *Congregations in Conflict.*

13. Drawing on an internal ELCA study and the U.S. Congregational Life Survey, Inskeep compared church members' denominational identity in 1991 and 2001 and found that about 80 percent of those surveyed claimed "it is important for me to be a member of a Lutheran Church"; another 60–70 percent claimed that it is important to be an ELCA congregation. See Kenneth W. Inskeep, "The Context for Mission and Ministry in the Evangelical Lutheran Church in America" (Evangelical Lutheran Church in America, Chicago, 2003, unpublished paper). Data from the Faith Communities Today Survey indicate that about 80 percent of those surveyed claimed that their "congregation clearly expresses its Lutheran heritage" either very well or quite well; FACT data accessed from http://www.elca.org/re/ccsp/ccspfreq.pdf (accessed March 10, 2006).

14. See Roof, *Spiritual Marketplace;* Nancy Ammerman, "New Life for Denominationalism," *Christian Century,* March 15, 2000, 302–7; Ammerman, *Pillars of Faith;* Kenneth W. Inskeep, "Religious Commitment in the Evangelical Lutheran Church in America" (Evangelical Lutheran Church in America, Chicago, 2001, unpublished paper).

15. Data on "fast-growing" ELCA congregations comes from Martin H. Smith, "Exploring the Differences between Fast-Growing and Randomly Selected ELCA Congregations" (Evangelical Lutheran Church in America, Chicago, 2002, unpublished paper). Drawing on data from the U.S. Congregational Life Survey, Smith reports that 22.2 percent of fast-growing congregations prefer contemporary worship, compared with 16.3 percent of randomly selected congregations; 42.7 percent use drums or electric guitar (vs. 16.3 percent of other congregations); 25.2 percent use visual projection equipment (vs. 6.5 percent of other congregations); and in 13 percent of the fast-growing congregations people routinely raise their hands in praise (vs. only 3.6 percent in other congregations). Data on fast-growing PCUSA congregations come from Deborah Bruce and Cynthia Woolever, "The U.S. Congregational Life Survey: Fastest Growing Presbyterian Churches" (Research Services of the Presbyterian Church, U.S.A., Louisville, 2003, unpublished paper). Bruce and Woolever report similar differences between the fast-growing churches and those with slow growth, no growth, or decline. Growth rates ranged from 25 to 75 percent, with an average growth rate of 33 percent in the ELCA congregations and 36 percent in the PCUSA congregations. See Kenneth W. Inskeep and Jeffrey L. Drake, "Worship Attendance in the Evangelical Lutheran Church in

America: Faith Communities Today," Evangelical Lutheran Church in America, Chicago, 2001, http://www.elca.org/re/reports/ccspwrspl.pdf (accessed March 10, 2006); David A. Roozen, "Three Sources of American Religious Renewal," Hartford Institute for Religion Research, http://fact.hartsem.edu/research/fact2000/topical_article1.htm (accessed March 10, 2006).

16. See Thumma and Petersen, "Goliaths in Our Midst," 102–24; Inskeep "Denominational Identity in the Evangelical Lutheran Church in America; Scott Thumma, "Denominational Identity and Church Vitality," Hartford Institute for Religion Research, 2000, http://fact.hartsem.edu/research/fact2000/topical_article4.htm (accessed March 10, 2006).

17. James K. Wellman, "The Churching of the Pacific Northwest: The Rise of Sectarian Entrepreneurs," in *Religion and Public Life in the Pacific Northwest: The None Zone,* ed. Patricia O'Connell Killen and Mark Silk (Walnut Creek, CA: Alta Mira Press, 2004), 79–106.

18. David A. Roozen, "Four Mega-trends Changing America's Religious Landscape," Hartford Institute for Religion Research, 2001, http://fact.hartsem.edu/research/fact2000/topical_article11.htm (accessed March 10, 2006).

19. Robert D. Putnam, *Bowling Alone* (New York: Simon and Schuster, 2000); Robert Wuthnow, *Loose Connections* (Cambridge, MA: Harvard University Press, 1998); Theda Skocpol, *Diminished Democracy* (Norman: University of Oklahoma Press, 2003); Paul Lichterman, *The Search for Political Community* (New York: Cambridge University Press, 1996). For an overview of the concept of community, see Suzanne Keller, *Community* (Princeton: Princeton University Press, 2003), 1–48.

20. The terms "community of memory" and "community of interest" are from Robert Bellah et al., *Habits of the Heart,* 134, 153–54. The term "communities of limited liability" refers to communities characterized by weak ties and easy entrance and exit; see Morris Janowitz, *The Community Press in an Urban Setting* (Chicago: University of Chicago Press, 1967).

21. Bellah et al., *Habits of the Heart,* 228–34.

22. John A. Coleman, S.J., "Selling God in America: American Commercial Culture as a Climate of Hospitality to Religion," in *Meaning and Modernity,* ed. Richard Madsen, William A. Sullivan, Ann Swidler, and Steven M. Tipton (Berkeley and Los Angeles: University of California Press, 2002), 147–48.

23. Swidler, "Culture in Action."

24. On religious tradition, see Carroll, *Mainline to the Future;* on religious conflict, see John Seidler and Katherine Meyer, *Conflict and Change in the Catholic Church* (New Brunswick, NJ: Rutgers University Press, 1989); on congregational change, see Ammerman, *Congregation and Community.*

25. Chaves, "Ordaining Women and Organizational Innovation." Fligstein makes a similar argument in an essay about organizational change: "environments are murky; thus actors have to provide interpretations of them. These accounts are a function of actors' interests and position in any given organization. Solutions to problems from this perspective require a construction of that problem as well as a course of action consistent with it. This gives rise to the importance of two issues: cognition or perception, and

the role of power in organizational change" ("Structural Transformation of American Industry," 315). See also Royston Greenwood and C. R. Hinings, "Understanding Radical Organizational Change," *Academy of Management Review* 21, no. 4 (1996): 1024.

26. Nina Eliasoph and Paul Lichterman, "Culture in Interaction," *American Journal of Sociology* 108, no. 4 (2003): 735–94.

27. Bass, "Congregations and the Bearing of Tradition."

28. Chaves, *Congregations in America*, 153–57. Chaves self-consciously draws on Stanley Lieberson's insights into the nature of change in names and fashion. Lieberson argues that culture, whether children's names or dress styles, changes in continuity with existing tastes. One mechanism he discusses is "incremental replacement," in which one or a few elements of existing tastes are changed, and as the new tastes are established, other elements are changed. Over time, fashion changes radically through the succession of small changes. See Stanley Lieberson, *A Matter of Taste: How Names, Fashions, and Culture Change* (New Haven, CT: Yale University Press, 2000), 114–15.

29. Penny Edgell encouraged me to consider how Bourdieu's insight into the relationship between orthodox and heterodox culture might apply to the congregations in my study.

Appendix

1. Active members include individuals who hold elected office, serve on committees, regularly teach or attend classes, sing in the choir, or attend worship at least twice each month. I wanted to talk with members who knew the history of the congregation or were well informed about what was happening in the church at the time of the study. Throughout the book, I use the term "congregational leaders" to refer to both clergy and this group of active church members in the nine congregations.

REFERENCES

Alexander, Jeffrey. "Citizen and Enemy as Symbolic Classification: On the Polarizing Discourse of Civil Society." In *Cultivating Differences,* ed. Michèlle Lamont and Marcel Fournier, 289–308. Chicago: University of Chicago Press, 1992.

Alexander, Jeffrey C., and Philip Smith. "The Discourse of American Civil Society: A New Proposal for Cultural Studies." *Theory and Society* 22 (1993): 151–207.

Almen, Lowell G. *One Great Cloud of Witnesses.* Minneapolis: Augsburg Fortress, 1997.

Ammerman, Nancy. *Congregation and Community.* New Brunswick, NJ: Rutgers University Press, 1997.

————. "Golden Rule Christianity: Lived Religion in the American Mainstream." In *Lived Religion in America: Toward a History of Practice,* ed. David Hall, 196–216. Princeton: Princeton University Press, 1997.

————. "New Life for Denominationalism." *Christian Century,* March 15, 2000, 302–7.

————. *Pillars of Faith: American Congregations and Their Partners.* Berkeley and Los Angeles: University of California Press, 2005.

The Augsburg Confession. St. Louis: Concordia Publishing House, 1906.

Aune, Michael B. "The Corporate and Confessional Character of Worship: The Common Service Debate." *Word and World* 8 (Winter 1988): 32–41.

————. "Liturgy Interest Group." In *Guide to Introducing the "Lutheran Book of Worship,"* ed. Henry J. Ehlen et al., 19–38. Minneapolis: Augsburg Publishing House; Philadelphia: Board of Publications, Lutheran Church in America, 1978.

————. "*Lutheran Book of Worship:* Relic or Resource?" *Dialog* 33, no. 3 (1994): 174–82.

Barna, George. *The Habits of Highly Effective Churches.* Ventura, CA: Regal, 1999.

Bartkowski, John P. "Breaking Walls, Raising Fences: Masculinity, Intimacy, and Accountability among the Promise Keepers." *Sociology of Religion* 61, no. 1 (2000): 33–54.

————. *Remaking the Godly Marriage: Gender Negotiation in Evangelical Families.* New Brunswick, NJ: Rutgers University Press, 2001.

Bass, Dorothy C. "Congregations and the Bearing of Tradition." In *American Congregations,* vol. 2, ed. James P. Wind and James W. Lewis, 169–91. Chicago: University of Chicago Press, 1994.

Bauman, Zygmunt. *Life in Fragments: Essays in Postmodern Morality.* Cambridge, MA: Blackwell, 1995.

Becker, Penny Edgel. *Congregations in Conflict.* London and New York: Cambridge University Press, 1999.

———. "Making Inclusive Communities: Congregations and the 'Problem of Race.'" *Social Problems* 45 (1998): 451–72.

Bell, Catherine. *Ritual: Perspectives and Dimensions.* New York: Oxford University Press, 1997.

Bellah, Robert N., Richard Madsen, William M. Sullivan, Ann Swidler, and Steven M. Tipton. *Habits of the Heart.* 1st California pbk. ed. Berkeley and Los Angeles: University of California Press, 1996.

Benford, Robert D. "An Insider's Critique of the Social Movement Framing Perspective." *Sociological Inquiry* 67 (1997): 409–30.

Berezin, Mabel. "Cultural Form and Political Meaning: State-Subsidized Theater, Ideology, and the Language of Style in Fascist Italy." *American Journal of Sociology* 99 (1994): 1237–86.

Best, Joel. *Threatened Children: Rhetoric and Concern about Child-Victims.* Chicago: University of Chicago Press, 1990.

Billingsley, Andrew. *Mighty Like a River: The Black Church and Social Reform.* New York: Oxford University Press, 1999.

Blain, Michael. "Fighting Words: What We Can Learn from Hitler's Hyperbole." *Symbolic Interaction* 11 (1988): 257–76.

Bloch, Jon. "The New and Improved Clint Eastwood: Change and Persistence in Promise Keepers Self-Help Literature." *Sociology of Religion* 61, no. 1 (2000): 11–32.

Bourdieu, Pierre. *Language and Symbolic Power.* Cambridge, MA: Harvard University Press, 1991.

———. *Outline of a Theory of Practice.* New York: Cambridge University Press, 1977.

Braaten, Carl. *Principles of Lutheran Theology.* Philadelphia: Fortress Press, 1983.

Braaten, Carl E., and Robert W. Jenson, eds. *Christian Dogmatics.* 2 vols. Philadelphia: Fortress Press, 1984.

Bruce, Deborah, and Cynthia Woolever. "The U.S. Congregational Life Survey: Fastest Growing Presbyterian Churches." Research Services of the Presbyterian Church, U.S.A., Louisville, 2003. Unpublished paper.

Burke, Kenneth. *A Rhetoric of Motives.* Berkeley and Los Angeles: University of California Press, 1969.

Burstein, Paul, and Marie Bricher. "Problem Definition and Public Policy: Congressional Committees Confront Work, Family, and Gender, 1945–1990." *Social Forces* 75, no. 4 (1997): 135–69.

Caplow, Theodore. "Rule Enforcement without Visible Means: Christmas Gift Giving in Middletown." *American Journal of Sociology* 89, no. 6 (1984): 1306–23.

Carroll, Jackson W. *Mainline to the Future: Congregations for the 21st Century.* Louisville, KY: Westminster John Knox Press, 2000.

Chaves, Mark. *Congregations in America.* Cambridge, MA: Harvard University Press, 2004.

―――. "Ordaining Women and Organizational Innovation." *American Journal of Sociology* 101 (1997): 840–73.

Cimino, Richard, and Don Lattin. *Shopping for Faith: American Religion in the New Millennium.* San Francisco: Jossey-Bass, 1998.

Clark, Linda. "'Songs That My Mother Taught Me': Hymns as Transmitters of Faith." In *Beyond Establishment: Protestant Identity in a Post-Protestant Age,* ed. Paul F. Bradshaw and Lawrence A. Hoffman, 99–105. South Bend, IN: University of Notre Dame Press, 1993.

Clemens, Elisabeth S., and James M. Cook. "Politics and Institutionalism: Explaining Durability and Change." *Annual Review of Sociology* 25 (1999): 441–66.

Coleman, James William. *The New Buddhism: The Western Transformation of an Ancient Tradition.* New York: Oxford University Press, 2001.

Coleman, John A., S.J. "Selling God in America: American Commercial Culture as a Climate of Hospitality to Religion." In *Meaning and Modernity,* ed. Richard Madsen, William A. Sullivan, Ann Swidler, and Steven M. Tipton, 136–49. Berkeley and Los Angeles: University of California Press, 2002.

The Common Worship Lectionary: New Revised Standard Version, Anglicized Edition. Desk Edition. Ed. Martin Manser, Kenneth Stevenson, and Martin Kitchen. Oxford: Oxford University Press, 1999.

Crapanzano, Vincent. *Serving the Word: Literalism in America from the Pulpit to the Bench.* New York: New Press, 2000.

Davidman, Lynn. *Tradition in a Rootless World.* New Brunswick, NJ: Rutgers University Press, 1991.

Dechow, Jon F. "Mission West: A History of the Association of Evangelical Lutheran Churches (AELC) in the West." 1988. Sierra Pacific Synod Archives, Berkeley, CA.

Dillon, Michele. *Catholic Identity.* New York: Cambridge University Press, 1999.

DiMaggio, Paul J., and Walter W. Powell. "The Iron Cage Revisited: Institutional Isomorphism and Collective Rationality." In *The New Institutionalism in Organizational Analysis,* ed. Walter W. Powell and Paul S. DiMaggio, 63–82. Chicago: University of Chicago Press, 1991.

Easum, William M. *Sacred Cows Make Gourmet Burgers.* Nashville: Abingdon Press, 1995.

Easum, William M., and Thomas G. Bandy. *Growing Spiritual Redwoods.* Nashville: Abingdon Press, 1997.

Eiseland, Nancy L. *A Particular Place: Urban Restructuring and Religious Ecology in a Southern Suburb.* New Brunswick, NJ: Rutgers University Press, 2000.

Eliasoph, Nina, and Paul Lichterman. "Culture in Interaction." *American Journal of Sociology* 108, no. 4 (2003): 735–94.

Emerson, Michael O., and Karen Chai Kim. "Multiracial Congregations: An Analysis of Their Development and a Typology." *Journal for the Scientific Study of Religion* 42 (2003): 217–27.

Erlander, Daniel. *Baptized We Live: Lutheranism as a Way of Life.* Self-published, 1981.

Ernst, Eldon. "American Religious History from a Pacific Coast Perspective." In *Religion and Society in the American West: Historical Essays,* edited by Carl Guarneri and David Alvarez, 3–39. Lanham, MD: University Press of America, 1987.

Ewick, Patricia, and Susan S. Silbey. "Subversive Stories and Hegemonic Tales: Toward a Sociology of Narrative." *Law and Society Review* 29 (1995): 197–226.

Fine, Gary Alan. "Negotiated Orders and Organizational Cultures." *Annual Review of Sociology* 10 (1984): 239–62.

———. "Public Narration and Group Culture: Discerning Discourse in Social Movements." In *Social Movements and Culture*, ed. Hank Johnston and Bert Klandermans, 127–43. Minneapolis: University of Minnesota Press, 1995.

Finke, Roger. "The Consequences of Religious Competition: Supply-Side Explanations for Religious Change." In *Rational Choice Theory and Religion: Summary and Assessment*, ed. Lawrence R. Young, 45–64. New Brunswick, NJ: Rutgers University Press, 1997.

———. "Innovative Returns to Tradition: Using Core Teachings as the Foundation for Innovative Accommodation." *Journal for the Scientific Study of Religion* 43, no. 1 (2004): 19–34.

Finke, Roger, and Rodney Stark. *The Churching of America, 1776–1990: Winners and Losers in Our Religious Economy.* New Brunswick, NJ: Rutgers University Press, 1992.

———. "The New Holy Clubs: Testing Church-to-Sect Propositions." *Sociology of Religion* 62 (2001): 175–89.

Fiske, John. "Audiencing: A Cultural Studies Approach to Watching Television." *Poetics* 21 (1992): 345–59.

Fligstein, Neil. "The Structural Transformation of American Industry: An Institutional Account of the Causes of Diversification in the Largest Firms, 1919–1979." In *The New Institutionalism in Organizational Analysis*, ed. Walter W. Powell and Paul S. DiMaggio, 311–36. Chicago: University of Chicago Press, 1991.

Frankiel, Sandra Sizer. *California's Spiritual Frontiers: Religious Alternatives in Anglo-Protestantism, 1850–1910.* Berkeley and Los Angeles: University of California Press, 1988.

Frye, Northrup. *Anatomy of Criticism.* Princeton: Princeton University Press, 1957.

Gallup, George, Jr., and Timothy K. Jones. *The Next American Spirituality: Finding God in the Twenty-first Century.* Colorado Springs: Cook Communications, 2000.

Gallup, George, Jr., and D. Michael Lindsay. *Surveying the Religious Landscape.* Harrisburg, PA: Morehouse Publishing, 1999.

Geertz, Clifford. *The Interpretation of Cultures.* New York: Basic Books, 1973.

Giddens, Anthony. *Modernity and Self-Identity.* Stanford: Stanford University Press, 1991.

Gilkes, Cheryl Townsend. "Plenty Good Room: Adaptation in a Changing Black Church." *Annals of the American Academy of Political and Social Sciences* 558 (1998): 101–21.

Goffman, Erving. *Frame Analysis.* Boston: Northeastern University Press, 1986.

Graverock, Paul J. "Liturgy for Life: The Liturgy and Adult Instruction for Lutheran Congregations." DMin diss., San Francisco Theological Seminary, 1990.

Greenwood, Royston, and C. R. Hinings. "Understanding Radical Organizational Change." *Academy of Management Review* 21, no. 4 (1996): 1022–54.

Griswold, Wendy. "Formulaic Fiction: The Author as Agent of Elective Affinity." In *Comparative Social Research*, vol. 11, ed. Craig Calhoun, 75–130. Greenwich, CT: JAI Press, 1989.

———. *Renaissance Revivals*. Chicago: University of Chicago Press, 1986.

Gritsch, Eric W., and Robert W. Jenson. *Lutheranism: The Theological Movement and Its Confessional Writings*. Philadelphia: Fortress Press, 1976.

Gusfield, Joseph R. *The Culture of Public Problems: Drinking-Driving and the Symbolic Order*. Chicago: University of Chicago Press, 1981.

Hadaway, C. Kirk, and Pennly Long Marler. "All in the Family: Religious Mobility in America." *Review of Religious Research* 35, no. 2 (1993): 97–117.

Hall, Stuart. "Encoding/Decoding." In *Popular Culture: Production and Consumption*, ed. Lee C. Harrington and Denise D. Bielby, 123–32. Malden, MA: Blackwell Publishers, 2000.

Hammond, Philip E. "The Market Paradigm and the Future of Religious Organizations." In *The Dynamics of Religious Organizations*, 32–47. New York: Oxford University Press, 2000.

Hart, Darryl G. *The Lost Soul of American Protestantism*. Oxford: Rowman and Littlefield Publishers, 2002.

Hatch, Nathan O. "The Appeal of American Evangelicalism." In *The Appeal of American Evangelicalism*, 9–20. Concordia Seminary Monograph Series, Symposium Papers. St. Louis: Concordia Seminary, 1993.

Hawkins, Robert D. "Whither Now Lutherans?" *Alleluia: Worship Newsletter* (North Carolina Synod, ELCA), Spring 1993, 4–6.

Heelas, Paul, Scott Lash, and Paul Morris, eds. *Detraditionalization*. Cambridge, MA: Blackwell Publishers, 1996.

Hilgartner, Stephen, and Charles L. Bosk. "The Rise and Fall of Social Problems: A Public Arenas Model." *American Journal of Sociology* 94 (1988): 53–78.

Hoge, Dean R., Benton Johnson, and Donald A. Luidens. *Vanishing Boundaries: The Religion of Mainline Protestant Baby Boomers*. Louisville, KY: Westminster/John Knox Press, 1994.

Hoover, Stuart M. "The Cross at Willow Creek: Seeker Religion and the Contemporary Marketplace." In *Religion and Popular Culture in America*, ed. Bruce David Forbes and Jeffrey H. Mahan, 145–60. Berkeley and Los Angeles: University of California Press, 2000.

Hunt, Lynn. *Politics, Culture, and Class in the French Revolution*. Berkeley and Los Angeles: University of California Press, 1986.

Iannaccone, Laurence R. "Rational Choice: Framework for the Scientific Study of Religion." In *Rational Choice Theory and Religion: Summary and Assessment*, ed. Lawrence R. Young, 25–44. New Brunswick, NJ: Rutgers University Press, 1997.

Ingram, Paul, and Karen Clay. "The Choice-within-Constraints New Institutionalism and Implications for Sociology." *Annual Review of Sociology* 26 (2000): 525–46.

Inskeep, Kenneth W. "The Context for Mission and Ministry in the Evangelical Lutheran Church in America." Evangelical Lutheran Church in America, Chicago, 2003. Unpublished paper.

———. "Denominational Identity in the Evangelical Lutheran Church in America." Department for Research and Evaluation, Evangelical Lutheran Church in America, Chicago, 2001. Unpublished paper.

———. "Religious Commitment in the Evangelical Lutheran Church in America." Evangelical Lutheran Church in America, Chicago, 2001. unpublished paper.

Inskeep, Kenneth W., and Jeffrey L. Drake. "Worship Attendance in the Evangelical Lutheran Church in America: Faith Communities Today." Evangelical Lutheran Church in America, Chicago, 2001. http://www.elca.org/re/reports/ccspwrsp1.pdf.

Janowitz, Morris. *The Community Press in an Urban Setting.* Chicago: University of Chicago Press, 1967.

Johnson, Benton. "On Church and Sect." *American Sociological Review* 28 (1963): 539–49.

Jordahl, Leigh D. "Folk Church, Liturgy, and Ceremony: Or Can We Avoid Disaster?" *Dialog* 14 (1975): 114–21.

———. "Schmucker and Walther: A Study of Christian Response to American Culture." In *The Future of the American Church*, ed. Philip J. Hefner, 71–90. Philadelphia: Fortress Press, 1968.

Keller, Suzanne. *Community.* Princeton: Princeton University Press, 2003.

Killen, Patricia. "Christianity in the Western United States." *Span*, Summer 2002, 6–7, 25, 28.

Klein, Christa Resmeyer. "Lutherans, Merger and the Loss of History." *Christian Century*, January 2–9, 1985, 18–20.

Kolb, Robert. *The Christian Faith: A Lutheran Exposition.* St. Louis: Concordia Publishing House, 1993.

Kosmin, Barry A., and Seymour P. Lachman. *One Nation under God: Religion in Contemporary American Society.* New York: Harmony Books, 1993.

Kraatz, Matthew S., and Edward J. Zajac. "Exploring the Limits of the New Institutionalism: The Causes and Consequences of Illegitimate Organizational Change." *American Sociological Review* 61 (1996): 812–36.

Kuenning, Paul P. *The Rise and Fall of American Lutheran Pietism: The Rejection of an Activist Heritage.* Macon, GA: Mercer University Press, 1988.

Lagerquist, L. DeAnne. *In America the Men Milk the Cows: Factors of Gender, Ethnicity, and Religion in the Americanization of Norwegian-American Women.* Brooklyn: Carlson Publishing, 1991.

———. *The Lutherans.* Westport, CT: Greenwood Press, 1999.

Lathrop, Gordon. "A Contemporary Lutheran Approach to Worship and Culture: Sorting Out Critical Principles." In *Worship and Culture in Dialogue*, ed. S. Anita Stauffer, 137–51. LWF Studies. Geneva, Switzerland: Department for Theology and Studies, Lutheran World Federation, 1994.

———. "New Pentecost or Joseph's Britches? Reflections on the History and Meaning of the Worship Ordo in the Megachurches." *Worship* 76, no. 6 (2001): 521–38.

———. "The Shape of the Liturgy: A Framework for Contextualization." In *Christian Worship: Unity in Cultural Diversity*, ed. S. Anita Stauffer, 67–75. LWF Studies. Geneva, Switzerland: Department for Theology and Studies, Lutheran World Federation, 1996.

———. *What Are the Essentials of Christian Worship?* Minneapolis: Augsburg Fortress Press, 1994.

Lectionary for the Common Mass (Lectionary for Mass). Collegeville, MN: Liturgical Press, 1970.

Leitch, Thomas M. *What Stories Are.* University Park, PA: Pennsylvania State University Press, 1986.

Lichterman, Paul. *The Search for Political Community.* New York: Cambridge University Press, 1996.

———. "Self-Help Reading as a Thin Culture." *Media, Culture, and Society* 14 (1992): 421–47.

Lieberson, Stanley. *A Matter of Taste: How Names, Fashions, and Culture Change.* New Haven, CT: Yale University Press, 2000.

Liebman, Charles S. "The Reappropriation of Jewish Tradition in the Modern Era." In *The Uses of Tradition*, ed. Jack Wertheimer, 471–77. Cambridge, MA: Harvard University Press, 1992.

Long, Elizabeth. "Women, Reading, and Cultural Authority: Some Implications of the Audience Perspective in Cultural Studies." *American Quarterly* 38 (1986): 591–612.

Long, Thomas G. *Beyond the Worship Wars: Building Vital and Faithful Worship.* Bethesda, MD: Alban Institute, 2001.

Lueker, Erwin L., ed. *Lutheran Cyclopedia.* St. Louis: Concordia Publishing House, 1954.

Luther, Martin. *The Small Catechism.* Minneapolis: Augsburg Publishing House; Philadelphia: Fortress Press, 1968.

The Lutheran Book of Worship. 10th ed. Minneapolis: Augsburg Publishing House; Philadelphia: Board of Publication, Lutheran Church in America, 1990.

Lyon, David. *Jesus in Disneyland.* Cambridge, UK: Polity Press, 2000.

MacIntyre, Alasdair. *After Virtue.* 2d ed. Notre Dame, IN: University of Notre Dame Press, 1984.

Marx, Karl. *The 18th Brumaire of Louis Bonaparte.* 1869. New York: International Publishers, 1963.

McIntosh, Gary. *One Size Doesn't Fit All.* Grand Rapids, MI: Revell Books, 1999.

McLoughlin, William G. *Revivals, Awakenings, and Reform.* Chicago: University of Chicago Press, 1978.

McRoberts, Omar M. "Understanding the 'New' Black Pentecostal Activism: Lessons from Ecumenical Urban Ministries in Boston." *Sociology of Religion* 60, no. 1 (1999): 47–70.

Miller, Donald E. *Reinventing American Protestantism: Christianity in the New Millennium.* Berkeley and Los Angeles: University of California Press, 1997.

Miller, Kent D. "Competitive Strategies for Religious Organizations." *Strategic Management Journal* 23 (2002): 435–56.

Moore, R. Laurence. *Selling God.* New York: Oxford University Press, 1994.

Nelson, E. Cliford, ed. *The Lutherans in North America.* Rev. ed. Philadelphia: Fortress Press, 1980.

Nichol, Todd. *All These Lutherans: Three Paths toward a New Lutheran Church.* Minneapolis: Augsburg Publishing House, 1986.

Niebuhr, H. Richard. *Christ and Culture.* New York: Harper and Row, 1951.

Noll, Mark A. "The Lutheran Difference." *First Things* 20 (February 1992): 31–40.

Nordquist, Philip A. "Lutherans in the West and Northwest." In *New Partners, Old Roots: A History of Merging Lutheran Churches in the Pacific Northwest*, ed. Heidi Emerson,

Milton Nesvig, Philip A. Nordquist, and Roland Swanson, 3–18. Tacoma, WA: North Pacific and Rocky Mountain Districts of the American Lutheran Church, the Pacific Northwest Synod of the Lutheran Church in America, and the Pacific Regional Synod of the Association of Evangelical Lutheran Churches, 1986.

Peterson, Richard A. "Six Constraints on the Production of Literary Works." *Poetics* 14 (1985): 45–67.

Polletta, Francesca. "'It Was Like a Fever. . .': Narrative and Identity in Social Protest." *Social Problems* 45 (1998): 137–59.

Press, Andrea. "The Sociology of Cultural Reception: Notes toward an Emerging Paradigm." In *The Sociology of Culture,* ed. Diana Crane, 221–46. Cambridge, MA: Blackstone, 1994.

Putnam, Robert D. *Bowling Alone.* New York: Simon and Schuster, 2000.

Quinn, D. Michael. "Religion in the American West." In *Under Open Sky: Rethinking America's Western Past,* ed. George Miles and Jay Gitlin, 145–64. New York and London: W. W. Norton and Co., 1992.

Reiff, Philip. *The Triumph of the Therapeutic.* New York: Harper Torchbooks, 1966.

Roof, Wade Clark. *A Generation of Seekers.* San Francisco: HarperCollins, 1993.

———. *Spiritual Marketplace.* Princeton: Princeton University Press, 1999.

Roof, Wade Clark, and William McKinney. *American Mainline Religion.* New Brunswick, NJ: Rutgers University Press, 1987.

Roozen, David A. "Four Mega-trends Changing America's Religious Landscape." Hartford Institute for Religion Research, 2001. http://fact.hartsem.edu/research/fact2000/topical_article11.htm.

———. "Three Sources of American Religious Renewal." Hartford Institute for Religion Research. http://fact.hartsem.edu/research/fact2000/topical_article1.htm.

Roozen, David A., and C. Kirk Hadaway, eds. *Church and Denominational Growth.* Nashville: Abingdon Press, 1993.

Roozen, David A., William McKinney, and Jackson W. Carroll. *Varieties of Religious Presence.* New York: Pilgrim Press, 1988.

Sargeant, Kimon Howland. *Seeker Churches: Promoting Traditional Religion in a Nontraditional Way.* New Brunswick, NJ: Rutgers University Press, 2000.

Schalk, Carl F. "Sketches of Lutheran Worship." In *A Handbook of Church Music,* ed. Carl Halter and Carl F. Schalk, 57–105. St. Louis: Concordia Publishing House, 1978.

Schaller, Lyle. *Discontinuity and Hope.* Nashville: Abingdon Press, 1999.

———. *Innovations in Ministry.* Nashville: Abingdon Press, 1994.

Schmauk, Theodore E., and C. Theodore Benze. *The Confessional Principle and the Confessions of the Lutheran Church as Embodying the Evangelical Confession of the Christian Church.* Philadelphia: General Council Publications Board, 1911.

Scholz, Robert F. "Henry Melchior Muhlenberg's Relation to the Ongoing Pietist Tradition." In *Lutheranism and Pietism: Essays and Reports,* vol. 14, ed. Aug R. Seulflow, 40–66. St. Louis: Lutheran Historical Conference, 1992.

Schudson, Michael. "How Culture Works: Perspectives from Media Studies on the Efficacy of Symbols." *Theory and Society* 18 (1989): 153–80.

Schuler, Rhoda. "Worship among American Lutherans: A House Divided." *Studia Liturgica* 25 (1995): 174–91.

Seidler, John, and Katherine Meyer. *Conflict and Change in the Catholic Church.* New Brunswick, NJ: Rutgers University Press, 1989.

Seligman, Adam B. *Authority, the Self, and Transcendence.* Princeton: Princeton University Press, 2000.

Senn, Frank C. "'Worship Alive': An Analysis and Critique of 'Alternative Worship Services.'" *Worship* 69, no. 3 (1995): 194–224.

Severton, Ansle. "Norwegian Lutherans in the Pacific Southwest." Berkeley, 1987. Unpublished paper.

———. "South Pacific District, the American Lutheran Church." Berkeley, 1989. Unpublished paper.

Sewell, William H., Jr. "A Theory of Structure: Duality, Agency, and Transformation." *American Journal of Sociology* 98, no. 1 (1992): 1–29.

Shibley, Mark A. "Contemporary Evangelicals: Born-Again and World Affirming." *Annals of the American Academy of the Political and Social Sciences* 558 (1998): 67–87.

Shils, Edward. *Tradition.* Chicago: University of Chicago Press, 1981.

Sikkink, David. "'I Just Say I'm Christian': Symbolic Boundaries and Identity Formation among Church-going Protestants." In *Re-forming the Center: American Protestantism, 1900 to the Present,* ed. Douglas Jacobsen and William Vance Trollinger Jr., 49–71. Grand Rapids, MI: Eerdmans, 1998.

Simmel, Georg. *The Sociology of Georg Simmel.* Trans., ed., and with an introduction by Kurt H. Wolff. New York: Free Press, 1964.

Skocpol, Theda. *Diminished Democracy.* Norman: University of Oklahoma Press, 2003.

Smith, Christian. *American Evangelicalism: Embattled and Thriving.* Chicago: University of Chicago Press, 1998.

Smith, Martin H. "Exploring the Differences between Fast-Growing and Randomly Selected ELCA Congregations." Evangelical Lutheran Church in America, Chicago, 2002. Unpublished paper.

Smith, Timothy L. *Revivalism and Social Reform: American Protestantism on the Eve of the Civil War.* Baltimore: Johns Hopkins University Press, 1980.

Spillman, Lynn. "Culture, Social Structures, and Discursive Fields." In *Current Perspectives in Social Theory,* vol. 15, ed. Ben Agger, 129–54. Greenwich, CT: JAI Press, 1995.

Spong, John Shelby. *Why Christianity Must Change or Die.* San Francisco: Harper, 1999.

Stark, Rodney, and William Sims Bainbridge. "Of Churches, Sects, and Cults: Preliminary Concepts for a Theory of Religious Movements." *Journal for the Scientific Study of Religion* 18, no. 2 (1979): 117–33.

Stone, Deborah A. "Causal Stories and the Formation of Policy Agendas." *Political Science Quarterly* 104 (1989): 281–300.

Strauss, Anselm. *Negotiations.* San Francisco: Jossey-Bass, 1978.

Sweet, Leonard. *AquaChurch.* Loveland, CO: Group, 1999.

———. *The Jesus Prescription for a Healthy Life.* Nashville: Abingdon Press, 1996.

Swidler, Ann. "Culture in Action: Symbols and Strategies." *American Sociological Review* 51 (1986): 273–86.

———. *Talk of Love*. Chicago: University of Chicago Press, 2001.

Szasz, Ferenc M. "'New Thought'and the American West." In *Religion in the West*, ed. Ferenc M. Szasz, 83–90. Manhattan, KS: Sunflower University Press, 1984.

———. *Religion in the Modern American West*. Tucson: University of Arizona Press, 2000.

Thompson, John B. "Tradition and the Self in a Mediated World." In *Detraditionalization*, ed. Paul Heelas, Scott Lash, and Paul Morris, 89–108. Cambridge, MA: Blackwell, 1996.

Thumma, Scott. "Denominational Identity and Church Vitality." Hartford Institute for Religion Research, 2000. http://fact.hartsem.edu/research/fact2000/topical_ article4.htm.

———. "Exploring the Megachurch Phenomena: Their Characteristics and Cultural Context." Hartford Institute for Religion Research, 2003. http://hirr.hartsem.edu/ bookshelf/thumma_article2.html.

Thumma, Scott, and Jim Petersen. "Goliaths in Our Midst: Megachurches in the ELCA." In *Lutherans Today: American Lutheran Identity in the 21st Century*, ed. Richard Cimino, 102–24. Grand Rapids, MI: Eerdmans, 2003.

Wagner-Pacifici, Robin. *The Moro Morality Play*. Chicago: University of Chicago Press, 1986.

Warner, R. Stephen. *New Wine in Old Wineskins: Evangelicals and Liberals in a Small-Town Church*. Berkeley and Los Angeles: University of California Press, 1988.

———. "The Place of the Congregation in the Contemporary American Religious Configuration." In *American Congregations*, vol. 2, ed. James P. Wind and James W. Lewis, 54–99. Chicago: University of Chicago Press, 1994.

Warren, Rick. *The Purpose-Driven Church*. Grand Rapids, MI: Zondervan, 1995.

Weber, Max. "The Social Psychology of World Religions." In *From Max Weber: Essays in Sociology*, ed. H. H. Gerth and C. Wright Mills, 267–301. New York: Oxford University Press, 1968.

Wellman, James K. "The Churching of the Pacific Northwest: The Rise of Sectarian Entrepreneurs." In *Religion and Public Life in the Pacific Northwest: The None Zone*, ed. Patricia O'Connell Killen and Mark Silk, 79–106. Walnut Creek, CA: Alta Mira Press, 2004.

Wentz, Abdel Ross. *The Lutheran Church in American History*. Philadelphia: United Lutheran Publication House, 1923.

White, Hayden V. *Metahistory*. Baltimore: Johns Hopkins University Press, 1973.

White, James F. *Christian Worship in North America*. Collegeville, MN: Liturgical Press, 1997.

———. *Protestant Worship*. Louisville, KY: Westminster/John Knox Press, 1989.

Witten, Marsha. *All Is Forgiven*. Princeton: Princeton University Press, 1993.

Wolfe, Alan. *The Transformation of American Religion*. New York: Free Press, 2003.

Wuthnow, Robert. *After Heaven*. Berkeley and Los Angeles: University of California Press, 1998.

————. *Communities of Discourse: Ideology and Social Structure in the Reformation, the Enlightenment, and European Socialism.* Cambridge, MA: Harvard University Press, 1989.

————. *Loose Connections.* Cambridge, MA: Harvard University Press, 1998.

————. *Meaning and Moral Order: Explorations in Cultural Analysis.* Berkeley and Los Angeles: University of California Press, 1987.

————. *The Restructuring of American Religion.* Princeton: Princeton University Press, 1988.

————. "Sources of Doctrinal Unity and Diversity." In *Views from the Pews,* ed. Roger A. Johnson, 33–56. Philadelphia: Fortress Press, 1983.

Yang, Fenggang, and Helen Rose Ebaugh. "Transformations in New Immigrant Religions and Their Global Implications." *American Sociological Review* 66, no. 2 (2001): 269–88.

Young, Lawrence A., ed. *Rational Choice Theory and Religion.* New York: Routledge, 1997.

INDEX